Left, the earliest known tea pot with the spout set at an angle to the leather covered handle. London, 1670, maker's mark TL. Right, the earliest known coffee pot. London, 1681, probably by George Garthorne. (See also p. 107.) Courtesy the Victoria and Albert Museum.

Starting to Collect
SILVER

John Luddington

Antique Collectors' Club

British Library Cataloguing in Publication Data
A catalogue record for this book is
available from the British Library

Printed in England on Consort Royal Satin
from Donside Mills, Aberdeen, by
the Antique Collectors' Club Ltd., 5 Church Street,
Woodbridge, Suffolk IP12 1DS

Antique Collectors' Club

The Antique Collectors' Club was formed in 1966 and now has a five figure membership spread throughout the world. It publishes the only independently run monthly antiques magazine *Antique Collecting* which caters for those collectors who are interested in widening their knowledge of antiques, both by greater awareness of quality and by discussion of the factors which influence the price that is likely to be asked. The Antique Collectors' Club pioneered the provision of information on prices for collectors and the magazine still leads in the provision of detailed articles on a variety of subjects.

It was in response to the enormous demand for information on 'what to pay' that the price guide series was introduced in 1968 with the first edition of *The Price Guide to Antique Furniture* (completely revised, 1978 and 1989), a book which broke new ground by illustrating the more common types of antique furniture, the sort that collectors could buy in shops and at auctions rather than the rare museum pieces which had previously been used (and still to a large extent are used) to make up the limited amount of illustrations in books published by commercial publishers. Many other price guides have followed, all copiously illustrated, and greatly appreciated by collectors for the valuable information they contain, quite apart from prices. The Antique Collectors' Club also publishes other books on antiques, including horology and art reference works, and a full book list is available.

Club membership, which is open to all collectors, costs little. Members receive free of charge *Antique Collecting*, the Club's magazine (published ten times a year), which contains well-illustrated articles dealing with the practical aspects of collecting not normally dealt with by magazines. Prices, features of value, investment potential, fakes and forgeries are all given prominence in the magazine.

Among other facilities available to members are private buying and selling facilities, the longest list of 'For Sales' of any antiques magazine, an annual ceramics conference and the opportunity to meet other collectors at their local antique collectors' clubs. There are over eighty in Britain and more than a dozen overseas. Members may also buy the Club's publications at special pre-publication prices.

As its motto implies, the Club is an amateur organisation designed to help collectors get the most out of their hobby: it is informal and friendly and gives enormous enjoyment to all concerned.

For Collectors – By Collectors – About Collecting

The Antique Collectors' Club, 5 Church Street, Woodbridge, Suffolk

Acknowledgements

I am deeply grateful to the following kind people; some of them have given me many hours of their time and all have co-operated most generously:

Miss Judy Wentworth
Mr. Eric Delieb
Mr. and Mrs. Ernst Schuckmann
Mr. J.E. Aspin
Mr. and Mrs. Michael Graeme Macdonald
Mr. and Mrs. Brian Fraser-Smith
Captain and Mrs. John Milner
Dr. and Mrs. Colin McDonald
Miss R.M. Coffin
Miss Susan Hare
Captain J.D. Norie
Trinity Hall, Cambridge
The Directors of Layard Enterprises Inc.
Miss Anneke Bambery
Ward & Chowen
Mr. Michael Ingham
Dr. David Fermont

Mr. and Mrs. Kent Karslake
Mr. C.B. Ryall
Mr. Martin Gubbins
Mr. and Dr. David Bayliss
Dr. D.L. Serventy
Dr. Graham Hulley
Mrs. L.T. Burrough
Mrs. Charles Tarr
Miss Celia Wiernik
Miss Marie Carousis
Mr. Douglas Sweet
Mr. R. Finlay McCance
Mr. T. Alun Davies
Mr. G.N. Mainwaring
Mr. G.S. Sanders
Mr. M. Walecki
Messrs Harvey and Gore

Mr. Lyn and Mrs. Jenny Jenner Antiques

I would also like to thank the following photographers for their expertise and care:

N. Keith Macdonald
Brian Stevenson
Edgar W. Morse

P.J. Gates
Colin Mason
Mrs. Harriet Crowder

Edward Leigh

as well as all those photographers whose names I do not know but whose work is represented in this book.

Some of the illustrations in Chapter 12 have previously appeared in articles in *Antique Collecting* by Ian Harris, Hubert Chesshyre and Gale Saunders-Davies, and I would like to thank both them and the Antique Collectors' Club for making it possible to reproduce these.

Last, but by no means least, I am grateful to all those friends and institutions who made photographs available or allowed photographs to be taken for this book. They are individually acknowledged in the captions to the photographs.

Contents

Preface

This book attempts to guide those who are totally ignorant of antique silver to a reasonable standard of knowledge at an early stage. It caters also for the average collector who wishes to avoid making further, often costly, mistakes whilst developing a wider discernment of quality. Those few who possess the resolution and inclination to complete the course of study (Chapter 9) should acquire a good understanding of the subject in six months. While it is hoped that these pages will assist anyone interested in silver, they are primarily designed to help the buyer, whether he be dealer or amateur, more directly than the seller of silver.

Rare vinaigrette in the form of a cornucopia. The realistic ram's horn is surmounted by a lid in the form of a bowl overflowing with flowers, fruit and corn. Birmingham, 1826, by John Betteridge, 3.75cm long, 12dwt. Victorian reproductions are less rare and lack the quality of this cast example.

In a sense, we are all beginners even if we began to collect silver many decades ago. We continue to learn or relearn, but whereas the complete novice should learn something new and exciting from most of the numerous items which he *must inspect intelligently* each week, the specialist is not so fortunate, for he may only meet with the same number of interesting discoveries in the course of a year.

Together, we will explore *all* the treacherous paths of the jungle, and if these tracks are memorised the student should orientate himself quickly and thoroughly. The most important aspects of our subject will be *hammered incessantly* throughout these pages until, it is hoped, such points, like nails, are firmly fixed.

As brains are liable to stall if overwhelmed by too many facts without intermission, anecdotes sometimes pop up surprisingly. These may remind you of hazards along the path whilst affording some light relief in your studies and, at the same time, introducing novices to the generally informal, happy and friendly atmosphere associated with the pursuit of antique silver.

Two egg cups from a set of six. Although a set of egg cups in a basket is recorded, made by Peter Archambo some twenty-five years earlier, this set may otherwise be the earliest known. London, 1770, by Aldridge & Green, bowl diameter 6.5cm, 6oz. 18dwt. (six). As the diameter of the bases exceeds those of the bowls, making it impossible for the cups to be positioned in a cruet frame with circular cup holders, it is difficult to believe that this set was contained in a cruet. Possibly this half dozen was part of a much larger set and reduced to the six by family divisions.

Rare wooden-backed livery badge chased with a turkey cock displaying and pricked with foliage and flowers, oval. London, 1693, maker's mark R.C. in monogram, 19.2cm long. The Strickland family of Boynton, Yorkshire, were credited with the introduction of the turkey into England, and in arms granted in 1560 the turkey cock is embraced 'in his pride proper'. Courtesy Sotheby's.

Humour is a rare feature in the decoration of antique silver, especially in the eighteenth century (though early nineteenth century drinking and eating club badges sometimes have humorous decoration). Cream jug by Thomas Satchwell, London, 1779. On one side a cock treads a hen whilst other birds take flight. The other side shows a parrot which appears to be giving a running commentary of events to a little dog who seems to be laughing. Courtesy the Dr. D.L. Serventy Collection, Australia.

This work embraces much of my first book, *Antique Silver: A Guide for Would-be Connoisseurs,* published in 1971, but in the light of more than a decade's additional experience, the old work has been revised and much extended. The number of illustrations has been greatly increased for the purposes of instruction as well as interest.

Typical of the simpler styles of the late eighteenth century, a pair of salt cellars with beaded edges and four hoof feet. London, 1786, by Hester Bateman, 10.2cm wide. Helmet-shaped jug with reeded borders on square plinth. London, 1794, by Peter and Anne Bateman, 18cm high. Courtesy Sotheby's.

Typical bright-cut decoration of the late eighteenth century. Oval tea pot, the ribbed body bright-cut with festoons and wrigglework enrichment. London, 1788, by Hester Bateman, 14cm high, 13.2oz. (a trifle light for size). Courtesy Sotheby's.

My first book gave satisfaction to good dealers but naturally it was deplored by the more dubious members of our trade. This work delves even deeper into irresponsible trade practices; indeed, some of the revelations may be thought to be detrimental to the business activities of both average and bad traders alike. Basically, my intention is, in the long run, to up-grade the standing of dealers so that, in the eyes of the public, they are dedicated practitioners, jealous both for the welfare of their customers and for their colleagues in the trade. In the meantime, my aim is to steer collectors towards the assistance of far fewer but highly conscientious and knowledgeable traders, thus to be spared those initial bitter experiences which, in the past, have so often terminated interest in the subject. Collectors of silver — *if they will develop their knowledge of the subject* — could gradually expel and certainly discourage all charlatans and crooks from our business.

It must be stressed that, although this book is dedicated to quality to the exclusion of all other considerations, apart from exceptional rarity, many *excellent* dealers are obliged to stock mediocre as well as good silver. This position is inevitable because the public, in general, neither understands nor requires the best quality, with its higher price tags. Indeed, should readers contemplate buying silver only for the rough and tumble of everyday use by a young family or their friends, it would be most unsuitable if they were to purchase items of importance. However, there are certain justifications for buying second-rate silver, which can still give much pleasure for many years.

Left, tankard of baluster form. London, 1759, by Fuller White. Right, tankard of tapered cylindrical form (straight-sided). London, 1788, by Charles Wright. Courtesy Sotheby's.

Within wide but rigid guide lines, beginners and more advanced collectors will be encouraged to formulate their own preferences in silver, and to be influenced neither by current fashions, almost invariably associated with inflated prices, nor by the many who proclaim, as if with authority, that, for example, straight-sided tankards are preferable to baluster specimens (see illustration), bright-cut decoration more valuable than plain surfaces, and one particular maker or origin of manufacture better than any other. You should be buying good silver to suit your own taste and which you will therefore enjoy throughout your life.

It would be foolish if I were not to make use of the vast store of expertise to be found among my friends, some of whose collections are amongst the most important and/or interesting in the world. Several people have allowed us to enjoy illustrations of some of their pieces and others have contributed their specialised knowledge. In order to extract the maximum interest and instruction from Michael Ingham's valuable Chapter 12 on armorial engraving, the beginner is advised to postpone his serious study of it until he has acquired a fair knowledge of antique silver. However, even from the outset, this chapter may enable him not only to determine the rank or standing of the original owner of his silver pieces, provided they bear a

Christening mug engraved with children in the style of Kate Greenaway, parcel (partly) gilt. London, 1880, by Thomas Bradbury and John Henderson, 8.9cm high. Courtesy the Worshipful Company of Goldsmiths.

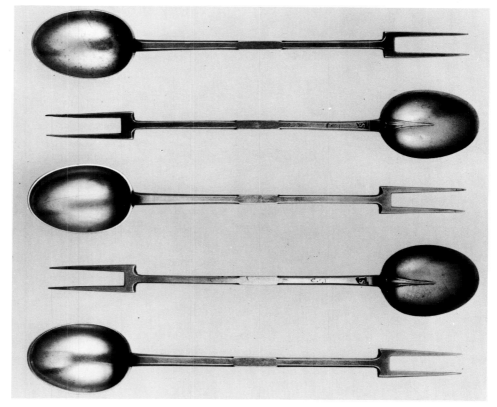

A set of sucket spoons and forks with hexagonal stems. London, c.1685, maker's mark IS with crown above. In the centre of each stem a bar for holding the rat-tailed spoon and two-prong fork at either end. Courtesy Phillips.

genuine contemporary coat of arms (in some cases merely from crests alone), but also to be able to determine their approximate date of manufacture, even if they be completely unmarked, and before he has learned to date his silver by the style of design, decoration or other considerations.

Recommendations for additional reading on most aspects of silver are given in this book, but because of the continual uncertainty as to whether even the best books are still available in the shops — or even if rumoured intentions of reprints and revisions will materialise before this book is published — readers may have to resort to libraries or search for secondhand copies. The work to be used for constant reference in this book (referred to in future as Jackson) is Sir Charles Jackson's *English Goldsmiths and Their Marks*, second edition. As this monumental work was first published in 1887, the revised edition appearing in 1921, it is inevitable that it contains many errors, some serious, and important omissions.* Nevertheless, it still provides a reliable guide to the hallmarks of the major assay offices, together with a multitude of makers' marks. Important errors and some omissions in Jackson are explained within these pages.

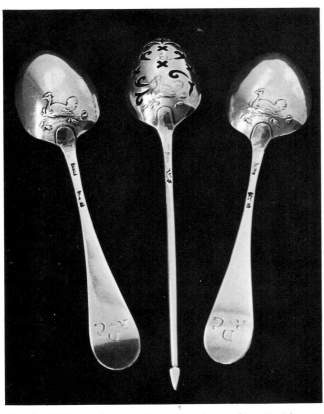

A pair of Hanoverian type tea spoons (part of a set) with mote spoon, all pieces stamped on back of bowl with a hen and four chicks. London, c.1756, by R. Swanson. Courtesy the Captain and Mrs. John Milner Collection.

A trophy for hunter-chasers, the campana-shaped body with lobing, gadroon borders, spreading foot and reeded handles rising from bacchanalian masks. Sheffield, 1805, by Roberts, Cadnam & Co. (also famous for their Sheffield plate), 33.5cm high, 56oz. 2dwt. 'Charles James Fox' ('Charlie' for short) sits on the lobing on the cover. The inscription reads: 'Thorpe Salvin Races, March 26th, 1806. Off-She-Goes.' Courtesy Sotheby's.

* The Antique Collectors' Club revised edition of Jackson's *English Goldsmiths and Their Marks* is now in preparation and will contain many hundreds of emendations and additions.

Under no circumstances should readers enter the silver jungle casually, without planning and self-discipline; nor should they emulate the apprenticeship of the author, whose sudden interest in silver was so disgracefully unplanned, but rewarded by such good fortune that a brief account of this puerile muddle must be worth any novice collectors' consideration, if only to show them how not to go about things.

Having successfully trained racehorses round the perimeter of the airfield on which I was stationed early in the war, I was in possession of a little spare money. I spoke to a colleague who told me to invest my money in antique silver and I took his advice for want of something better to do. The first shop I entered was situated on a steep hill in Lincoln; the medieval oak beams were scented by the smoke from centuries of log fires. An old man, with butterfly collar, black tie and pearl tie pin, advanced to greet me with a smile and manner as gracious as his shop. Without the slightest trepidation, I placed myself in his hands.

"I know nothing about silver," I began, "but I want to start collecting it. I was thinking of some small piece that I will never grow tired of. Will you help me, please?"

He thought for a moment and then pulled from a drawer a number of table spoons. He handled them all carefully before making his decision. "This is your piece. It is a rat-tailed spoon of the Queen Anne period and bears the full set of Britannia standard Chester Assay marks for the year 1712. It weighs almost three ounces and is of magnificent quality. The maker is ..."

I could not wait to listen to further details. I had no idea that such magnificent spoons existed and, even today, I doubt if I have seen better. I didn't enquire how much it was, but said: "Thank you very much indeed. What do I owe you?"

What a fortunate shop to find at random. What a start!

Armed with this perfect piece as a model, and still without a guide to hallmarks, I toured through the Lincolnshire towns searching for further spoons. I bought a few but, as my standards were so fortuitously high from the outset, I already had some competence to reject the second class. Unconsciously, too, because of the superb patina on my first and subsequent spoons, I was already instinctively suspicious of spoons of a different colour. I had no reason for this suspicion: I had no idea that this different colour was probably caused by repaired shanks, reshaped bowls or erased initials, but I did appreciate that they were unsuitable companions for my own spoons.

The next important step — also a fantastic stroke of luck — occurred while I was on leave in Northamptonshire. I entered a shop full of antiques of every description and asked an extremely dissipated looking old dealer if he had any silver. He said he had a Victorian coffee pot and, because he placed it in my hands before I had time to say I wasn't interested in Victoriana, I felt compelled to examine it. It had the same soft colour and simple lines as my spoons. On the lid was a strange finial that opened and shut on a hinge. The marks seemed to me to be London, Britannia standard period, like most of my spoons.

"Isn't it early eighteenth century?" I enquired.

"No, no, my boy. It's Dublin, Victorian."

A rare egg timer, enclosing grey sand. London, 1809, 9.5cm high. The two ends and the three baluster supports are all detachable by screws and all parts are marked. Although the maker's mark is rubbed on this example, there is no doubt that this was one of a small batch made by Emes & Barnard in 1809. The sand takes two and a half minutes to run through, suggesting that hens and their eggs were smaller in days gone by. An identical example with a clear maker's mark was stolen from the author in 1971.

"Well, anyhow, I like it," I replied, only half convinced by his correction, "how much is it?"

"Eleven pounds to you, my boy."

I was inclined to ask how much it would have been to others, but respect for such a venerable dissipation restrained me. I paid up and departed.

Immediately I got home, I consulted my recently acquired guide to hall-marks, and confirmed that the date of my pot was London, 1719. On opening Jackson, a recent gift, I discovered that the maker was Augustin Courtauld. A picture in my scrap book of illustrations and descriptions of silver indicated that the 'coffee' pot was actually a chocolate pot. This explained the hinged finial (similar to the one in the illustration) that would allow some slender instrument to be inserted to stir the chocolate. It seemed possible that I had obtained an interesting piece for a modest outlay.

Some days later, I had an introduction to visit Mr. Frederick Bradbury, the well-known authority on Sheffield plate and antique silver. He was a charming old man and only too pleased to help a poor chap in the R.A.F. He showed me his collection and then I showed him my chocolate pot.

"What a pity," he said "that the coat of arms engraved on this applied shield is of a slightly later date. The shield probably conceals the original coat underneath and it shouldn't be there. We'll have to get it off for you. It will spoil the patina, of course, but it will be more valuable without the shield."

Chocolate pot showing the hinged finial on domed lid. The curved spout is at right angles to the handle. London, 1703, by Seth Lofthouse, 24.2cm high, 23oz. 7dwt. Marked on body and in lid. Courtesy Sotheby's.

As I have already explained, although I had already recognised it, I didn't know what patina meant, and forgot or was too ashamed of my ignorance to ask. I accepted Mr. Bradbury's advice without question. In retrospect, at a much later date, I believe the removal of the applied shield was unjustified. The substituted coat, as Mr. Bradbury had told me, was only of slightly later date. I think he wanted to have a look at the original coat underneath.

When the pot arrived back, I was dismayed. I could scarcely bear to look at it. A few days before I had owned an object of beauty and now even its simple, graceful lines were forgotten under the garish shimmer of high polish.

But even this misfortune proved as valuable experience as any beginner could have had. In disgust, and without bothering to ascertain its value, I advertised to sell the offending piece in *The Times:* "Chocolate pot, London, 1719, by Augustin Courtauld. £30". During lunch on the same day the advertisement appeared an enormous car pulled up at the door. A dealer from London, one hundred and fifty miles away, had arrived to buy. The alacrity of this powerful car's arrival, when petrol was so strictly rationed, suggested to me that I had undervalued my pot. Besides, I took an instinctive dislike to this dealer. I fobbed him off and then sent the pot to auction where it fetched £80.

I suppose a chocolate pot of 1719 would have fetched £200 in those far off days if in good condition and so, considering that the patina of my pot was completely ruined and that the traces of the original coat were unsightly, the figure of £80 checks quite reasonably with the conclusions in Chapter 5: How quality affects value.

Realising now that even 'ruined' silver was worth money, my standards dropped for a considerable time and, instead of collecting fine specimens, I began searching for bargains. I did not enjoy myself as much, and I was insufficiently experienced to avoid burning my fingers. But my early experiences had shown me what I wanted for my personal collection and this is why I was such a fortunate man. I still sometimes recall the aroma of those oak beams in Lincoln when I spot a piece of outstanding quality.

John Luddington

CHAPTER 1

Background to the market place

The market over the last two decades

One of the key problems with antique collecting is to separate an interest in money from the pure aesthetic enjoyment derived from owning a piece. When you look at your favourite antique does it please you because it is worth many times what you paid for it, or because its line or form delights your eye? Put the question another way, if the value of your favourite piece was affected by a severe general depression in value so that it was worth only half what you paid for it, would you make a point of seeking out other examples in the hope that you might find a better one?

The sad truth is that far too many people fool themselves into believing that they like their favourite piece for its quality, whereas all too often they like it principally because it cost them less than it should have done and thus reminds them of their own success. Often the sensible thing would be to sell it and use the profit to buy something really worth having, even if that costs full price. Too many people prefer the silent flattery of the not so good item that they bought for a bargain.

Fine and rare baluster knop spoon of heavy gauge, the tapering hexagonal stem surmounted by cast silver gilt knop of baluster form with gadroon and ball finial, the fig-shape bowl curved. London, 1553, with maker's mark of a crescent enclosing a mullet, 17.5cm. Courtesy Phillips.

A particularly fine tankard assayed in the first year of the reign of William and Mary, with a contemporary widow's coat of arms and volute thumb piece. Marked on body, lid and handle. London, 1689, maker's mark JS in script, 19.1cm high, 34oz. 6dwt. Note the impressive weight for size. Courtesy Sotheby's.

It would be a good idea if right at the start you worked out your reason for keeping some of the not so good pieces. If one of these has sentimental value and reminds you of happy days then, of course, you must keep it; but if the amount you paid for it springs too readily to mind and if your home contains many such pieces then beware — you are likely to have a difficult time making an objective assessment either of this, or possibly even other items.

The first lesson to learn must be to let the piece you are looking at speak, as far as possible, for itself. At first what it is trying to tell you will have to be translated for you by someone who speaks the language. But as you see more

A fine unmarked late seventeenth century terrapin shell box with silver mounts, hinged and possibly intended for snuff. Engraved 'John Neilson aught [sic] this box, September 27 Anno Domini 1696', 7.9cm long, 7cm deep. Courtesy Phillips.

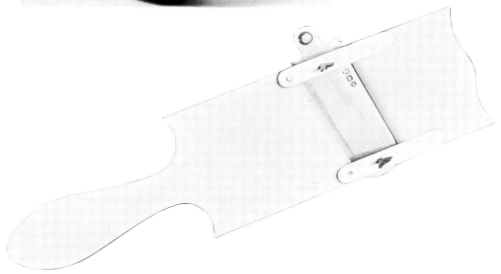

Cucumber slicer set in ivory. The setting of adjustable screws means slices of different thicknesses can be cut. London, 1808, by Phipps & Robinson, 23cm long. Courtesy Phillips.

pieces you will develop comparative standards by which to judge quality which is, after all, what true collecting and this book is all about. When you become more knowledgeable you will gradually close your ears to most of what you hear and rely on what you see. Bernard Shaw's comment: if you want to understand what a woman is thinking you should look at her and not listen to what she is saying, applies equally to antiques and those who try to sell them.

Probably the greatest example of lemming-like cupidity came to a sudden and sharp end at an auction of silver in spring 1969. Instead of more record prices being realised some ninety per cent of the antique silver on offer was unsold. An investment bubble that had gradually been inflated since the early 1960s burst.

It was an instructive time for the observer of the behaviour of antique markets. Silver was undervalued in the early 1960s, a fact which was

A good pair of unusually early butter shells, realistically fluted and chased, with applied cast shell feet. London, 1746, by George Wickes, 9.5cm wide. Courtesy the Mr. and Dr. David Bayliss Collection, Hong Kong.

gradually appreciated by investors who, however much they liked to flatter themselves, had a very high cupidity factor and a minimal aesthetic interest. Like many such exercises before it the silver boom fed initially on itself. Prices were rising, but then of course they would, as investment money comes in large lumps and the supply of silver coming on to the market was relatively slow even with the attendant publicity of high prices. As silver moved up in price more quickly the supply became shorter and the quality of what was on offer declined.

Around this time a new breed of dealer appeared, often young and usually without too much knowledge and even less morals, to whom low quality did not matter so long as he had something to sell. As for the average, none too intelligent, investor, used to dealing in carefully defined shares and commodities, a George II teapot was as clear a description as a tonne of copper or an ICI share — it was there in the auctioneer's catalogue, just as share and commodity prices are quoted in the daily press.

All in all, here was a situation bound to blow up in the faces of the new investors. To understand why the end came so sharply one needs only to skim through the headlines of *The Times* for a few weeks during the critical time.

> Only Bank of England selling prevents the pound from falling below its floor of $2.3825
>
> $3,000M pours into Germany
>
> Stalemate at No. 10 talks for reform of the unions
>
> Heavy falls in shares
>
> Manufacturers' orders shrink as squeeze hits high street
>
> 'Your Government is going on' — Wilson

Sitting on a large theoretical profit, some silver investors understandably decided to get out. At this point a problem arose which might not previously have occurred to them. Whereas in the share, money and commodity markets getting out entails only a telephone call, in the world of antiques disposal is more complicated. The dealers who had been shovelling out whatever they could find to meet the investment market were not anxious to buy back what they had recently sold at a good profit, so auction was the best hope for disposal.

Unlike share and commodity markets, auctions take place at widely spaced intervals, so that by the time the weekly/fortnightly/monthly sales

The arms of the Duke of Grafton engraved on a pair of standing dishes. London, 1684, by Ralph Leake. Various forms of gadrooning, as on feet and rims, were popular even until the reign of William IV. Courtesy the Worshipful Company of Goldsmiths.

Punch bowl and cover with ladle, gilt. Standing on three dolphin feet the lower part of the body is chased with gadroons (or convex flutes) alternating with bands of husks. Cover with similar decoration and surmounted by pineapple finial. Presented to the Corporation of Stamford in 1685 by Charles Bertie M.P. and bearing his arms. Marked only by the maker PR, two pellets above, a rose below, diameter 40.3cm, capacity 3.5 gallons. But for the cylindrical stem of the ladle, the style has many similarities with the 1740-50 period. Courtesy the Worshipful Company of Goldsmiths.

Set of three open work tea caddies with blue liners in silver-mounted shagreen casket. London, 1771, by Thomas Heming, 32.9cm high. The set is decorated with figures copied from contemporary theatrical engravings against an architectural background. Courtesy the Worshipful Company of Goldsmiths.

21

occurred word had passed round the investors that it was time to get out of silver, and the rush was on. Needless to say prices slumped. Candlesticks and coffee pots — the blue chips of the silver world — slumped in price, and the difference between a poor quality piece bought from a none too scrupulous dealer at retail price and sold without reserve at auction after the slump could have been as much as seventy-five per cent.

As so often happens, the price of good quality pieces also suffered in the general stampede. However, within a matter of months the trade and genuine collector element started buying so that items of quality began to recover in price. Indeed the really fine pieces probably did not suffer greatly because they were too expensive for the unknowledgeable speculator.

In retrospect, after more than a decade has elapsed, the slump turned out to be in the best long-term interests of collectors and trade alike for two reasons: it engendered a lingering nervousness in the antique silver market which has helped to steady prices and, above all, discerning traders and collectors became more selective and better aware of the value and desirability of quality. Although it must be admitted that prices for good and

Although a number of replicas of a Roman bath were made early in the second half of the eighteenth century in other materials, this souvenir made in silver is rare. London, 1768, by George Smith, 3.5cm high. Courtesy the R.M. Coffin Collection, U.S.A.

The marks on the miniature Roman bath.

interesting silver have now moved ahead again, and may continue to do so particularly when inflation is rampant, silver is still underpriced in comparison with almost everything else and must, from every point of view, prove a rewarding investment, but only for those who love it.

Prior to the last two decades, Continental silver — a subject fraught with even more dangers than English silver — was, except for important pieces, generally unconsidered both here and overseas, but as prices and interest in English silver increased, the Continentals followed our lead and displayed belated interest in their local heirlooms. Today, the prices of Continental silver in many European countries have rocketed and, because of its scarcity rather than its universal excellence, it is now far more expensive than its often more desirable English counterpart.

Preliminary cautions

I have mentioned varying degrees of quality of antique silver. But what about fakes?

Because of the heavy penalties to be risked, *mass* forgeries of silver articles are unknown, but there are always a few rogue silversmiths and their runners anxious for easy profits from deceit, and some of them nowadays are dangerously knowledgeable. Few of them seem to get caught and this may be because very many small dealers neither keep proper books nor bother about receipts for goods which they buy for cash. They argue that taxes are too punitive and they have a point.

The fakers, who sometimes confine themselves to enhancing the value of a legitimate article by applying fashionable decoration in an antique style, and the forgers with their spurious assay marks and alterations (all these deceits will be explained as the book progresses), usually work to a predictable plan. They reproduce or embellish a fast-selling line of goods which is in short supply and market them to inexperienced or dishonest dealers. As such items find their way into the hands of more reputable dealers, they are recognised as fakes and the trade is alerted. The fakers then switch to another popular line and the process is repeated. Each batch of fakes abounds in the market stalls and small fairs for about two months after which time most of them have been sold to the public. For the next few decades they keep popping up occasionally, usually at small auctions and in junk shops.

In the last twenty years we have seen the work of a forger who converted many worn out Georgian tea spoons, which he had bought for about 50p each, into caddy spoons of normal size. He removed a section of the stem, leaving the hallmarks untouched, and then joined the stem together again; the worn out bowl was reshaped, probably embossed with fruit and foliage and, in some cases, the 'new' spoon was gilt, not only to conceal the join on the stem but also to increase the item's appeal. A cleverer version — because the results seemed better balanced and quite attractive — entailed the removal of the top of any small, top-marked spoon with hallmarks, leaving sufficient length beneath the marks to divide the lower part of the remaining shank into two sections or tendrils (see left). The tendrils were then soldered neatly to either side of any suitable bowl available, in the manner of many an authentic caddy spoon.

Modern hallmarks stamped and Georgian Irish marks cancelled on a forged caddy spoon as described in the text. The piece has been assayed and found to be of sterling standard; although the new set of marks makes the object lawful, it is of no interest as an antique.

Other machinations include the fitting of fashionable castle top plaques into the lids of vinaigrettes and snuff boxes; the simple conversion of table spoons into the more valuable marrow spoons; the stamping of spurious reproductions of very rare assay or guild marks, such as Plymouth, Bristol or Colchester, on new spoons which have been pitted and scratched (perhaps shaken with lead shot) in an attempt to suggest genuine antiquity; refashioning punch ladles with broken stems, and therefore valueless, into cream boats by adding a handle and legs; the erasure of a maker's mark and its substitution with the spurious mark of another maker whose production is much sought after and valuable. All this should suffice to put the novice collector on his guard. The next decade or so may not be quite as dangerous thanks to the increasingly effective liaison between the officials at the London Assay Office and the comparatively new Antiques Fraud Squad at Scotland Yard.

It is sad to see members of the public who try to invest in silver with little available capital, starting off and usually continuing out of step. Perhaps they think, quite erroneously, that the long established dealers do not want to be bothered with them.

Instead of putting themselves in reliable hands and making an occasional small but worthwhile investment, they tend to fritter their money away on flimsy, mass-produced, silver knick-knacks often devoid of any merit whatsoever. At best, or maybe at worst, they purchase what was once a genuine article long since worn out — a spoon for example, with its bowl reshaped, embossed within the last few months or years in a crude design of fruits and leafage and called in the trade a 'berry' spoon. The original hallmarks are still visible and so, thinks the customer, it is a genuine antique. Tourists from overseas are also prone to buy this ornate nonsense.

In the numerous antique markets and fairs, both outdoor and indoor, there are many honest dealers, but there is still only a sprinkling of expertise; and it is in such places that the experienced eye can very occasionally spot an interesting bargain. They are light-hearted friendly places and well worth visiting, but the inexperienced collector would be chancing his luck if he attempted to buy antique silver from inexperienced or unknown dealers. The same warning must apply to many shops all over the country unless they are long- and well-established.

As one walks through the markets, one often encounters little groups of dealers and customers, all trying to help each other, as they peer backwards and forwards between their guide to English hallmarks and, for example, a late nineteenth century Continental article. An enthusiastic suggestion (?guess): London, 1710, is countered by a gloomy: Birmingham, 1925.

Unless purchased from a reliable source, I cannot emphasise too strongly that it is highly dangerous for anyone, dealer or collector, to purchase any item of antique silver if they still feel the need of a guide to hallmarks before they can recognise, almost at first glance, the origin and approximate date of any silver item.

Except for a few auction houses, of which Christie's, Sotheby's and Phillips are the best known (as I will explain later), it is extremely risky for the inexperienced to buy at auctions. It is at auctions that many dealers get rid of their sub-standard stock. Some years ago, a woman stallholder in the Portobello Road came to me with a table spoon by Hester Bateman. She wanted £6 for it. The marks were satisfactory, but I have never seen a spoon with a bowl so startling; nor shall I ever forget it. In shape and quality it resembled a flying saucer in imminent danger of disintegration.

"Oh, no," I said, "I can't hold myself responsible for this thing."

"Nor can I," she replied.

Thus there was an understanding between us and I thought of a way to help her.

"I'm selling some junk at auction in the country next week," I said, "and I'll get them to take this spoon for you. There are a lot of new dealers down there and they'll buy anything by Hester. I'm certain that even this spoon will fetch £7 or £8." In fact it fetched some £20; bought by the daughter of a well-known local family, who had just taken up the fashionable game of 'antique dealing'.

"One fool will usually find another in a country auction", said one dealer to whom I told the story.

Although the number of dealers in antique silver has increased dramatically in the last two decades, there may be fewer than one hundred real experts in the world and many of these are based in London. There are many dealers with brains like ready reckoners and eyes like hawks who can assess the value and condition of the usual or popular items in a flash and with amazing accuracy, but they are often out of their depth when confronted by the unusual.

Mr. X is one of the biggest and most popular dealers in the world and much of his stock is of superb quality. Unfortunately, because of his very

An interesting whistle and rattle, c.1740, maker's mark JR in script. Instead of the usual child's coral teether there is a contemporary stopper with suspensory loop, suggesting that a parent or growing child had the item changed into a useful device for controlling dogs. Courtesy the James Aspin Collection, South Africa.

Monograms can be just as attractive and interesting as coats of arms and more informative than crests. The engraving on this small mug, London, 1725, by William Spackman, 9cm high, 7oz., was probably applied to celebrate a silver wedding in 1750. Courtesy the Captain and Mrs. John Milner Collection.

considerable interests overseas, where collectors are even less particular than in London, he deals also in second and third quality goods. He has been buying and selling enormous quantities of silver every day for about fifty years. He 'thinks silver' all day long and probably dreams of it. Nevertheless, I would hesitate to consider Mr. X, with whom I happened to be dining in a provincial hotel, as among the leading hundred experts in the world.

"I suppose, by now," I said, "you must know everything there is to know about silver."

Mr. X did not even pause to think: "Good God, no! I pick up something new every week."

Later that same evening, Mr. X told me a curious tale that worries me still as I try to follow the processes of his mind.

"I had a good customer who wanted a James II lidded tankard," Mr. X began, "and all I had in stock was one which the Victorians had embossed and which I had had beaten out flat again for overseas. I could have let this go for £1,000, but I reckoned that my customer would think that too cheap, and would be worried there was something wrong with it. He was an old customer and I wanted him satisfied so I charged him £3,000. Some months later, he came back to return it, rather cross because some friend had told him that it had been dechased. He even started lecturing me about hammer marks and then found a complete bacchanalian grape against the rim that had got missed out.

"You try and do your best for customers," Mr. X added in a pained voice "and that's all the thanks you get..."

Mr. X's modest admission that even after fifty years he was still learning about silver led to an amusing sequel a few weeks later. I was trying to explain some point of interest about an early spoon to a youth in his late teens.

"As a matter of fact, I happen to know all about silver," he said.

"How very interesting! And may I ask you where you work?"

"I'm with Mr. X."

I pursued the matter no further, but I might have replied: "In your present frame of mind it may be several years before you are fit to do anything but clean Mr. X's silver."

But we should excuse the boy's unwarranted confidence. I went through the same silly stage of 'knowing it all', and I believe that almost all collectors experience the same infantile and often very painful teething troubles. It is only when we are aware of the abysmal depths of our ignorance that we begin to understand the wide scope of our subject and really start to learn. All this is odd because in our first year we are humble and diffident enough: then something awful happens. Perhaps we are overwhelmed with glee in picking up an exciting bargain from someone many years our senior in experience. We are in danger as great as the boy who is unlucky enough to enjoy a large win on the horses with his first bet.

Where to learn

At this early stage in our book, if you have not been frightened away from antique silver altogether, it would be surprising if you did not feel confused. Actually, even before you have begun your course of study, you are gradually acquiring an innate sense of the dangers associated with collecting antiques of every type and in this respect you are already better equipped than many collectors. Perhaps, you are already wondering where you can find further practical help, how to start your collection and, not unnaturally, if there are still bargains to be found after two decades of intense activity in the search for antique silver. You need not worry, interesting pieces are constantly turning up, but only for those who are prepared to put some effort into learning.

At Christie's and Sotheby's auction rooms in London, where I hope you will be able to spend many happy hours in pursuing the policy and advice offered in the course of study, there is expert advice 'on tap', of which you

Pairs of fruit knives and forks (often cased for travelling) with mother-of-pearl handles with silver mounts, and usually made at Sheffield and struck only with a king's head and a lion passant, are common and pleasant little items. This version, which locks together to form one unit when not in use (as shown below), is comparatively rare. Sheffield, c.1800, by T. Gray.

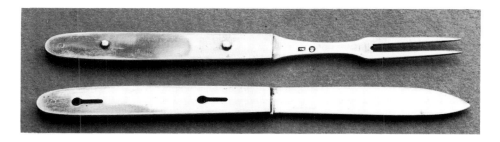

The knife and fork as one unit.

Interesting silver handled snuffers with guillotine cutter in steel. The style of the cast handles would suggest a date of c.1760 but they were assayed at London in 1830. About 18cm long. Courtesy the Michael Graeme Macdonald Collection, U.S.A.

Pair of snuffers. London, c.1702, by Matthew Cooper, 12cm long, 2oz. 1dwt., maker's mark and lion's head erased. Courtesy the Ernst and Patricia Schuckmann Collection, Colombia.

should make use if you wish to make purchases before you are reasonably experienced. At most auctions you are going to pay a buyer's premium on your purchase price, so do insist on getting satisfactory answers. But don't waste the true expert's time in asking elementary questions to which you should know the answers before starting to buy. The experts of the top auctioneers are very sound in their judgements and you will find them most helpful and kindly, despite the fact they are extremely busy. Just occasionally somebody may not wish you to bother the expert and you may find yourself palmed off with a novice: be careful.

The occasional specialised sales of small collectors' pieces conducted by the fast-growing London auction house of Phillips are also well worth your inspection even although I must warn you that at any important sale in London or the provinces it is, far more often than not, folly to buy but astute to sell. The keenest and wealthiest collectors from many parts of the world are drawn to such events, like children to lollipops. Amidst such competitive excitement unrealistic prices are often obtained. At one such auction I remember sitting next to a perfectly rational looking gentleman who was unsuccessfully bidding well over £100 each for quite ordinary mid-eighteenth century mote spoons. I was sorely tempted to offer him rather better specimens at about half the price.

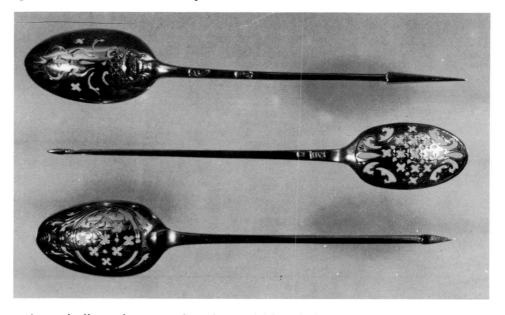

Three fine mote spoons of the mid-eighteenth century, the top specimen die-stamped on back of bowl with a double-headed eagle. Courtesy the James Aspin Collection, South Africa.

At a similar sale, a vendor changed his mind at the last moment about parting with a somewhat vulgar heavily decorated silver gilt three-piece place setting for fruit of the William IV period, one of the three utensils being struck with the mark of Paul Storr. In order not to risk losing his possession, it being then too late to withdraw the entry from auction, the vendor increased his reserve from £800 to £1,200, a ridiculous figure. Nevertheless, the item still sold at the reserve figure and the distraught vendor 'cried all the way to the bank'! It is amusing to conjecture at what figure the bidder would have given up the chase had the reserve been even higher.

There have always been obvious psychological reasons causing some dealers to outbid their rivals and it now seems that many traders, because of the acute shortage of good stock, are buying silver for short term hoarding before releasing it at further inflated prices. Add to these conditions the formidable influx, even into the provincial rooms, of many foreign traders and the spate of competitive, usually foolhardy amateurs, and you will appreciate how difficult auctions have become. Often goods now fetch more at auctions than in shops, one of the most peculiar developments of the last two decades.

A wig duster or powderer, a rare article in silver. London, 1804, maker WP (probably William Parkyns), 11.3cm high, 3oz. 15dwt. Soap boxes are of almost identical form, but would normally be rather larger. At this period (c.1800) one would expect the piercing on the lid of a soap box to be less simple in design, but a few earlier specimens have no piercing whatsoever. Courtesy the Michael Graeme Macdonald Collection, U.S.A.

Amateurs seem to believe that, should they be allowed to make a purchase at an auction, they must be winning their prize at just one bid above that of a shrewd dealer. Actually, more often than not, they are buying, at the price of a dealer's optimistic reserve, goods which he is unable to sell in his shop. It is possible that this farcical position may correct itself in due course, with amateurs wisely drifting back to reputable shops and with auctions reverting to the traditional role of supplying dealers; but such a change is unlikely to occur for some years. Nowadays, an interesting item may go through half a dozen or more dealers' hands before reaching either a collector, a West End shop or a London auction. It should be the collector's purpose, but certainly not before he is experienced, to intercept such an item quite early in its trade career and before it has become very expensive. The passing of goods from one dealer to another is due to several considerations; not the least of which is the small dealer's necessity to cash in quickly and to reinvest his money without the delays of selling at an auction house, which may take up to six months to pay.

To sum up on auction houses: they are excellent places of learning for the amateur collector, but not always the best places for purchasing.

Another way to learn about silver is to look for expert opinions on pieces you already own.

The metalwork department at the Victoria and Albert Museum, London, is a real boon to silver enthusiasts, whether dealers or amateurs. The experts will examine and offer an opinion on any item that you care to take them.

There is no charge for this splendid service, but (very correctly) they will never make valuations. You can either make an appointment to see them or call in during specified periods.

You can learn much from the best museums and books, as will be shown in your course of study but, above all, never be frightened of entering the very largest and most expensive London shops and asking to speak to the principal. A good dealer will be delighted — business considerations apart — to meet a new collector and to share some of his experience with you.

Remember, too, that you should always be prepared to contribute financially for your knowledge. A small purchase of an item recommended

Wine cup on pedestal foot. London, 1813, by W. Fountain, 11.3cm high, 4oz. 15dwt. Many symbols of patriotism were engraved on silver during this bellicose and victorious period of British history.

A playing card hand holder presumably made for a wealthy victim of the Napoleonic Wars. The practicality of this ingenious and very rare implement is self evident. Made in London, 1817, by Benjamin Smith, Senior, and Benjamin Smith, Junior. Courtesy the Worshipful Company of Goldsmiths.

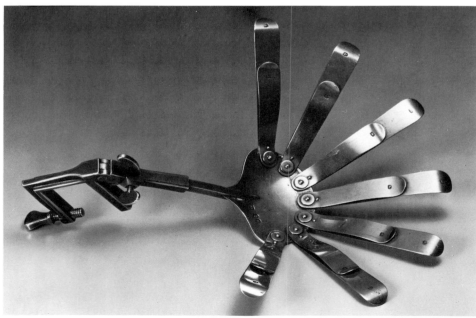

by a good dealer plus some helpful tips should together tot up to a sound investment.

However much a collector — or dealer — learns, strange situations still arise to confound his knowledge! Recently, one of the biggest London dealers bought a very plain medicine or caddy spoon of heavy gauge and fine quality, enclosed in a delightful contemporary shagreen case, for £80. It was of the mid-eighteenth century and although without hallmarks it bore the marks of a respected goldsmith. The dealer sold it for £120 and it reappeared soon afterwards in a big specialised sale of small pieces where it fetched almost £900. As I was prepared to bid up to £350 for this same spoon at the auction, I cannot believe that it was not a great bargain when it had been sold in an impressive London emporium at about one seventh of what it obtained under the hammer.

As a very general rule (and remember rules are dangerous things) poor quality pieces tend to cost less in a London shop than in a provincial shop or auction, while the reverse is true of items of real quality — which is why the latter so often find their way to London or into the collections of the discerning who intercept them on their way.

Are there still bargains?

But for the general ignorance throughout the trade — and don't forget fashionable 'dollies' or 'after tea dealers' playing at antique dealing and sometimes affording their relatives a considerable disservice by selling their silver on commission — I very much doubt if a specialist with a sense of responsibility to his customers could make a living; he must know more about his subject than his neighbours and be in a position to spot a bargain.

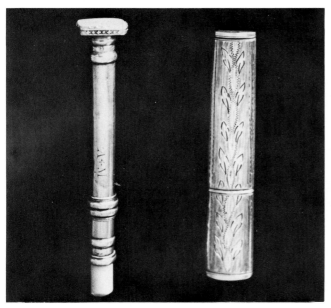

There are still plenty of genuine little collectors' pieces to find. A sealing wax holder with a crayon now fitted instead of the wax, the seal at the other end cut in blue stone. Birmingham, 1817, by John Betteridge, 8.5cm long, and a bodkin holder by Samuel Pemberton, Birmingham, c.1800, 8.8cm long. Courtesy the Charles Tarr Collection, U.S.A.

Mid-Victorian etui housed in a portmanteau-like case. London, 1870, by SM, 5.5cm long, with fitments for needlework: two bobbins (white and black cotton), spindle and needle holder. Courtesy the Dr. Colin McDonald Collection, Australia.

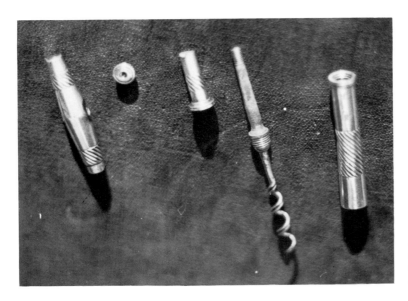

A corkscrew, all components detached, of unusual construction. Birmingham, c.1800, by J. Taylor, 8.5cm long when in use. Courtesy the Dr. Colin McDonald Collection, Australia.

A pair of circular swivelling plaques, with the likeness of Mrs. Pankhurst in high relief and stamped 'E Pluribus. Unum...1909', attached to steel pins. Birmingham, 1909, maker's mark AJS, 3.4cm diameter, 33cm long.

In the search for treasures no stone should be left unturned but, since none of us has either the resolution or life span to go to such extreme lengths, we must do the best we can. It should be remembered that every abortive expedition is one step nearer your next bargain. It is as foolish to be depressed by failure as to be unduly elated and made over-confident by success. If you keep on hunting you will be well rewarded every now and then and usually when you are least expecting it.

Many years ago I went to a country auction and arrived rather too early. Having inspected the silver on view, and to while away the time, I started fiddling with things — it irritates me when casual shoppers do the same with my stock — and happened to open the lid of one of those nineteenth century leather dressing cases. Today, such items can be worth many hundred pounds but at that time there was no value attached to them beyond the silver content of the silver-mounted and lidded glass containers, worth about 15s. in those days. From the recesses of the case my idle fingers removed a drawer and inside the drawer was a box that rattled. Amongst a quantity of hairpins I saw a silver ruler with a glorious patination. A beautifully engraved inscription in Latin upon this unmarked treasure revealed that the ruler was donated by a royal tutor to a prince upon the occasion of the latter's birthday in 1639. After looking furtively over my shoulder to see that I was not observed I replaced the box and the drawer and shut the lid of the case. I noted the lot (number 140) in my catalogue, and then repaired to the nearby hostelry.

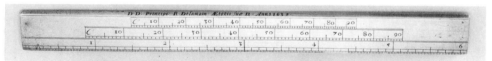

A Charles I instrument for measuring geometric chords, and embracing a six-inch ruler, engraved 'D.D: Principi: R. Delamain. Aetatis Suae 12 Anno 1639'. Later engraving on the other side 'John Harvey Esqr 1732'. Richard Delamain, a mathematician, dedicated his Grammelogia *to King Charles and was appointed tutor to the King in mathematics. Delamain presented a silver ring sundial to the Duke of York but the recipient of the gift illustrated remains untraced. Courtesy R. Finlay McCance.*

Some ninety minutes later I tore myself away from the inn, with a belated recognition that time had flown, and arrived back at the auction in a panic to hear the auctioneer calling lot 138. Lot 140 was offered and was bought by me for 15s., but before I had had time to congratulate myself the auctioneer was offering another dressing case, exactly the same, unlisted in the catalogue and termed lot 140A. Alas! Very many more of these identical dressing cases were to follow and I was obliged to buy all of them because of my uncertainty as to which one contained the ruler. By the time lot 140K had been sold the auctioneer was knocking them down to me automatically and I, not so ugly in those far off days, and perhaps a trifle effeminate in appearance, had become the butt of all the wags in the tent.

I can't remember exactly how many of those damned dressing cases I bought, but I do recall that I was stopped by the police on my return journey for my car was both overloaded and without proper visibility. It was a very

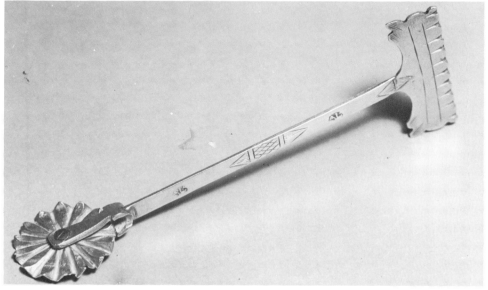

A rare pastry crimper with maker's mark only, AL, struck twice, c.1680, 18cm long. Silver is not a suitable metal for hard-used kitchen tools and I know of only one other surviving example of this early date. There are, of course, numerous eighteenth and nineteenth century examples in brass. Courtesy the Mr. and Dr. David Bayliss Collection, Hong Kong.

sobering experience, but my treasure afforded me great pleasure before it went the same way as most of the other interesting things that dealers buy...

In one respect, the private collector has an advantage over a dealer. There are a number of provincial dealers, usually sour, middle-aged spinsters, who refuse to part with anything if they suspect one is 'trade'. Knowing little or nothing themselves, they work on the principle that 'if it's worth that to him it's probably worth more to me'. Probably they're right! And yet, on the other hand, many provincial dealers of this type are inverted snobs who prefer to sell cheaply to a so-called collector — who then boasts all over town

Posset cup on spreading foot, moulded ·border and with unusually shaped handle. London, 1728, by James Goodwin, 5.8cm high, 2oz. 11dwt. Courtesy the R.M. Coffin Collection, U.S.A.

of the ignorance of the country dealer — than sell at a fair price to a dealer, who would return regularly for more interesting articles. In these circumstances, such dealers are remarkably short sighted.

The experienced collector can enter the most expensive shops and somewhere amongst the stock he is likely to find the odd something considerably below its market value: everyone slips up occasionally and sometimes dealers forget to mark up old stock in keeping with inflation.

The provincial shop specialising in furniture or porcelain, but carrying a little silver, is a highly promising covert to draw, especially if you're in time to catch the proprietor when he's just back from a private 'buy'.

There are occasional bargains to be picked up in the street markets such as Bermondsey and Portobello, on Fridays and Saturdays respectively, where some small dealers commence their activities at about 4 a.m. Nothing would induce me to attempt to buy silver by torchlight nor would I choose to rise so early. Such hours and conditions must be unsuitable to the average collector unless he is prepared to gamble in the dark.

The larger antique fairs around the country are sometimes rewarding. On the final day of such an event, I paused at the first display case on entering the hall. My eyes, which are no longer very keen ones, shot to a small circular lidded box because I was thrilled by the *warmth of its patination* even before I had scrabbled for my glasses. When you have completed your course of study, you too should be galvanised when you spot this particular quality on

Top, corkscrew with inlaid ivory handle, Birmingham, c.1790, by Samuel Pemberton. Centre (left), small porringer (toy, sample or apprentice piece) of heavy gauge, scroll handles, fully marked, London, 1795, by IG (without a shield enclosing), overall 6.5cm wide, 2.1cm high. Centre (right), caddy spoon of heavy gauge, Birmingham, 1834, by Taylor & Perry. Bottom, unmarked silver apple corer with green ivory handle, c.1790, 15cm. The use of green ivory was very popular for handles between 1788 and 1800. Courtesy The Eagle Collection, Devon.

an item lying unrecognised by others amongst a mass of junk. It is as compelling to the eyes as a sudden shaft of sunlight through a dreary mist. It is not merely avarice that sparks the thrill; it is equally the instant recognition that you would have as a parent when you have found your much loved and long lost child.

The item that I had noticed was an unmarked silver pyx of the mid-seventeenth century.

"It's only plate," the lady in charge told me, "the price is £4."

"£4?" I queried, fearful that my ears were deceiving me.

"Well, £3," she suggested.

During my life I have suffered far too many disappointments with women and, fearful that I might lose this latest prize through my customary rude over eagerness combined with a stupid diffidence, I did not behave as a gentleman and suggest a fairer price.

Instead, I said craftily, "It's really quite pretty," paid up the £3 and bolted out of the fair with my pyx without even inspecting the other stalls.

Charity shops, bazaars and white elephant stalls produce occasional bargains even though local dealers, in the hope of getting a first picking of the goods donated for sale, vie with each other to get on the list of voluntary helpers. Recently, I have seen a good Queen Anne snuff box and a George III bread basket both sold as plate. Then there is the story of the collector who bought a single George III cast candlestick in a charity shop for £10. As the assistant was wrapping it up she added a pertinent afterthought: "We've got another three of them in the back". This collector, at least, had the decency to send a handsome donation to the charity concerned.

But, please, *never forget that any very beautiful or interesting piece of silver, if in exceptionally fine condition, is always a bargain if you love it.*

What to look for

As a dealer, if the requisite funds were available, I have invariably succumbed to the temptation to pay over the odds for items which I judged to be particularly desirable from every consideration excepting price. Unbusinesslike as my actions were, and will continue to be, I have consoled myself in the knowledge of the pride and joy that their possession will certainly afford me even supposing that I were unable to sell them. In retrospect — although I do allow that inflation may have been responsible — I realise that in no such transaction have I ever lost money although, in a few cases I did not take my profit before many pleasurable months of ownership had passed. Customers have often found me looking rather gloomy.

"I've just sold one of my nicest pieces," I explain.

"Isn't that what you want to do?"

"No, but I have to. However, I think it's gone to a good home." We depart for a drink and the world then looks rosier.

In the course of my travels in pursuit of silver, I have inspected innumerable stocks in shops and antique fairs throughout the country, and have also seen a number of private collections. I think it would be useful to present my observations and comments on the type of stock I have come across in statistical form. With this before our eyes, we can discuss it. I have not seen many stocks overseas, but I have watched what the dealers from overseas buy in the United Kingdom.

Quality of silver items/stocks held by private individuals, dealers, antique fairs, etc.

	Average private collection in U.K.	Average dealer's stock in U.K.	Average dealer's stock in N. America	Average dealer's stock in Europe	Average stock in top class antique fair/ London shop
Forgeries	5%	5%	8%	10%	0%
Altered pieces	15%	15%	22%	30%	5%[1]
Serious repairs (visible)	5%	5%	0%	0%	5%[2]
Serious repairs (hidden)	25%	25%	25%	25%	5%
Lesser repairs or second quality	35%	35%	35%	30%	35%
Good quality	10%	10%	5%	5%	30%
Superb quality	5%	5%	5%	0%	20%

1 A number of later-decorated pieces might be stocked.
2 Exceptionally rare items in poor condition might be stocked.

Obviously, the amount of good quality silver remaining in this country (apart from that which is safely on display in museums or concealed in banks) is decreasing. It does not take many years of everyday rough use to reduce silver from a superb state to a secondary condition, and museums from overseas can often outbid everyone when important items come on the market (export licences are occasionally withheld from items of national importance). Knowledgeable or well-advised private collectors from all corners of the earth frequently by-pass their local retailers and buy direct from London. It is certain that really good English silver is already in desperately short supply and the demand for it is keen.

All of us must surely have had some experience of collecting, whether it be of postage stamps, butterflies or sea shells. If, as a true collector, you had the free choice of seventeen mediocre shells or of one superb specimen, which would you choose?

Your answer reflects the precise reason why, according to a recent sale catalogue, a very poor George II pear shaped cream jug was knocked down for £40 while a fine example of the same style obtained £700. However long you live, however important your collections may become, you will never tire of an outstanding example of old silver, even if it be nothing more than a humble mid-Georgian tea spoon which cost you £10.

New collectors are advised to develop their knowledge of silver on a broad basis and as comprehensively as their pockets and inclinations suggest. It must be a mistake to restrict your experiences by specialising in just one or two specific items, which are easily available and much collected, however appealing they may seem. Such fashionable items, and I am thinking of Victorian caddy spoons and vinaigrettes, etc., may seem to be very over-priced in comparison with much rarer and more interesting pieces. By reading this book, you are showing a willingness to bother to learn about our subject and thereby to benefit from the encouraging fact that rare items do not necessarily always obtain a realistic price until they are offered for sale before the expertise of an important London auction.

My confident advice to collectors is to buy the best, whatever it is and whenever you find it, either with good hallmarks, with maker's mark only or with no marks whatsoever, and don't worry too much about the price because *the best is rare.*

A rare condiment spoon of plain trifid form with rat tail bowl, thick gauge. London, c.1680, maker's mark only, probably by Francis Garthorne, 9.5cm. Courtesy Phillips.

CHAPTER 2

The evolution of style:
a pictorial record

Styles of silver — and by styles we think of the shapes of articles and their decoration — have never evolved throughout the ages as rapidly as, for example, the fashions pertaining to motor cars during the last nine decades or so. It is therefore much easier for someone who understands silver, even without glancing at the hallmarks, to recognise the approximate decade of any item of antique silver (unless it should be a faithful reproduction of an earlier style) than it is for the motor enthusiast to recognise the precise year of manufacture of a vintage car.

With silver, between the fruition and withering of each style and the budding of the next, there is almost invariably a transitional era as the developing idea of the morrow first intrudes on the vogue of today. These transitional periods, after a little study, are just as easy to recognise as established styles and, in a sense, they are often beautiful styles in their own right.

By the end of the Civil War, there was little early silver left in the country, but the evidence of its artistic merit, although scant, remains truly formidable. A number of events, all inevitably entailing the immediate or subsequent melting of plate, include the looting by William the Conqueror of his newly won territories, the Wars of the Roses in the fifteenth century, numerous compulsory loans demanded by Tudor and Stuart sovereigns, (Henry VIII being particularly rapacious), the Dissolution of the Monasteries when the sovereign seized all the monastic plate, the Civil War when both combatants, desperate through lack of funds, melted all the silver they could collect (the Roundheads even destroyed the crown and sceptre), and, in 1666, the Fire of London.

Changes of styles throughout the ages resulted in the refashioning of plate. Thus, for example, Romanesque silver, of which few examples remain, was presumably melted down and refashioned into Gothic style items, and these in turn altered to conform to the Renaissance taste. The attitude of past owners towards their secular plate also left much to be desired. Instead of regarding their treasures as works of art to be preserved and passed on to heirs, they were valued chiefly as investments superior to coins, which were sometimes counterfeit or chipped, and hoarded as an insurance against difficult times.

So it was human need and cupidity, common bedfellows, rather than the wear and tear of time, that denuded us of our plate. Apart from early spoons (see opposite), which often avoided seizure by concealment, and a few examples of ecclesiastical plate, even the resourceful collector is most unlikely to discover silver prior to the Civil War.

With the Restoration, the pre-eminence of goldsmiths seems to have faded, with some justification, even although there was an increased demand

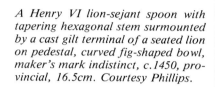

A Henry VI lion-sejant spoon with tapering hexagonal stem surmounted by a cast gilt terminal of a seated lion on pedestal, curved fig-shaped bowl, maker's mark indistinct, c.1450, provincial, 16.5cm. Courtesy Phillips.

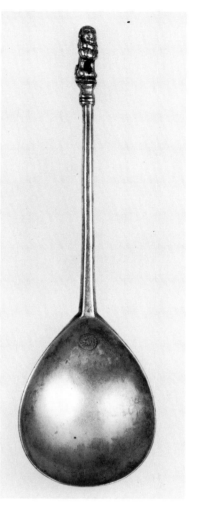

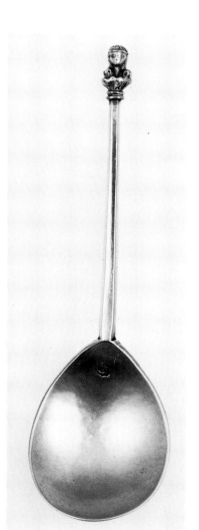

A late medieval English diamond point spoon with tapering hexagonal stem and diamond point finial, fig-shaped curved bowl, 15.2cm. Courtesy Phillips.

A Henry VIII maidenhead spoon with hexagonal tapering stem, possibly made by Lawrence Gilbert of Ipswich, c.1520, 16.3cm. Courtesy Phillips.

for their services. Denuded of their silver, the nobility, merchants, smaller landowners and gentry wished to restock their boards and there probably developed at this period, somewhat ironically, a new awareness of the desirability of retaining silver for aesthetic satisfaction (see below and opposite). The goldsmiths were undoubtedly in a difficult position because their metal (despite imports from South America which were augmented by the melting

Footed salver with porringer and cover chased with animals, acanthus leaves and tulips. London, 1668, diameter of dish 38cm. The inscription around the royal armorials relates to a presentation by King Charles II at the launching of His Majesty's ship The Royal Charles *on 5th April, 1668. Courtesy the Worshipful Company of Goldsmiths.*

of English, and sometimes foreign, coins — a cheaper and already refined source of silver) was in short supply and there were many orders to fulfil at speed. In consequence, many articles were fabricated from a thin gauge and there was often much hasty and frequently rather crude embossing to present a false impression of substance. Such work, although interesting, valuable and attractive to collectors, obviously lacked the quality of earlier silver.

How things would have continued is anyone's guess had not the revocation of the Edict of Nantes (1685) caused an influx of skilled craftsmen to Britain. These Huguenot refugees, working at first in bitter competition with the natives and thus forcing them to respond to the challenge, provided a favourable influence on our domestic silver. From the time of the Huguenots' arrival and throughout most of the eighteenth century many works of art were again created. Following the slightly fussy 'tulip and

A Restoration trinket box in memory of Charles I. This rare piece has nine English enamels inset on the lid of the box and one on the underside of the lid. These are probably emblematic of Charles' descendants and of his own death respectively. The filigree was probably worked by Italian craftsmen hired by English smiths when silver for solid items was in short supply. English, 4cm high, 7cm diameter, c.1665, unmarked. Courtesy the James Aspin Collection, South Africa.

The feet on the body of the trinket box, and a bird's eye view of the enamels (the heart shape below the central enamel is not in fact an enamel).

The macabre enamel on the underside of the lid of the trinket box.

acanthus' motif of the post-Restoration period, the popular taste turned to simplicity of design in the early years of the eighteenth century.

In due course the student may decide that after the middle of the eighteenth century the quality, design and craftsmanship of our goldsmiths began to deteriorate. Despite the magnificent creations of Paul Storr and several contemporary goldsmiths at the outset of the nineteenth century, a sterility of inspiration and a lack of quality usually associated with mass production seemed to set in. The artistry of John Edwards, who seems to me to be an underrated goldsmith, was not often equalled by his contemporaries (see below right). The feminine designs of Hester Bateman (see below left) are much prized throughout the world, but the craftsmanship of some of her multitudinous staff and apprentices, in a factory seemingly geared for quantity rather than perfection, was certainly often disappointing.

The Victorian age, meeting the demands of a newly rich society, produced the maximum ostentation for the minimum cost; as we have noticed, it was notorious, especially in the first quarter of the reign, for the pitiful ruination by fussy decoration of many fine earlier examples.

It is suggested that readers should now spend some time studying the illustrations between pages 43 and 65. A few examples of silver prior to the Restoration in 1660 are shown, but thereafter you will find a good selection of subsequent examples, especially of the late seventeenth century and eighteenth century, up to the mid-1800s. The examples are arranged, as far as is practical, by date. If you can remember all you see, you will then be in a good position to acquit yourself with distinction in the picture quiz in Chapter 13.

A distinctive and delightful mustard pot by Hester Bateman with urn motifs, garlands and bead edges, representing the popular taste of the period. London, 1780. Courtesy the Worshipful Company of Goldsmiths.

Tureen and cover. London, 1805, by John Edwards. The arms are for Chambers with Polhill in pretence. R.J. Chambers of Middle Temple married Elizabeth Polhill of Horbury Park, Yorkshire. Courtesy the M. Walecki Collection.

The bottom (left) of the Founder's Cup has a shield bearing Bishop Bateman's arms in coloured enamels, now considerably damaged. In each of the three spandrels between the arches surrounding the arms a winged dragon is depicted. The arms are repeated on the vessel's base (right).

Covered beaker presented to Trinity Hall, Cambridge, 1350, by William Bateman and known as the Founder's Cup. The vessel is 10.7cm high. The moulded foot and girdles are enriched with a tooth motif, while the cover has a battlemented rim, but the finial, once supposed to have contained a jewel, is incomplete. Courtesy Trinity Hall, Cambridge.

Ewer and basin, gilt. London, 1545, maker's mark a queen's head crowned within a shaped cartouche (the ewer made en suite at a later date), diameter of basin 45.7cm. The broad band of arabesques on the rim and the raised boss in the centre with the owner's coat of arms in enamels are the most typical features of the period. Courtesy the Worshipful Company of Goldsmiths.

Left, communion cup and cover with tapering bowl engraved with arabesques; knopped stem and pedestal foot; the cover has a flat finial upon which it can stand when removed from the cup. London, 1570, 21cm high, 12oz. Courtesy Sotheby's.

Right, standing cup. London, 1616, 31cm high. Fine baluster stem, hemispherical bowl and spreading foot. Courtesy the Worshipful Company of Goldsmiths.

A rare late Elizabethan casting bottle, unmarked, height from foot to top of domed screw cover 10.25cm. The bottle is formed from two silver-mounted cowrie shells, with a petalled flange above the spreading circular foot. The shells are supported by four reeded ribs surmounted by two grotesque mask loop handles with rings above presumably for attachment to a chatelaine. It is possible that this bottle was used to contain an absorbent sand, the precursor to blotting paper.

Three-footed lobed basin with cover and standing-finial of similar motif. With an internal spice strainer, this very rare article was used with mulled wine. London, 1640, 16.5cm high, diameter 30.5cm. Courtesy the Worshipful Company of Goldsmiths.

Tapering cylindrical beaker engraved with sprays of thistles and scrolling leafage, on rim foot. London, 1641, 12.7cm high, 8oz. 15dwt. Courtesy Sotheby's.

Sweetmeat dish embossed with panels surrounding floral motifs, the handles designed as shells. London, 1652, 19.2cm across the handles but weight only 2oz. 10dwt. Courtesy Sotheby's.

Small beaker flat chased with tulip motifs. London, 1656, by Gilbert Shepherd, 5cm, 1oz. 5dwt. Courtesy Sotheby's.

Caudle cup and cover with disc (standing) finial, chased with fruit, flowers and foliage, scroll and bead handles. London, 1663, 12cm high, 11oz. 12dwt. Courtesy Sotheby's.

An early snuffer tray chased with stylised foliage and acanthus leaves. London, 1669, 23.5cm wide. Snuffers, London, c.1680. Combined weight 10oz. 16dwt. The tray is attractive and seemingly perfect, and the two pieces may possibly be worth five figures in a few years. Courtesy Sotheby's.

The Hanbury Cup and Cover. London, 1665, by Arthur Mainwaring. The spreading foot is less domed than it was likely to have been some twenty years earlier. Courtesy the Worshipful Company of Goldsmiths.

Campaign or travelling set of knife, fork, marrow spoon and fitted filigree case. London, c.1670, maker's mark II, about 13cm long. Courtesy the James Aspin Collection, South Africa.

Peg tankard. York, 1670, by Marmaduke Best. Each drinker was presumably expected to drink to the level of each peg, no further, before handing the vessel on to his immediate neighbour. This is the Scandinavian form of tankard (notice the pomegranate feet) found principally in York as a result of the North Sea trade. Courtesy the Worshipful Company of Goldsmiths.

Wine taster. London, 1674, with simple loop handles and chased with grapes and scrolls. A frail but pretty little piece with a repair beside one of the handles. Courtesy the Worshipful Company of Goldsmiths.

Tapered cylindrical tankard, the slightly domed lid chased with floral border and with cast twin dolphin thumb piece to scroll handle. London, 1679, maker's mark IC, 17.2cm high, 25oz. 3dwt. Not a large tankard so weight satisfactory. Courtesy Sotheby's.

Three porringers of a remarkably satisfactory weight for size in this period. They all afford typical examples of the chasing which was to remain a popular taste for another decade. Left, London, 1681, 9cm high, 7oz. 9dwt. Centre, London, 1683, 12cm high, 18oz. 18dwt. Right, London, 1683, 9.5cm, 10oz. This porringer has armorials with foliate mantling at the front and armorials within plumage mantling at the rear. Courtesy Sotheby's.

Tankard with curved body and cut card decoration, heavy lobed border to foot and rim, slightly domed cover with foliate knop, remarkable double scroll fluted handle. London, 1684, 12cm high. Notice the split centre top of body. Courtesy the Worshipful Company of Goldsmiths.

Mug of heavy gauge with tapering cylindrical body flat chased with chinoiseries between ribbed bands, beaded handle. London, 1682, by Benjamin Pyne, 9.5cm high, 11oz. 4dwt. Courtesy Sotheby's.

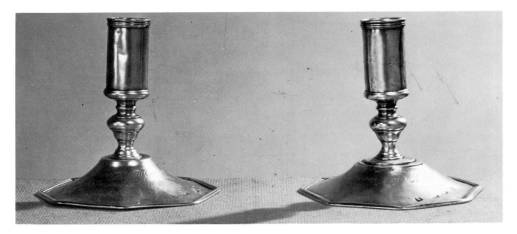

Pair of candlesticks from a toilet service, on spreading domed feet, baluster stems and cylindrical sconces. London, 1686, by George Garthorne, only 11.5cm high. Simpler than so many of the styles of this period, these delightful little pieces are scarcely instructional to the student of design except to indicate that we should be prepared for surprises in all periods of silver. Courtesy the Worshipful Company of Goldsmiths.

Monteith bowl chased into eight panels, flat chased with chinoiseries beneath an applied foliate rim. London, 1689, diameter 28.2cm, 31oz. 12dwt. Courtesy Sotheby's.

An early gilt teapot. London, 1690, by Sir Richard Hoare, 14cm high. The style has been frequently copied in this century. Courtesy the Victoria and Albert Museum.

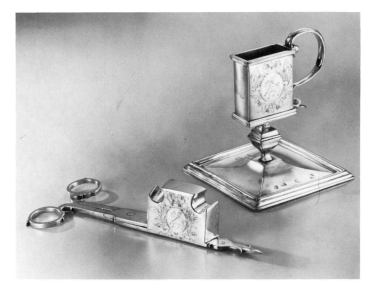

Pair of snuffers and stand, engraved with the device of the Middle Temple, with heavy applied mouldings on stand. The contemporary snuffers, without marks, fit into the stand. London, 1690, stand 10.1cm high. Courtesy the Worshipful Company of Goldsmiths.

Scotland produced much fine silver. A thistle-shaped mug with moulded girdles, straps and egg and disc decorated loop handle. Edinburgh, 1694, by James Cockburne, 7.6cm, 5oz. 12dwt. Courtesy Sotheby's.

English wine tasters in this form are rare; the domed centre and flared sides reveal the colour of the wine to the best advantage. London, 1695, diameter 10.10cm, 3oz. 3dwt. Courtesy Sotheby's.

Helmet-shaped ewer with the gadrooned girdle around upper body, further enriched by cut card work above gadrooning. London, 1697, by Pierre Harache, 26.7cm high. Courtesy the Worshipful Company of Goldsmiths.

The style of decoration on this tankard is common during this period. London, 1697, by Philip Roker, 23cm high, 42oz. 12dwt. Courtesy Sotheby's.

Fine tobacco box engraved with the arms of John Holles, Earl of Clare and Duke of Newcastle. London, 1702, by Nathaniel Lock, 8.8cm diameter, 6oz. Courtesy the Michael Graeme Macdonald Collection, U.S.A.

Rare set of three oblong-octagonal castors. London, 1703, by Matthew Cooper, 18.5cm and 15.5cm high, 16oz. Courtesy the Ernst and Patricia Schuckmann Collection, Colombia.

A particularly interesting silver mounted tortoise-shell tobacco box. The brickwork engraving which, when considered with the remainder of the scrolling ornamentation of the late seventeenth century, must date the box no later than c.1705, may be one of the earliest examples of brickwork engraving, which is normally associated with the 1710-30 era. Such boxes are usually opened by a simple squeeze action at both ends, but here we have an ingenious wrought-iron spring fastener which releases the lid when the silver-capped button is pressed. 9cm long. Courtesy the Ernst and Patricia Schuckmann Collection, Colombia.

Sugar castors on flared moulded pedestal feet with moulded girdles. The domed covers are delightfully pierced in foliate motifs below urn or bell-like finials. London, 1706, 15.5cm high, 13oz. 10dwt. Courtesy Sotheby, King and Chasemore.

Centre, octagonal castor of baluster form. London, 1717, by Glover Johnson, 17.8cm high, 6oz. 13dwt. Two pairs of cast octagonal matching table candlesticks, London, 1715, both pairs by Joseph Bird and Thomas Merry, 19.2cm high, 24oz. 6dwt. The two goldsmiths must have been working in conjunction. Courtesy Sotheby's.

Toilet box, gilt, c.1710, engraved with the arms of Calne, Wiltshire, within a contemporary cartouche. The sides and border of lid engraved at a later date, possibly c.1750, or possibly when this box was presented to the town by Lord Shelburne, M.P. for Calne from 1847 to 1856. Courtesy the Worshipful Company of Goldsmiths.

A chamber pot typical of the plain lines of the period. London, 1716, by Simon Pantin, 19.8cm in diameter. It is said that these 'nécessaires' were used in dining rooms rather than in bed chambers. Courtesy the Worshipful Company of Goldsmiths.

A tea pot in the pleasant octagonal style of the Britannia period, domed lid surmounted by wooden finial, wooden handle. Wood does not appear to have been used extensively with silver until the eighteenth century. London, 1715, by Samuel Wastell, 13.3cm high. Courtesy the Worshipful Company of Goldsmiths.

Salver of octafoil shape. London, 1729, by Abraham Buteux, diameter 48.9cm. The arms are those of the City of Chester within a baroque cartouche. Courtesy the Worshipful Company of Goldsmiths.

Salver engraved with arms in lozenge (for a woman), flanked by supporters and beneath a coronet (for Margaretta, Countess of Cadogan), the border engraved with masks and vases of flowers within a Chippendale rim. London, 1730, by Samuel Lea, diameter 30.5cm, 33oz. 2dwt. Courtesy Sotheby's.

An interesting spherical tea kettle showing conventional rocaille decoration in addition to floral pendant swags. We would not expect to see swags of this type at this period from anywhere but Ireland. Dublin, c.1735, by James West. Courtesy Sotheby's.

Flat chased decoration on a silver taper-stick. London, 1736, by Gawen Nash, 10.75cm high, 40oz. 5dwt. This type of decoration on silver 'sticks is rare, being more usual on brass examples of the period.

Bread basket with everted body pierced with diaper motifs, spreading base pierced with scrolls, swing handle, engraved with crest (usually armorials on most examples) within. London, 1737, by George Wickes, 37cm wide, 79oz. Courtesy the Worshipful Company of Goldsmiths.

Pair of candlesticks. London, 1737, by George Wickes. Notice the early rococo cartouches on the bases. About 21cm high. Courtesy the Worshipful Company of Goldsmiths.

Jacobite snuff mull formed by alternating strips of ivory and ebony, three-lug hinge. Unmarked, first half of eighteenth century, 8.3cm tall, 8.5cm wide at top. It is a common belief that these mulls provided a secret sign to establish recognition between adherents of the Jacobite cause. They were supposed to have been clasped in the palm of the hand with the thumb concealing the top of the box until the moment of disclosure.

Cup and cover of remarkably fine applied work and superlative balance, the cover and foot embossed and chased with scrolls, shells, grapes and leaves, vase finial overflowing with the produce of the vine. London, c.1739, by Frederick Kandler, struck only with the maker's mark four times on the base and twice on cover, 34.8cm high. Courtesy the Worshipful Company of Goldsmiths.

Rare baluster beer jug. Limerick, c.1740, by Joseph Johns, 19.7cm, 24oz. 6dwt. Joseph Johns was a Sheriff and Mayor of Limerick. The arms are for Singleton (John) impaling d'Alton (Marcella). Courtesy Sotheby's.

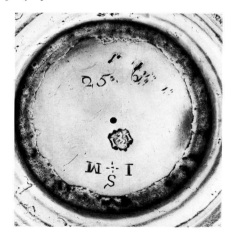

The base of the beer jug, showing the maker's mark, the original pricked weight (25oz. 6dwt.) and initials S over I.M. which must relate to John and Marcella Singleton.

A pair of heavy sauce boats on three volute feet headed by rococo heads, the body applied with cast swags beneath a waved gadroon border, scroll work handle. London, 1744, by Peter Archambo, 24.3cm wide, 47oz. 18dwt. Courtesy Sotheby's.

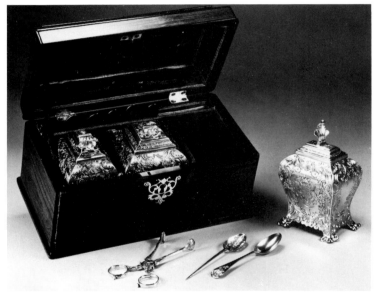

A pair of tea caddies and a sugar box in a fitted case with hinged finials to the lids. London, 1749, by Elizabeth Godfrey. Courtesy the Worshipful Company of Goldsmiths.

Tea caddy. London, 1747, by Paul de Lamerie, 14cm high. The body is embossed with Chinese rococo and the piece has all the magnificence of the master craftsman in this rocaille period. Courtesy the Worshipful Company of Goldsmiths.

This cream jug could come from nowhere but Ireland with its characteristic helmet shape on three lion mask and paw feet — unless it were a reproduction. Dublin, c.1750, by Samuel Walker. Courtesy the James Aspin Collection, South Africa.

A pair of tapersticks. London, 1749, by John Cafe, a specialist in the making of 'sticks, about 12.5cm tall, 9oz. By this date some 'sticks had detachable nozzles, perhaps to prevent wax falling on the hands whilst being carried. Courtesy the Eagle Collection, Devon.

Coffee pot. London, 1754, by Thomas Whipham, 34oz. This fine pot has a fluted bird's neck spout on an otherwise plain design. Courtesy the Michael Graeme Macdonald Collection, U.S.A.

Four fine and attractive table spoons of c.1755 with the backs of the bowls die-struck with shells, shell and scrolls and a basket of flowers. These are all quite common motifs and are well worth collecting. Ideally, each tablespoon should weigh at least 1oz. 15dwt.

Oval soup tureen and cover. Bulbous body on four hoof feet headed by bulls' masks, drop ring handles suspended from lions' masks, wolf crest finial above typical chased decoration. London, 1755, by William Cripps, 98oz. 16dwt. Courtesy Sotheby's.

Tankard. Newcastle, 1759, with maker's mark of Samuel James. Gadroon decoration was back again in favour. Courtesy the Worshipful Company of Goldsmiths.

A rare and large punch strainer. Dublin, c.1760, by Mathias Brown, with maker's mark, harp and Hibernia, 29.3cm across the handles. Courtesy the James Aspin Collection, South Africa.

Tea urn. London, 1760, by Samuel Courtauld. One of the last works of the late rocaille period when one might think that this style had become degenerate. Nevertheless, the piece remains balanced to the eye and devoid of the 'stiffness'' of the Victorians. Courtesy the Worshipful Company of Goldsmiths.

Four salt cellars. Dublin, c.1765, by J. Walker. Courtesy the James Aspin Collection, South Africa.

Pair of candlesticks. London, 1771, by John Cafe, 24.5cm high. Courtesy the James Aspin Collection, South Africa.

Pair of tapersticks. London, 1761, by William Cafe, 15.5cm high. Courtesy the Worshipful Company of Goldsmiths.

Gilt cup and cover. London, 1771, by Thomas Heming, 32.9cm high. An interesting transitional piece between rococo and classicism. Courtesy the Worshipful Company of Goldsmiths.

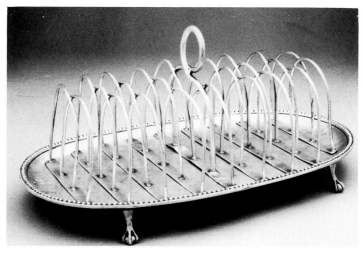

Cream jug. Dublin, c.1772, by Matthew West. Notice how the rococo is still found at this late date in Dublin. Courtesy the James Aspin Collection, South Africa.

Large oval toast rack. London, 1774, by Charles Aldridge and Henry Green. Each section of the toast rack is detachable for cleaning. Courtesy the Michael Graeme Macdonald Collection, U.S.A.

A pair of openwork coasters, each with ivory boss in centre of wooden base. London, 1775. Courtesy the Kent Karslake Collection.

Epergne formed as an open pagoda with classical columns, swags of laurels interspersed with the device of Liverpool (this fine piece belongs to the Corporation of the City of Liverpool). The baskets and dishes from lesser epergnes frequently appear on the market at reasonable prices and they are usually marked with a lion passant and maker's mark only. This fine specimen was made at London in 1775 by James Young. Courtesy the Worshipful Company of Goldsmiths.

A group of five pepper castors illustrating styles. Left to right, London, 1795. London, 1781 by Hester Bateman. London, 1783. London, 1754. London, 1763. Notice the worn beading on the central example and the patch in the side of the example second from right. Courtesy Sotheby, King and Chasemore.

These fine bread baskets made by Wakelin & Taylor of London between 1781 and 1785 are uncommon, but identical specimens appear in several important collections; this example is dated 1781 and weighs almost 40oz. The rim of the bowl is formed by three narrow bands of husks and the diameter is 27.25cm. Courtesy the James Aspin Collection, South Africa.

A wine cup on trumpet foot, London, 1785, by Hester Bateman, 15.2cm high, 5oz. A pair of wine coasters on wood backed silver bases, the sides pierced with geometric designs, London, 1773, by Philip Freeman, diameter 12.7cm. Courtesy Sotheby's.

Tea pot. London, 1784, by William Vincent. This is the standard form of tea pot during this period. Courtesy the Michael Graeme Macdonald Collection, U.S.A.

Sugar basket, London, 1785, by Robert Hennell. The initial in the bright cut cartouche is of later date. Helmet cream jug of typical form, London, 1784, by Benjamin Mountique. Courtesy the James Aspin Collection, South Africa.

Cup and cover. London, 1785, by Daniel Smith and Robert Sharp. Courtesy the Worshipful Company of Goldsmiths.

Salver with bead edge and bright cut decoration, the centre engraved with a monogram. London, 1785, by James Young, diameter 28cm. An illustration of the marks on this item appears on page 131. Courtesy the Worshipful Company of Goldsmiths.

A pioneer style. Many will decide that the tapering lines of this fine tankard, made some twelve years before the style was generally adopted, are superior to the later versions of the same motif. London, 1786, by Andrew Fogelberg (to whom Paul Storr was apprenticed) and Stephen Gilbert, 30oz., height (overall) 18.7cm.

A pair of wine cups, London, 1788, by John Denzilow, 14.5cm high, 12oz. 17dwt. Wine ewer, London, 1787, by John Schofield, 22.7cm high, 19oz. 14dwt. Courtesy Sotheby's.

Coffee pot. London, 1789, by Henry Chawner. Courtesy the Worshipful Company of Goldsmiths.

Vase-shaped hot water jug on reeded spreading foot, the lower part of the bowl with shallow bats' wing flutes and the lid surmounted with a finial of ostrich feathers. London, 1792, by Paul Storr. Courtesy Christie's.

Typical styles of the late eighteenth century: Left, boat-shaped sweetmeat basket marked on basket and handle, London, 1789, by Robert Hennell, 15.9cm wide, 4oz. 13dwt. Centre, boat-shaped sugar basket without the more usual swing handle, London, 1790, by Charles Hougham, 13.5cm wide, 6oz. 7dwt. Right, sweetmeat basket marked on base and handle, London, 1791, 13.3cm wide, 6oz. 4dwt., rather light for size. Courtesy Sotheby's.

An oval tray finely engraved below reeded rim with a band of interlaced bright cut foliage, the centre with armorials within drapery mantling. London, 1792, by Crouch & Hannam, 50.3cm wide overall, 48oz. 19dwt. Courtesy Sotheby's.

Globe inkstand hung with floral swags. The upper part swings back to reveal two silver-mounted wells, a pen and tablet. London, 1792, by John Robins, 16.6cm high. Courtesy Sotheby's.

Chamberstick with reeded rims and bright cut decoration on the stem and extinguisher. London, 1795, by Crouch & Hannam. Courtesy the Michael Graeme Macdonald Collection, U.S.A.

A heavy dish ring of about 17oz. Dublin, 1796, by John Power. Whereas in England dish crosses were normally used, this type of ring (incorrectly called a potato ring) was popular in Ireland from c.1760 and varied little in the general form of decoration. Courtesy the James Aspin Collection, South Africa.

A popular style from 1795 to c.1815 in the form of a tankard decorated with bands of fluting (mugs were more usual than tankards). London, 1797, by Peter and Anne Bateman, 18.5cm high, 26oz. 6dwt., a good average weight for size. Courtesy Sotheby's.

Coffee pot. London, 1802, by John Robins. Courtesy the Kent Karslake Collection.

A fine inkstand. London, 1803, by Digby Scott and Benjamin Smith, 35cm long. Courtesy the Worshipful Company of Goldsmiths.

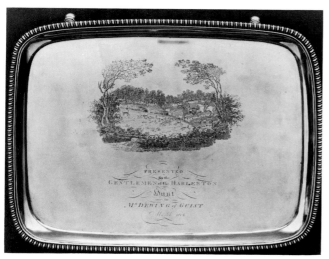

Sauce boats. London, 1812, by Crespin Fuller. Courtesy the Michael Graeme Macdonald Collection, U.S.A.

An oblong salver. Newcastle, 1808, by Anne Robertson. embracing an unusual gadrooned collar above the ball feet Engraved by Thomas Bewick with a scene depicting hounds moving on to draw a covert. Courtesy the Victoria and Albert Museum.

Scottish provincial plaid holder of pierced form, the border set with foiled crystal imitating amethysts and citrines, the centre with quatrefoil designs surrounding a domed rock crystal. Inverness, c.1815, by Robert Naughton, 11.5cm diameter. Courtesy Phillips.

One of a pair of seven light candelabra. London, 1814, by Paul Storr. Many years ago the author bought a very similar piece by the same maker at a London auction for 2s. per ounce, paying £70 in total. When he collected this massive piece, he found it so heavy that he soon tired of his burden and entering the nearest suitable shop sold it, with much relief, for 2s. 3d. per ounce. Courtesy the Worshipful Company of Goldsmiths.

Robert Naughton was a fine provincial silversmith of the early nineteenth century. With stylised leaves and flowers, this bell is an outstanding piece. Inverness, c.1815, marked on side of bell with maker's and town mark and with maker's mark struck on clapper. Courtesy the Michael Graeme Macdonald Collection, U.S.A.

Pair of heavy silver-gilt cast fruit serving spoons. London, 1816, by Edward Farrell, 21.5cm, 8oz. (the pair). It is interesting to note that this impressive goldsmith is omitted from Jackson.

Heavy Scottish punch ladle with turned wood handle. Edinburgh, 1822, by J. Mackay. Engraved in bowl, within a shell and scroll border, are the inscrutable words: 'To W.A. Ritchie, Esq., by the Exposers of — Nether Monynut, in Berwickshire, Nov. 1822'. Courtesy the Eagle Collection, Devon.

Mustard pot of fine quality with applied foliate border above strapwork and quatrefoil motifs. London, 1837, by Charles Fox (a good maker), 7.7cm high, 4oz. 12dwt. Courtesy Sotheby's.

A set of four candlesticks. London, 1839, by W. Garrard, 184oz. Courtesy Sotheby's.

One of the many attractive Victorian items, a very rare ortolan or wheatear basket. London, 1850, by Robert Hennell. Courtesy the Worshipful Company of Goldsmiths.

Pair of candlesticks. London, 1853, by C.T. Fox and G. Fox, 22cm high, 29oz. Courtesy the Ernst and Patricia Schuckmann Collection, Colombia.

Typical Victorian engraving and chasing on a milk jug. London, 1860. Courtesy the Kent Karslake Collection.

CHAPTER 3

Small collectable silver: late 17th century to c.1900

Let us now look at some of the various types of small collectable silver that are available to the collector. Many of these items will reflect the forms and decorations which we have seen in the previous chapter, and with which the reader may now be feeling more familiar.

Mote spoons range in date from c.1690-1790 and until a painting of about 1720 came to light, some forty years ago, showing a mote spoon (or mote strainer) positioned with other accoutrements for taking tea, this little item was thought to be — and was therefore used as — an olive spoon. The olive was a rare delicacy during the eighteenth and nineteenth centuries in this country and those few olive spoons that we find of English manufacture, although identical in style to the mote spoon were, like their French counterparts, very much larger, about the size of a small table spoon, and thus easily distinguishable. The olive spoon would have proved unsuitable for skimming small particles of leaf or dust floating in the tiny cups of the eighteenth century for their diameter is only marginally larger than the straining section of the olive spoon.

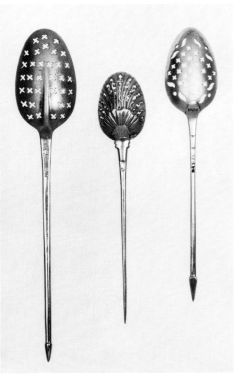

Mote spoons, from left to right: with rat-tailed bowl pierced with crosslet motifs, London, c.1726, by Edward Jennings, 17cm. The intermediate size of this example suggests that it might be an olive spoon rather than a mote spoon. It would be awkward, although not impossible, to skim period tea cups of small diameter with a bowl so large in comparison. Centre, a cast mote spoon, London, c.1745, 12.7cm. Right, a late fully marked mote spoon, London, 1785, by Hester Bateman, 13.7cm. This is the earliest fully marked mote spoon that the author has seen.

The mote spoon appeared some thirty years after the introduction into this country in 1657 of Chinese tea in bulk quantity. The earliest mote spoon that I have handled, dating about 1690, had a spike-like stem with simple perforations cut in its bowl, which was shaped like that of a trifid spoon of the period, but lacking the usual rat tail support. Not surprisingly, considering the slenderness of the stem, it was unmarked. During the Britannia period of silver, with mote spoons of very slightly sturdier proportions, we sometimes see successful or partially successful attempts to punch a lion's head erased on the slender stem. The punching of a harp was also bravely attempted at the Dublin Assay Office but without many 'bulls' eyes'!

From about 1719 most goldsmiths started to cut the perforations of the bowls in attractive designs; at the same time barbs, varying considerably in style, replaced the spiked terminals of earlier examples. These were probably intended not only to dislodge the clogging leaves but also to trap and remove the larger leaves from the tea after they had fully served their purpose. The precious tea leaves of the seventeenth and first part of the eighteenth centuries were, most probably, dried whole and, when infused, expanded to their original size. Drawn by the egress of the liquid as the tea was poured from the pot, the leaves must have caused a constant nuisance as they assembled over the grille at the base of the spout. Some grilles to spouts on the bullet-shaped tea pots (c.1720-40) were, although hidden from sight, attractively pierced in scrolls, etc., similar to the bowls of mote spoons but rather larger, and these would not have restrained leaves, if powdery, from entering the spout (see illustration opposite).

66

Bullet tea pot. London, 1729, by Thomas Tearle, 11.9cm high, 11oz. Courtesy the Ernst and Patricia Schuckmann Collection, Colombia.

The interior of the tea pot, showing the cut grille below the spout in the style of the piercing of a mote spoon bowl.

Mote spoons, throughout their period of use, were generally made *en suite* with tea spoons and thus, during the period 1740-80, they frequently had pictures stamped on the back of their bowls to match their set of tea spoons (see p. 14). As the delights of a 'cuppa' became enjoyed by far greater numbers towards the middle of the eighteenth century, the crating of entire leaves in bulk must have become rare because of its impracticability. This fact and the innovation of the tea strainer of modern form in about 1790, must have been the reasons why the mote spoon became obsolete, although a few fully marked examples of the early nineteenth century do still turn up occasionally.

Sugar nips have been manufactured ever since c.1675. Like mote spoons, they have appeared in many different styles to please the customer, but as many of the early types are completely unmarked it is impossible to guess their precise date. Undoubtedly, the andiron type of nips (see illustration p. 68) is the earliest style; these nips had a triple purpose: the rat-tailed pans picked up lumps of sugar whilst perforations in one or both of the pans enabled the tea to be skimmed in the cups; on some, a central spike, detachable by unscrewing, was used to dispel leaves if they clogged the spout. The earliest types were obviously copied from fire irons and numerous modifications of this style occurred during the first twenty years of the eighteenth century, until they evolved into the hinged scissor-type of sugar nips. With the advent of mote spoons, pierced pans for skimming had become obsolete on sugar nips. By 1720 the rat-tailed pan was disappearing too and was generally replaced by pans in the shape of shells.

Until 1740 it was customary at all assay offices for marks to be stamped in the pans, but subsequently marks were punched (lion or town and maker's mark) on both the circular thumb and finger grips. In the middle of the eighteenth century nips appeared sometimes in unusual forms such as Harlequin and such tastes appeared in the reigns of George IV and William IV. The Victorians produced many imaginative designs, both good and bad.

Three early sugar nips, c.1700-20. The central spike on the earliest example (left), known as the andiron type, unscrews and was used to remove tea leaves blocking the spout. The single perforated pan is used as a mote spoon. Courtesy the James Aspin Collection, South Africa.

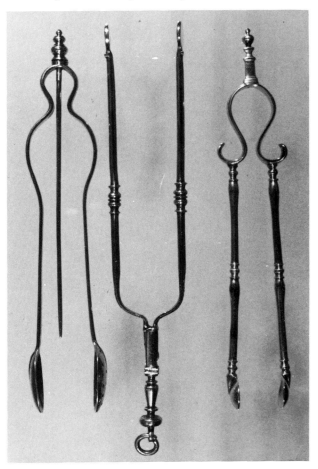

Three sturdy sugar nips. London, c.1725-40. Until 1739 or 1740 most of these examples appear to be marked with the lion passant and maker's mark in the pans; subsequently the marks moved to the thumb and finger grips at the other end. Courtesy the James Aspin Collection, South Africa.

Three examples of sugar nips of heavy gauge, all made between 1745 and 1755 in London. Courtesy the James Aspin Collection, South Africa.

Four attractive sugar nips assayed at Dublin, c.1750, all are marked with harp and makers' marks on ring handles. Compare the pronounced difference between the English taste seen in the illustrations on the left, and the Irish taste shown here. Courtesy the James Aspin Collection, South Africa.

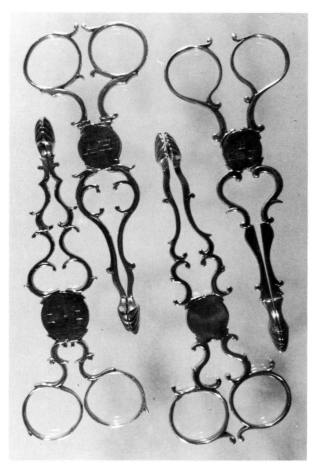

Four sugar nips. London, c.1759-1770. Normally, examples of this period are not of such robust form as those of earlier specimens. Courtesy the James Aspin Collection, South Africa.

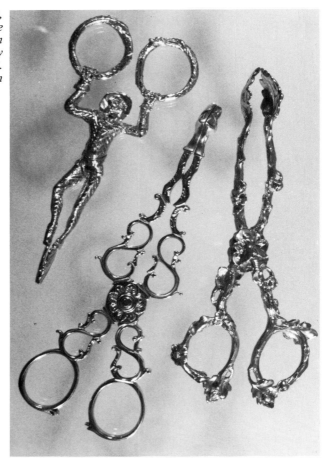

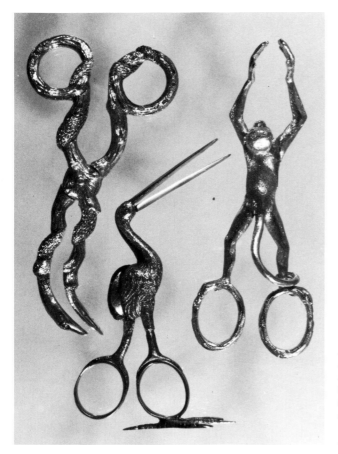

Sugar tongs made their appearance in about 1770 and soon became more popular than nips. Tongs provide an instructive and attractive record of the changing vogues in designs on silver until the Victorian era. Up to 1784 they were stamped with a town and maker's mark only but subsequently were more fully marked, although in London, where the majority were made, the date letter and/or town mark were frequently absent. I consider that these underpriced and surprisingly little-respected items, especially those made before the nineteenth century was far advanced, provide a sound purchase for new collectors.

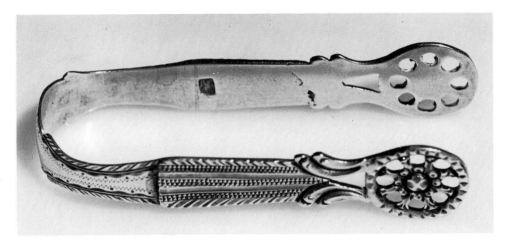

A rare pair of very small sugar tongs of thick gauge made in three parts, the two sides of which are cast. A minor casting fault and the soldering junction joining the side to the bow of the tongs (beside the lion passant) show clearly; beginners often consider these solder lines on the three part type of tongs are repairs. Exeter, c.1775, by Thomas Eustace, length 8cm. Courtesy the Mr. and Dr. David Bayliss Collection, Hong Kong.

Shoe buckles were worn as early as the fourteenth century, but I have found only four examples made prior to 1740. Presumably buckles either were being constantly refashioned to conform to changing styles or, after their purpose had been served, were discarded like dead men's boots. They were made in innumerable styles, few pairs being exactly alike, so they are quite interesting items to collect. Single specimens, which appear to me to be just as collectable as pairs, are not 'reckoned' in the trade and can still be obtained relatively cheaply. Do keep an eye open for a seventeenth century example and please let me know when you have found one.

Top, an early single buckle by Joshua Healey, c.1725, marked with lion passant and maker's mark. Bottom, single buckle, marked with lion passant and maker's mark, RC, London, c.1730. Left and right, a pair of buckles, Birmingham, 1800, by Matthew Boulton. These buckles are of curved steel covered with a fine grained Moroccan leather and with silver border. The back has a curved spring steel piece with very small sharp hooks. This enables the buckles to be pressed and hooked into the leather. Courtesy the Eagle Collection, Devon.

Shoe buckles. Top row, left to right, London, 1788, by Hester Bateman (note: buckles were not usually fully marked until c.1790). London, c.1765, maker's mark IFGL. London, c.1779, maker's mark PS. Middle row, London, c.1785, by T. Wallis. Newcastle, c.1788, by Langlands & Robertson. Dublin, c.1775, by Benjamin Wilson. Bottom row, Edinburgh, 1792, by Alexander Ziegler. London, c.1758, by J. Frost. London, c.1780, maker's mark JP. Courtesy the Eagle Collection, Devon.

Commemorative plaques, prizes, medals, buttons. When writing about small collectable items such as these, I certainly do not imply that their value is necessarily small. It does not require an experienced dealer's knowledge of the precise value per ounce of a massive centrepiece by Paul Storr to spot and buy unrecognised and small pieces of merit. More important is an inherent flair for identifying quality and historical significance.

If you are confident that you possess these attributes, back your own judgement with small, inexpensive items, no matter when or where you get the 'hunch', and even at the very outset of your collecting career. Although you may back many losers, the rewards from your winners could be very encouraging.

The two medals and the set of hunt buttons shown on this page started their careers in the trade at extremely modest prices and, when recently re-encountered, were changing hands for well over hundreds and thousands of pounds respectively.

Never allow an absence of competition to dampen your 'hunch' if the stakes are low and easily affordable.

Two medals in their original cases (not shown). London, 1823, maker's mark CR. Left, diameter 6.25cm, 1oz. 6dwt. Translation: The Rhuthun Welsh Society 1823. J. Blackwell. A member of the Society for his Poetry on the Birth of Edward II in Wales. Right, diameter 7cm, 1oz. 15dwt. The medal commemorates the prize winning ode at the 1823 Flintshire Eisteddfod, written by John Blackwell.

One of a set of eight hunt buttons for 'tails', which are still worn by a few hunting folk at major evening functions throughout the hunting season. These buttons, diameter about 3.3cm, are sewn on both sides (three and three) at the front of the coat and two more are added in the small of the back above the vent of its 'tails'. A smaller set of buttons is sewn on the cuffs.

Hunt buttons are normally made of gold, silver-gilt or brass, though the Bramham Moor Hunt in Yorkshire, to which these buttons relate, is the only hunt traditionally entitled to wear silver buttons.

The interesting York hallmark on the reverse of the hunt button shows the date letter for the year 1858/9 but Jackson records no letter later than V for 1856/7. The maker's mark, JB, will relate to James Barber or some other.

Following enquiries instituted by the Prime Warden of the Goldsmith's Company in 1854, the Assay Office in York was found to have disregarded regulations. The Office had not bothered to assay silver for several years and the chest containing the assay tools was covered with dust, the lock rusted and its key lost. The Office was closed in 1858 in disgrace. Very late date letters from the York Assay Office are worth a collector's interest.

Silver wine and spirit labels became popular soon after clear glass decanters became fashionable early in the eighteenth century; the parchment or wooden tickets used previously to identify the contents of opaque containers did not complement the coloured wines in clear glass decanters. The earliest type of silver wine label (c.1730) was the plain escutcheon type made by Sandylands Drinkwater, a London goldsmith, and copied soon afterwards by John Harvey, also of London. This design must have proved very popular for there are still quite a number of them to be found. Until the final quarter of the eighteenth century labels, if marked, were stamped only with a maker's mark, with or without a town mark and with or without a lion passant.

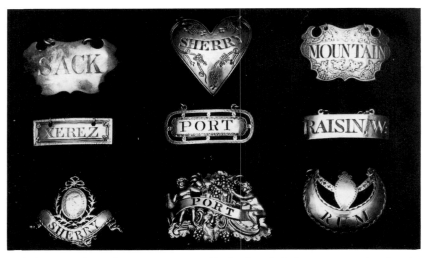

Top row, left to right, London, c.1750, by Sandylands Drinkwater. Unmarked, c.1770. London, c.1750, by Thomas Rush. Middle row, London, c.1764, by Margaret Binley. London, c.1795, by Henry Greenway. London, c.1762, by Richard Redbrick. Bottom row, London, c.1785, by T. Daniel. London, c.1798, by Phipps & Robinson. London, c.1788, by Turton & Walbank. Courtesy the R. Ryall Collection.

As news of the new London vogue travelled afar, labels were made also in Irish, Scottish and English provincial centres and the escutcheon type was often embellished with engraved decoration. A wide variety of pleasing designs developed subsequently and labels by Hester Bateman are particularly graceful.

By the nineteenth century, whilst many labels tended to become purely utilitarian and inexpensive, often of unexciting oblong form with reeded edges and canted corners, others were novel and some even grotesque, these latter groups being eagerly sought after by modern collectors. Ambitious goldsmiths such as Benjamin Smith and Paul Storr catered for affluent customers with massive cast creations, often of bacchanalian designs and sometimes weighing up to two ounces each. Later in the nineteenth century, many labels were designed as realistic vine leaves, some massive and expensive, others flimsy and cheap to produce.

The Grocers' Licensee Act of 1860 permitted stores to sell single bottles of wine providing they bore a paper label denoting the nature of the contents and, possibly for this reason, the manufacture of silver labels declined noticeably until the twentieth century.

Collectors of labels vie avidly with each other to collect rare designs, labels with rare names of wines, labels by fashionable makers and those from less usual sources of manufacture such as Limerick, Cork and the lesser Scottish centres. This enables others to obtain attractive but commonplace London examples on quite reasonable terms.

A collection of fourteen wine labels all made by members of the Bateman family between 1775 and 1810. Courtesy The Antique Collector.

An important pair of wine labels with the engraver producing a three dimensional effect. Edinburgh, 1818, by J. McKay, claret 6.5cm high, 16dwt., Madeira 5.6cm high, 14dwt. The owner is of the opinion that there was once a third label, for port, in the form of a hare, and collectors would be fortunate to find such a label. Courtesy the G.S. Sanders Collection.

A selection of eighteen labels. Top row, left to right, London, 1815, by Paul Storr. London, 1806, by R. & S. Hennell. London, 1841, by R. Garrard.

Second row, London, 1814, by Edward Farrell. London, 1810, by B. & J. Smith. London, 1817, by Edward Farrell.

Third row, London, 1833, by Rawlins & Sumner. London, 1843, by Rawlins & Sumner. London, 1829, by W. Reid.

Fourth row, unmarked, early nineteenth century. London, 1890, by J.N. Mappin. Unmarked, early nineteenth century.

Fifth row, London, 1818, by John Reilly. London, 1823, by John Reilly. London, 1835, by Charles and George Reilly.

Sixth row, London, 1845, by Charles and George Fox. Unmarked, mid-nineteenth century. London, 1835, by Charles and George Fox.

Courtesy The Antique Collector.

Group of nine labels all assayed at Birmingham in the nineteenth century and later. Top row, left to right, by Matthew Boulton. By George Unite, 1839. By Joseph Willmore, 1822. Middle row, by Joseph Taylor, 1820. By Gervais Wheeler, 1833. By Yapp & Woodward, 1856. Bottom row, by Nathaniel Mills, Junior, 1849. By Hilliard & Thomason, 1906. By Matthew Linwood, 1817.

The ugly label 'Mother's Ruin' is mercifully rare but it is valuable. Courtesy the R. Ryall Collection.

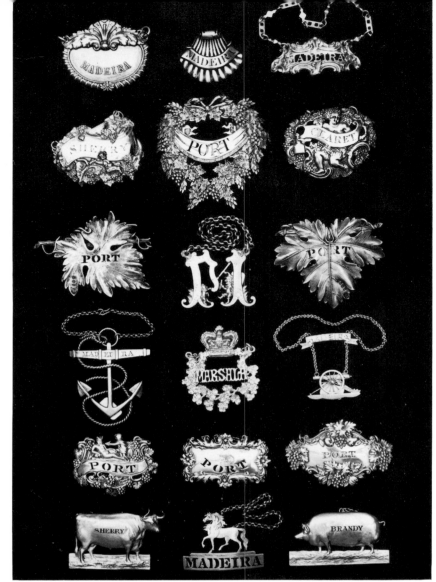

A flourishing club, the Wine Label Circle, has completed much research in recent years and unearthed the identity of virtually all the goldsmiths who made labels. However, as with all types of antique silver, there are still plenty of interesting discoveries to be made.

The rare but well illustrated 'pointer' labels (see Delieb, *Investing in Silver,* p. 146) are intriguing. These depict identical sporting dogs, possibly with a heraldic association, standing on narrow oblong bases, each of which is engraved with the name of a popular wine. The dog, depicted in an eager stance, appears to be winding and thus pointing towards game still concealed within a covert.

It has been stated that this type of label was introduced in Edinburgh in 1817, made by John McDonald, but I have recently discovered an identical example made by Hannah Northcote and assayed at London in 1800. Never having handled an example of this sporting label before, I was surprised to find how flimsy its construction is in relation to the boldness of the design. There is no evidence to suggest that Hannah Northcote (entered 1796) originated a design that seems to me to have more feel for the eighteenth than the nineteenth century.

Numerous names of wines, which are either engraved or pierced on the antique labels which we collect, are unheard of by the general public and wine merchants of today, due to the fact that many vineyards were destroyed and their wines lost for ever when plagues such as phylloxera attacked them. In order to assist collectors, Mr. C.B. Ryall, a past vice-president of the Wine Label Circle, has kindly allowed me to reproduce a summary of a paper which he wrote some years ago entitled 'A Note On Uncommon Wines'.

Alicante	A Spanish dessert wine — popular in the nineteenth century.
Bucellas	The name of a small town close to Lisbon which gave its name to á wine similar to Riesling. Very popular in the nineteenth century.
Calcavella	A sweet Portuguese wine popular at the end of the eighteenth century and beginning of the nineteenth century.
Canaria Seco	(Canary Sack). See Sack below.
Carlowitz	Hungarian wine which, with Tokay, forms the survival of the mid-Victorian Hungarian wines which were once so popular in England.
Constantia	One of the first South African wines to be imported from the Cape during the late eighteenth century.
Frontiniac	An incorrect rendering of Frontignan, the best French dessert wine from Languedoc. A popular drink in the late eighteenth century.
Geneva	An early spelling of gin, which consists of diluted alcohol flavoured with plant extracts. The original and still the principal added flavour is that of juniper, and it is from the first syllable of its Italian equivalent — Ginevra — that the drink gets its name. It was commonly known as 'Geneva' but has no connection with the Swiss city.
Hermitage	A red or white wine from the Rhône valley, famous in the

eighteenth and early nineteenth centuries. Named after a ruin on top of a hill near Valence supposed to have been a hermit's cell. It never recovered from the phylloxera scourge of 1870.

Hollands	A distinctive type of gin from Holland. Popular in the early nineteenth century.
Lisbon	Red and white wines from the valley of the Tagus; shipped to England in large quantities during the eighteenth century.
Malaga	A Spanish sweet wine from Eastern Andalusia — shipped from the port of Malaga.
Malvasia	A sweet fortified wine made in Madeira or the Canary Islands, normally known as Madeira, which name now embraces the different types of wine that come from that island.
Mountain	A sweet wine from the mountains of Malaga. Very popular during the eighteenth and early nineteenth centuries. Similar to Sherry.
Old Tom	Slang for unsweetened gin — named after a celebrated character of the early Victorian era, Old Thomas Chamberlain of Hodge's Distillery.
Pajarete or Paxarete	A sweet dark wine named after a famous monastery of the Jerez district of Spain. It never recovered from the phylloxera scourge of the late 1860s.
Pineapple Rum	At the beginning of the nineteenth century rum was drunk by almost everyone and pineapple juice was one of the most popular flavourings.
Rotta	Also known as Tent, Rota Tent or Tintilla de Rota. The darkest of all Spanish red wines produced in Alicante which was in vogue in Georgian and early Victorian times. Now chiefly used for blending.
Sack	A dry amber wine occasionally sweetened with honey or syrup. Referred to sometimes as Jerez Sack or Sherris Sack, to distinguish it from Canary Sack which ceased to be shipped in the middle of the nineteenth century. (See Tenerife below.) The Jerez or Sherris wines are now known as Sherry.
St. Perret	An alternative spelling for Saint-Péray, a famous wine producing commune of the Rhône valley.
Shrub	A home-made liqueur consisting of rum or brandy steeped with fruit and sugar.
Tenerife Vidonia	Wines from the Cape Verde Islands. In 1852 the crop was virtually destroyed by the white mildew known as Oidium Tuckeri. Some replanting took place, but the new vines were almost immediately wiped out by the phylloxera pest.

Caddy spoons and tea caddies. The name caddy is derived from the Malaysian measure of weight of just over a pound called a kati, but it is thought that tea canisters were not called caddies until quite late in the eighteenth century. Many of the observations made pertaining to wine and spirit labels apply also to caddy spoons. Again, it is the rare or special examples, of either design, origin or maker, that collectors seek; numerous attractive but ordinary specimens can still be obtained for the cost of a good dinner for two with wine.

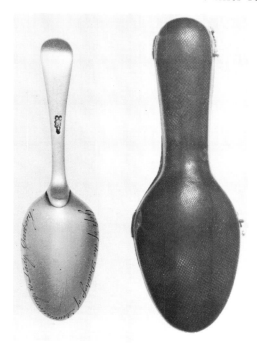

A rare medicine or caddy spoon of Hanoverian form and its original shagreen case with red velvet lining. London, c.1755, with the mark of Paul Callard, 9cm long. Engraved on bowl: 'Gift of the Dutchess of Queensberry'. Courtesy Phillips.

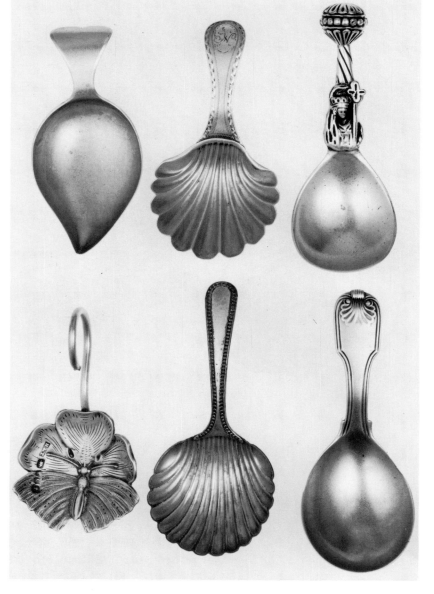

Group of caddy spoons. Top row, left to right, Birmingham, 1807, by William Pugh. London, 1792, by Peter and Anne Bateman. A strange spoon cast with a medieval saint, London, 1872, by George Fox. Bottom row, stamped as a butterfly, Birmingham, 1851, by Hilliard & Thomason. Old Sheffield plated example by Nathaniel Smith & Co., c.1790. London, 1821, by William Eley. Courtesy Phillips.

Before the arrival of the caddy spoon it is possible that the precious tea leaves were either deposited in the pot by shaking direct from the caddy, which might seem an extravagant manoeuvre or, as some suggest, the leaves were first placed in an open receptacle and from thence transferred carefully into the pot either with the fingers or by some other method. Whereas the small octagonal canisters, made up to c.1720, had a pull-off lid *without* a cylindrical cover, the more commodious oblong style, c.1710-40, had sliding removable lids or bases with the flat lid invariably surmounted by a cylindrical pull-off cover of a suitable size to measure and transfer the leaves into the pot; thus, in all likelihood, these cylindrical covers served the purpose of caddy spoons. Sets of tea caddies usually consisted of two tea containers and a sugar bowl and, frequently, the sets were augmented with teaspoons, a mote spoon and a pair of sugar nips.

Right, a rare cast caddy or sugar spoon in the form of Harlequin. London, 1822, by Edward Fennell, width of bowl 3.5cm, spoon 12cm long. Courtesy the L.T. Burrough Collection, U.S.A.

Far right, the reverse of the spoon.

With the increasing popularity of tea as the eighteenth century progressed and with some easing of its price, most of it would have been imported in fragmented form in order to achieve the maximum content in each chest and thus economise on shipping space. When towards the middle of the eighteenth century a number of pear-shaped tea caddy sets appeared without a removable lid or base but with circular open tops and covers of quite a small diameter, it seems certain that the majority of tea leaves arrived in a size no larger than some of our popular brands of today; otherwise it would have been difficult to fill the caddies.

Medicine spoons with a simple bowl and a short shank, made in small numbers from c.1740, and supplied with shagreen cases, were thought, until some twenty years ago, to be early caddy spoons (see illustration p. 79). They were ideally suited for this latter purpose and one is forced to wonder if, in this respect, modern ideas are incorrect. The last so-called medicine spoon that I handled bore a contemporary inscription which indicated that it had

An early caddy spoon (centre) and two sugar sifter spoons cast in the Onslow style, Irish, c.1745. The larger sifter 11.3cm long, 1oz. 17dwt., the paired spoons 10.7cm long, 19dwt. each.

The crest on the caddy spoon, possibly for the O'Neill family, depicts the 'Red Hand of Ulster'. All three spoons have identical turn-over suspensory supports (see text below), but the larger sifter spoon (matching caddy spoon missing) comes from a different tea caddy set.

been a loving gift to a dear friend. A strange present.

A recent discovery provides a 'missing link' (in addition to the so-called medicine spoon discussed in the previous paragraph) between the domed, cylindrical lift-off cover of earlier tea caddies and the conventional tea caddy spoon of modern form which was made in considerable numbers from about 1760.

In about 1740 the domed cylindrical lift off covers on tea caddy lids drifted out of fashion (apart from some types of the pear-shaped caddy) and were replaced by numerous and greatly varied lid finials. These were designed only for artistic effect and made no provision for measuring and then transferring the tea leaves.

The 'missing link' is represented by the two smaller spoons shown in the illustration above: one is an early example of a caddy spoon and the other a sugar sifter *en suite*. They were constructed to hang from the sides of a tea caddy and sugar bowl (in the Dutch fashion) after the removal of lids. Whether or not there was usually a second caddy spoon (subsequently lost) to hang from a second tea caddy is, of course, conjectural but just one caddy spoon would have sufficed for both. (One theory, that 'missing link' caddy spoons are, in fact, condiment spoons, is a good example of the sort of issue which can confuse students. You must be prepared to encounter such doubts and contradictions, weigh the evidence over a period of time, and make your own decision.)

To sum up on the complex matter of caddy spoons: in the period between 1740 and 1760, after which conventional caddy spoons became plentiful, we have three probable utensils for transferring tea from caddy to pot and all three options probably had their devotees:

1. The domed lift-off cover of those tea caddies that still retained them.
2. The rare so-called medicine spoon.
3. The true caddy spoon as seen in the illustration.

The inclusion of a larger sifter spoon (at the top of the illustration) of the same period and style as the spoons *en suite*, is important because (even without its caddy spoon) it provides additional evidence that should refute current theories that the sugar bowl associated with caddies was primarily used as a mixing bowl for blending teas.

Traditionally, the first caddy spoons of c.1755-70 were fashioned in the Onslow pattern. Although sometimes unmarked, most of them bore a maker's mark and/or a lion passant. Caddy spoons became very plentiful in about 1775 and many delightful patterns emerged, those with shell bowls being initially the most popular. I am told that the first fully marked example was assayed at London in 1778, and recently a fully marked example from the Sheffield Assay Office, with shell bowl and bright cut stem, made by Thomas Law in 1779, passed through my hands. Hester Bateman was responsible for several charming designs.

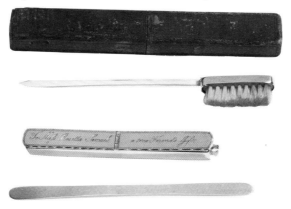

Tooth brush set consisting of leather case, the tooth brush with removable brush, a tongue scraper and a delightful powder box. Birmingham, 1800, by S. Taylor. The double compartment box with bright cut engraving around the edge is engraved 'To Miss Rosetta Samuels a True Friend's Gift'. Courtesy the Eagle Collection, Devon.

Medical items. All implements used internally or externally upon the human body for medical, surgical, hygienic or personal reasons appear to be classified in the medical group, but few such examples survive prior to the second half of the eighteenth century apart from such items as babies' teething sticks and rattles, pap boats (feeding vessels for invalids and infants) and lancets.

So-called silver bleeding bowls (a form of porringer, perhaps) seem likely to have been made usually for pleasanter purposes both because of their shape and because of the invariable absence of any engraved scale by which to measure the quantity of blood drawn. One of these vessels was presented as a racing trophy at Hanstead Plains in America on March 25th, 1668. Was this prize intended to bleed bookmakers or their erstwhile equivalents? However, these conclusions do not infer that these bowls were never used for medical purposes.

Although some amusement may be gained nowadays by suddenly producing an antique silver ear trumpet, I cannot believe that the normal collector of silver has any anticipated personal use for nipple guards, tongue scrapers, castor oil spoons, forceps, catheters and saws for amputating limbs, etc., and anyway most of these objects are unattractive both to the eye and to the imagination. But, very naturally, members of the medical profession find such antiques of absorbing interest and in consequence their prices are high.

I have neither the qualifications nor inclination to discuss medical implements and I have avoided illustrations with gruesome associations. The little box for powder, which is delightful, in the tooth brush set, like the detachable brush, has never been used so far as I can tell.

A bleeding bowl or porringer. London, 1689, 17.2cm across handle, 4oz. 9dwt. Courtesy Sotheby's.

Card cases, 1825-1914. These articles for holding visiting cards, have always seemed to me to be a classic example of snobbery. Yet in their normal usage they merely indicated good neighbourliness, albeit for the privileged classes only.

The earlier card cases made in Birmingham and London, especially those of Nathaniel Mills, Senior (see overleaf), were mostly of fine quality. Many, during the first twenty-five years of their use, had repoussé plaques inserted into their lids with views of famous palaces, castles, mansions, monuments and public buildings which, rather lazily, are nowadays lumped together under the classification of 'castle tops'. Views of Windsor Castle and Abbotsford House, the home of Sir Walter Scott, were particularly popular. Some of these boxes had engraved decoration of similar scenes or of beauty spots, real and imaginary.

As the nineteenth century advanced and card cases were used by an increasing number of the middle and upper-middle classes, their quality and construction, usually from a thinner gauge, deteriorated, as did their designs. Towards the end of the century and at the beginning of the twentieth century, many examples in silver were produced in shoddy form whilst others were made of ivory, tortoiseshell and mother-of-pearl, with or without silver mounts.

Card cases. Top row, left to right, with a view of St. Paul's in high relief, Birmingham, 1858. View of Windsor Castle in relief, Birmingham, 1856, by Frederick Marston. Bottom row, a Victorian host box, Birmingham, 1853, by I. Key. A card case engraved with sprays of flowers and a bird in flight, Birmingham, 1885, maker's mark T.M. & Co. Courtesy Phillips.

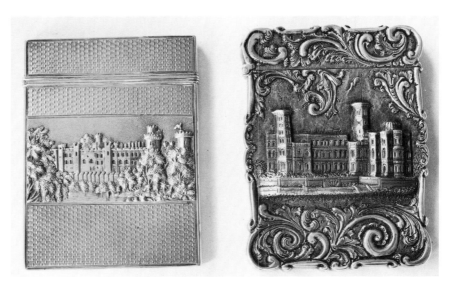

Left, a card case, Birmingham, 1836, by Nathaniel Mills, Senior, with engine turned decoration and with two different plaques (one on either side) of Warwick Castle in low relief. This box, 9.2cm × 6.5cm, 2oz. 11dwt., is typical of earlier specimens and of better quality than most of the later examples. Right, a card case, Birmingham, 1849, by Edward Smith, 9.75cm × 7cm, 2oz. 1½dwt. It depicts a rather rare view of Osborne House, Isle of Wight, beloved by Queen Victoria and Prince Albert.

The advent of the telephone and the changed social conditions following the First World War put an end to the manufacture of card cases, but the custom of calling and leaving cards, with or without cases, carried on with diminishing significance and frequency.

On the market, the card case of any period was scarcely worth its weight for melting until about 1960 when collectors started buying them; today a fine example with one of the rarer repoussé 'castle tops' might command £300 or more.

Group of vinaigrettes. Left column, top to bottom, purse shape, Birmingham, 1820, by John Lawrence & Co., 2.5cm wide. Birmingham, 1815, by J. Willmore. Birmingham, 1816, by Joseph Taylor, silver gilt, in form of watch. Birmingham, 1828, by Nathaniel Mills, Senior. Birmingham, 1828, by Nathaniel Mills, Senior.

Centre column, top to bottom, mussel shell, London, 1876, by S. Mordan & Co. London, 1799, by Thomas Holland, the ring hoop possibly added at a later date. Articulated fish, Birmingham, 1817, by W. Lea & Co. Birmingham, 1815, by J. Willmore. Silver-gilt example showing fox leaving covert and inscribed 'Talio', Birmingham, 1821, by Samuel Pemberton. Lid cast with scene of shepherd playing flute, Birmingham, 1813, by J. Willmore.

Right column, top to bottom, Birmingham, c.1820, by Ledsam, Vale & Wheeler. Birmingham, 1814, by J. Willmore. Birmingham, 1824, by J. Willmore. Birmingham, 1828, by Thomas Shaw, silver-gilt. Birmingham, 1826, by WS, silver-gilt.

Group of vinaigrettes all assayed at Birmingham. Left column, top to bottom, 1829, by Nathaniel Mills, Senior, with a view of Abbotsford House, 4cm long. In form of purse, 1816, by Matthew Linwood. 1830, by John Betteridge.

Centre column, 1838, by Nathaniel Mills, Senior, with a view of Windsor Castle. 1845, by Nathaniel Mills, Junior, 4.5cm long. 1845, by Nathaniel Mills, Junior, with engraved view of private house, possibly Houghton House, Northants., demolished like so many other large places c.1930.

Right column, 1845, by Nathaniel Mills, Junior, with unusual view of Warwick Castle. 1819, by T. Simpson & Son. 1850, by F. & Co.

All boxes with 'castle tops' are popular. Courtesy Phillips.

Vinaigrettes. Although there are accounts from early in the seventeenth century of vinaigrettes fitted to the tops of gentlemen's walking canes, supposedly neutralising germs as well as unpleasant odours, the box-like vinaigrette (successor to the apple-shaped pomander), which is still in such plentiful supply today, was not generally used by ladies until the final quarter of the eighteenth century when the female mode of stiflingly tight apparel tended to cause swooning and dizziness.

These numerous later vinaigrettes, the quarry of so many modern-day collectors' keen pursuit, contained, under the grilles inside the boxes, sponges or sheep's wool soaked in aromatic vinegars contrived from diverse recipes usually containing cloves, cinnamon or nutmeg blended with the essence of fruit and flowers.

The interiors of silver vinaigrettes were protected from acidification by gilding, and those boxes which have subsequently suffered repairs and lost this original mercury fire-gilding have usually been electro-gilded to compensate.

Birmingham and London were the main sources for the manufacture of these boxes, the former centre producing the greatest number and the most original creations and the latter tending to concentrate on quality products. Examples produced elsewhere are scarce and, if they can be found, command high prices.

Late eighteenth century grilles have simple piercing without embellishment but early in the nineteenth century their designs became varied and artistic. As the Victorian era advanced, most examples degenerated into crude and formal scrolls of leafage. Particularly attractive or interesting grilles fetch high prices and these same considerations govern both the value and the popularity of the embellishment on the lids of the vinaigrettes. Some of the most sought-after examples commemorate events or people, for example Lord Nelson, some having cast lids such as 'Little Boy Blue' of the nursery rhyme, 'Hare Feeding in Corn', sporting subjects and 'castle tops'. Vinaigrettes in the form of books and those with interesting or attractive engraved designs (such as masonic emblems and the symbols of magic) are also popular and pricey.

Two rare vinaigrettes. Left, variation in the form of a miner's lamp, c.1870-80, by S. Mordan & Co., 7.7cm high. The cover houses the vinaigrette and the glass windshield opens to reveal another container possibly intended for vestas. The flame of the candle is enamelled red, simulating flames. S. Mordan & Co. appear to have been a law unto themselves for the box is not hallmarked but the maker's name is engraved across the front of the article in the same style as those of the manufacturers of real miners' lamps. Right, vinaigrette in the form of a snail by Matthew Linwood, Birmingham, 1804.

Snuff boxes (not Sheffield plated examples) were traditionally hinged so that the box could be held in one hand leaving the other free to take pinches of the powder. Considerations relating to the particular popularity of nine-

Left, cowrie shell snuff box with integral hinge and rather crude provincial Scottish engraving, marked on rim INS (town) and RN (maker), Inverness, c.1760. The maker's mark, in the same form as for Robert Naughton of Inverness who was working at this centre from c.1800 to 1840, might indicate that RN had a father, unrecorded as a silversmith, who also worked at Inverness and perhaps at Dundee as well. A similar RN is noted in Jackson for Dundee, c.1776.

Right, a fine cowrie shell box with disguised integral hinge, showing typical Scottish engraving of the c.1780 period above typically distinctive Scottish initialling. The fine engraving suggests that this item was probably made in Edinburgh, c.1775-90.

teenth century snuff boxes are similar to those sought in vinaigrettes, and neither type of box should be ignored by the discerning collector should they appear quite ordinary and yet represent the finest quality. It should be a sobering thought to collectors of nineteenth century boxes that late seventeenth century pomanders, spice or amatory boxes, wine tasters, spoons or nutmeg graters, for example, can usually be obtained less expensively than many of the most popular Victorian boxes.

Top, silver-gilt snuff box made in the form of a book with various musical instruments overlaid on the lid. London, 1809, by A.J. Strachan, 8.3cm wide.

Below left, snuff box with the cover in low relief of a Roman judgement in a courtyard, an executioner stands by and the wrongdoers grovel at the foot of a dais. Birmingham, 1827, by John Betteridge, 8.2cm wide, 5oz. 14dwt.

Below right, snuff box with coursing scene, the cover repoussé in low relief. Birmingham, 1827, by John Lawrence & Co., 8.9cm wide. Courtesy Sotheby's.

A stirring naval scene cast on a snuff box. London, 1837, by T. Eley, 8cm long, 5oz. Courtesy the Dr. David Fermont Collection.

Left, snuff box with green-grey and red-brown agate lid, inset into the side a rectangular area for striking vesta matches. Birmingham, 1855, by Gervaise Wheeler, 10cm long. Right, a silver mounted and hinged snuff box formed from a stag's antler, the silver lid following the lines of the horn. London, 1812, by John Robins. Courtesy the Eagle Collection, Devon.

Picture back and fancy back tea spoons, c.1740-80. These small items prove a constant delight and interest for those who collect them. Common varieties in perfect state with the backs of the bowls die-struck with scrolls, shells and baskets of flowers can still be bought reasonably. Specimens, even of rare examples which by reason of long and honest use have worn bowls and pictures, can be obtained very cheaply and despite their imperfections they should still interest collectors, especially those of modest means. However, care should be taken to avoid specimens with reshaped bowls which are, therefore, unrepresentative of their period.

Three picture back table spoons die-struck with (left to right) a double headed eagle crowned, a squirrel in a tree and a dolphin or whale, all assayed at London, c.1750-60. Courtesy Phillips.

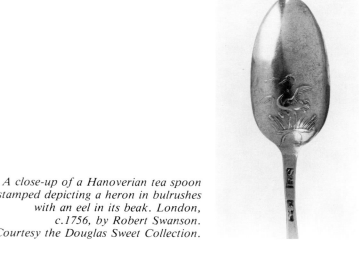

A close-up of a Hanoverian tea spoon stamped depicting a heron in bulrushes with an eel in its beak. London, c.1756, by Robert Swanson. Courtesy the Douglas Sweet Collection.

Some of the subjects depicted on the bowls of these spoons are purely ornamental and others have indisputable political connections: the picture showing a sheaf of corn beneath the word 'plenty' must, for example, relate to the Corn Laws of the period. Others seem to have Jacobite associations, for this cause had many loyal adherents throughout the United Kingdom.

The experiences of just one man, even when assembled over a long period of time, may produce conflicting, incomplete and unbalanced conclusions, but in order to make a guess concerning the relative scarcity or abundance of the numerous types of picture back spoons, I list overleaf those that I have seen or heard of and the frequency with which they occur.

A splendid set of six tea spoons die-struck on bowls with a sailing ship. London, c.1760, maker's mark WC. Courtesy the Eagle Collection, Devon.

Type of picture back	Comment
Pierrot	Very rare
Broken bagpipes	Very rare
Hen with more than two chicks	Rare
Heron in bulrushes	Rare
A cock crowing	Rare
Milkmaid with pails	Rare
Swan	Rare
Parrot	Rare
Stag	Rare
Tea pot	Rather rare
Masonic emblems	Rather rare
Cockerel	Rather rare
Squirrel	Rather rare
Hen with two chicks	Rather rare
Double-headed eagle	Rather rare
Prince of Wales' feathers	Rather rare
Crown	Rather rare
Burning heart	Rather rare
Hearts of oak	Rather rare
Dolphin	Rather rare
Sheaf of corn and word 'plenty'	Not too hard to find
Cage below 'I love liberty'	Not too hard to find
Ship	Not too hard to find
Dove and olive branch	Not too hard to find
Flower arrangements	Common
Shell	Common
Scroll	Common
Shell and scroll	Common

Picture backs appear less frequently on table spoons and they are quite scarce on dessert spoons. Some tea spoons, in addition to decorated bowls, have designs (often figures from mythology) upon their shanks.

Nutmeg graters for carrying about on one's person appeared with the introduction of pockets in the last quarter of the seventeenth century. The early specimens are of heart-shaped form, large enough to contain a nutmeg and house a steel grater (the cylindrical so-called nutmeg graters of the same period with silver graters may in reality have been tobacco or other rasps). Early nutmeg graters are usually stamped only with a maker's mark and it is perhaps for this reason that many collectors are more interested in the much later and commoner fully marked examples which are to be found in a variety of shapes and sizes, some with attractive engraved decoration.

Although the point may be of academic interest rather than importance, a common error when displaying small tubular examples (c.1800) with a lift-off cover at either end, one domed and the other flat, is to place the domed end directly over the grater. The domed cover must have been intended to collect particles of nutmeg after grating and, to substantiate the point, a few examples of the type of box described have a wider diameter at one end of the tubular body, which fits only the domed cover, while its flat counterpart fits only the base directly below the grater.

Nutmeg grater with steel rasp within hinged base. London, 1786, by Phipps & Robinson, 5.7cm wide. Courtesy Sotheby's.

A humble yet attractive little patch box with bright-cut engraving, lift-off cover. London, 1799, maker's mark RB, 3.2cm long. Courtesy Christie's.

Circular box with lift-off lid, possibly used as a patch box. London, 1684, marked on base and cover, maker's mark RG beneath star, 5cm in diameter. Courtesy Sotheby's.

Patch boxes. Ladies of fashion bedecked their faces with patches of remarkable designs and sizes from early on in the seventeenth century, though we do not find surviving examples of patch boxes until the second half of that century. The Puritans considered these adornments to be immoral and entered a bill in 1650 suppressing their use. Patches regained their popularity with the Restoration and were commonly used well into the nineteenth century.

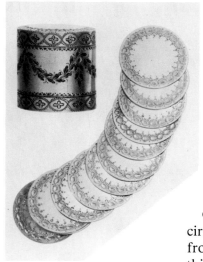

A cylindrical silver counter box, the body engraved with garlands, containing twelve counters with borders engraved to match the container. Unmarked, c.1795, 2.8cm high. Courtesy Christie's.

Counter boxes are often confused with patch boxes. The former are all circular, so far as I know, and these larger boxes of tubular form, dating from the Restoration into the reign of George II, contained numerous wafer-thin medallions usually depicting the sovereign of the period. Thomas Kedder produced a great quantity of these boxes in varying sizes early in the eighteenth century which were, I think, invariably without hallmarks. He usually struck the pull-off lids with a likeness of the current sovereign. After all these years, it is understandable that the tiny counters from the smaller boxes are usually missing.

There was a revival in the popularity of gambling with counters towards the end of the eighteenth century, and the fact that ladies participated in this activity accounts for the numerous elegant little boxes of the period.

Spice boxes appeared in the second half of the seventeenth century and were possibly intended chiefly to carry grated nutmeg. They are usually of oval form and hinged. These boxes are opened by squeezing the two extremities of the oval; this releases a clasp on the lid from its lock on the body. There is another circular type of spice box, and this, with its pull-off lid, closely resembles a patch box, but is usually slightly smaller than seventeenth century examples of the latter.

A typical oval spice box engraved with scroll leafage and a bird. The pinch ends for opening are just visible. Unmarked, c.1690, 4.4cm long. Courtesy Christie's.

Taper holder complete with extinguisher, Birmingham, 1827, by Joseph Willmore. Pair of pepper castors, London, 1872, length 10cm.

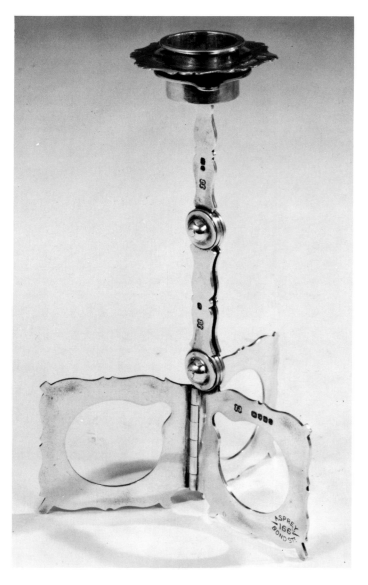

Typical of Victorian ingenuity and practicability is this travelling candlestick here shown expanded. London, 1867, maker's mark JJ, 13cm high, 12oz. Courtesy the Eagle Collection, Devon.

The candlestick closed.

Pair of greyhound collars inscribed between moulded borders and joined by a chain and clasps. Edinburgh, 1829, by WC (not identified), 17oz. 16dwt. Courtesy Sotheby's.

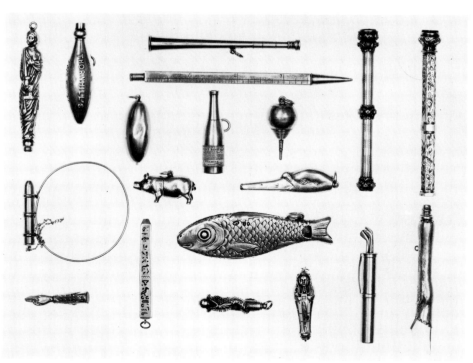

A group of nineteen propelling pencils of imaginative form made in the period 1850-1910. Courtesy Sotheby's Belgravia.

So far I have only touched on some of the more common types of traditionally collected smaller items. The range is, of course, vast and one of the enjoyments of collecting these small pieces is to find curious objects, such as those opposite and above, and attempt to work out what they were used for — take, for example, the travelling candlestick or greyhound collars (illustrated). There are also, for example, small fittings once used to clip the napkin to the jacket so that the juices which ran down the chin did not stain the clothes.

Remember too, particularly if you do not have much spare money, that there are a number of relatively modern silver pieces. The propelling pencil, for example, is fast becoming unfashionable but combines a wide range of designs (see previous page) with the generally good quality of workmanship associated with much pre-war work. These are nearer the 'antiques of the future' than many of the objects currently being manufactured and sold under that title.

Another area of interest is found with miniature items which often reflect the taste of the period when they were made, and a selection of these is shown below.

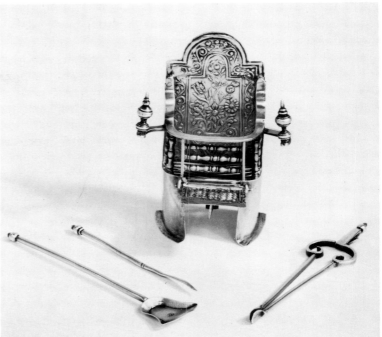

Miniature George I fire grate, 9.5cm high, and a set of fire irons, the back plate stamped with stylised flowers and scrolling foliage. The grate has an adjustable draught slide. All pieces by David Clayton, the fire grate fully marked, London, 1719, other items with maker's mark only. Courtesy Christie's.

A group of miniature items with, at the rear, a pear-shaped tea kettle and stand, overall 9cm high, London, 1715, by David Clayton; a chocolate pot, London, c.1725, maker's mark and lion passant; set of eight dinner plates, 3.5cm diameter, c.1740, by David Clayton; set of eight tea bowls and covers and a sugar bowl and cover, c.1710, all by David Clayton. Courtesy Christie's.

CHAPTER 4

The effects of time and the recognition of patina

Often, as we inspect an item of antique silver, we read its original scratched weight, sometimes carefully engraved, on a concealed part of the article. Not only can we thus identify outselves quite closely with the diligence and concern of the craftsman who made it, but also, by comparing the original weight with the current weight, we can glean useful information. Should the latter weight be in excess of the former, we are immediately alerted because something must have been added to the article since it was made. Assuming slight loss of weight over the years from wear, then if the weights of yesteryear and today are identical we must also be suspicious for this could either indicate a small subsequent addition or provide evidence of recent electroplating (adding to the weight of the item) in an attempt to conceal a serious repair. Very soon, as you begin to recognise patination (a protective coating gradually building up on a surface), you will spot plated silver at your first offended glance.

In due course, you may agree with me that the average loss of weight on an item of silver subjected to normal wear and tear during its passage through time is around 2½% for every hundred years. Accordingly, the anticipated loss of weight on a two hundred year old piece would be 5% and so an item weighing 20oz. in 1780 would balance at 19oz. today. But if this same item now weighed only 18oz., representing double the average loss of weight for age, you would either expect to find some small part broken off, a replacement of some part by a lighter substitute or evidence of heavy wear and probable erasures. (Remember: weights of silver have always been measured by the troy scale, not avoirdupois scale as, for example, in cooking.)

These losses of weight may not seem very significant to the inexperienced — and a small majority of silver items have no original weight scratched on them — but the chief purpose in offering such statistics at this stage in the book is to point out to you that the age of an antique is no real criterion of its desirability. Over the course of years indignities, both terrible and slight, have been inflicted on the vast majority of antique silver articles on the market, and with this in mind it is an idea to give some preliminary thought to what type of collection, or collections, you may wish to form. (You may already have received some preliminary advice in the form of personal views which are not necessarily in accordance with the ideas of most dealers.)

Will you concentrate on real collectors' pieces and enjoy their beauty under the protection of glass, where their loss of weight will be nil or negligible and their quality unimpaired, or do you wish to enjoy your silver in everyday use, thereby subjecting it to additional wear and decreasing its desirability very slightly as the years progress? You have the option, too, of making two collections, one for the cabinet and another for use. Those items intended for use should obviously be of a robust gauge and free of all serious defects and nasty modern repairs. It is not suggested, nor is it desirable in the interests of posterity, that items for use should be of a rare quality or interest.

Having briefly reviewed some of the detrimental effects of time upon silver, we must now consider how it has also enhanced its appeal in the minds and eyes of connoisseurs. So far as I am aware no other writer, prior to my previous book, has ever stressed the vital importance of patination on silver and the damage that can be done by removing it. For most serious dealers and collectors it is a key factor in determining the quality of silver and it is essential that you understand what it is and what it looks like.

The beauty of antique silver is only 'skin deep'. At first the finished article has a glittering, perhaps ostentatious polish without depth and without appeal to the connoisseur. As the years go by, there develops gradually, with slight progress from one decade to another, a beautiful mellowness not unlike heavily frosted hedgerows glowing in the waning winter sunshine. By reason of the diversity of opinions as to the cause, I have remained slightly uncertain about the chemical explanation of patination — some say it is the result of the action of oxygen on the silver; others believe that it is the gradual carbonisation of the alloys mixed with the silver; some say it is all caused by gentle cleaning over long periods of time; others say it is nothing more than myriads of usually indiscernible scratches on the surface.

There may be a germ of truth in all those explanations as to the development of patination, but I feel hopeful that now, at last, the basic secret of this phenomenon is revealed by indisputable logic. Ernst Schuckmann, a senior executive of the world's largest company associated with the study of metals, inevitably became interested in patination, shortly after starting his important collection of antique silver. Accordingly, I am very grateful to him for agreeing to give his views on this vital aspect of our subject and for allowing me to reproduce them in this book.

> One popular theory of the patina, or colour, of old silver is that it is created by the reflection of light on the myriad nicks and scratches on its surface which have accumulated over the years. However, there is old silver with a relatively smooth surface and very good patina as well as silver with many nicks and scratches and no colour at all. So this theory does not completely satisfy; nor does it explain why silver with good patination does not seem to tarnish rapidly when left in the normal 'polluted' atmosphere of most of our industrial cities. Silver with very good patina can be exposed to this same atmosphere for a very much longer time without tarnishing. When it finally does show signs of tarnish, this can be removed by merely wiping with a soft cloth. Silver without patina exposed for the same length of time to the same air usually has to be cleaned with a commercial cleaner to restore its brilliance.

> All of this seems to indicate that patinated silver is covered by some form of protective coating. Another indication that this is so is that the much coveted colour of old silver is not truly the colour of the metal, not even alloyed with copper in the usual propor-

One of a set of eight circular sugar bowls chased with the arms of the City of London, the lid with applied vine ornamentation below its terminal of a coiled snake, the body with cast and chased decoration featuring cornucopias on matted ground, female term heads to handles. London, 1803, by Scott & Smith, 14.8cm high. Courtesy the Worshipful Company of Goldsmiths.

A boldly marked tankard, flat-chased with chinoiserie decoration. London, 1683, 16cm high. Courtesy the Worshipful Company of Goldsmiths.

Cup engraved with the arms of the City of Hereford (facing), with those of the donor on the reverse, extensively embossed with acanthus foliage, original cover missing. London, 1675, 33cm high. Courtesy the Worshipful Company of Goldsmiths.

A splendid two-handled cup and cover with applied cast decoration and engraved with the arms of J.G. Bridge, of the firm of Rundell & Bridge (goldsmiths), Prime Warden of the Worshipful Company of Goldsmiths in 1839. London, 1739, by Paul de Lamerie, 34.4cm high. Courtesy the Worshipful Company of Goldsmiths.

tions. Silver, or the normal alloys of silver used in England, looks white or what is traditionally called silver-white, while old silver with patina has a bluish hue, almost like the colour of chromium. In other words, with patinated silver we are looking through a very thin coat of something else with a different colour which changes the colour of silver.

What is the most likely explanation of all this? It must be that this coat is silver oxide. Silver does not oxidise easily and for this reason is considered to be a precious metal. The normal tarnish encountered on silver is not silver oxide, but rather silver sulphide. This is caused by sulphur-containing contaminents in the air, sometimes also by the same element present in certain foods, such as eggs. Silver sulphide can be removed easily with a commercial silver polish which uses a chemical together with a slight mechanical action. While silver does not oxidise perceptibly, it may do so gradually over a period of a hundred and fifty to two hundred years or more. Since silver oxide is highly resistant to further chemical action it would not be affected by a commercial cleaner. There would be a very gradual build-up of a micro-scopically thin coating of silver oxide which would protect the silver underneath against other chemical attacks such as the above mentioned sulphur-containing air pollutants. The only way this protective coat of silver oxide could be removed would be with a mechanical polishing wheel. Silver oxide is black. A micro-scopically thin film of a black substance would make the silver underneath look bluish, the very colour of old silver.

It is well known that old Sheffield plate may also develop par-ticularly good patina. It may be that as the silver begins to wear down and gets close to the copper, copper oxide may start to form. Copper naturally oxidises much more readily than silver, and its oxide is also black, thus contributing to the film that gives the bluish colour of old Sheffield plate.

Quite often one examines a surface with a basically fine patination but notices also that it is extensively discoloured by darker blotches (see illustration opposite). Although many reputable traders make light of this condition, factually and perfectly legitimately explaining that the blotches are nothing more sinister than original fire stains, I, like some others, find this condition displeasing to the eye. The discoloration is caused by the alloy mixed with silver of the sterling standard emerging to the surface. These fire stains can, of course, be removed today by a polishing wheel, but in such drastic action the patination of centuries is destroyed and the item's finished state is far worse than the original. Patina at its best has an apparently fathomless depth of beauty and, by the way, it hardly ever seems to need a clean. But burnish it, thus destroying the skin of patination, and it will elude you for very many decades.

When butlers became redundant after the 'Kaiser' war and uncleaned silver was left in chests and attics, later to emerge so black that it was dispatched to be polished professionally, much fine silver was reduced to a secondary condition. The surfaces of such pieces, although they may be free

Discoloration (somewhat exaggerated) on a late eighteenth century tea pot. Courtesy Sotheby's.

of repairs, are covered with innumerable faint scratches, roughly circular in shape, inflicted by a buffing-wheel which necessarily removed the skin of patination. To ensure that patina is not damaged in this way, collectors who are obliged to store their silver should make certain it is wrapped in acid-free material and that it is not put away with fingerprints remaining.

Many modern repairers and dealers think that they can produce a good patina on articles even after they have been subjected to intense heat and acid treatment. They talk nonsense, probably thinking that a dull polish instead of a bright one will produce a pleasant colour. Some misguided dealers instruct their repairers to conceal restorations with an 'antique finish' achieved by 'dark plating'; another trick is to shake a restored surface in a bag of lead shot. But these processes cannot produce a convincing antique patina and those who say otherwise have never learned to recognise it.

Patina, once it is acquired and remains free of mishaps, continues to improve as the centuries pass. It is, perhaps, at its most magnificent on items of thick construction of the Britannia standard era, and almost equally as good as a background to the arabesque engravings of the Elizabethan period. In fact, we should insist on it for all antique silver.

My personal appreciation of patina, even although it was only a sub-conscious understanding, came almost at the outset of my interest in silver (as is related in the preface of this book), so there is no reason why readers should not be infected within a week or two by my apparent fetish about it. But be warned: even after achieving recognition, unless you possess a perfect example of patination readily available for your comparison, you will have temporary lapses of forgetfulness caused, perhaps, by the tricks of light or wishful thinking.

My personal confidence in the recognition of a good patina — in which case, of course, there is no question of a modern repair or forgery — tends to make me lazy in my routine inspection (Chapter 10) and in consequence I fail sometimes to notice a minor antique repair. But then, I don't really worry much about very small faults providing they are themselves antique.

When customers come to me and the conversation turns to patina, I am able to demonstrate the difference between good and bad patina. But to my disappointment they may not immediately thrill to the fine example because it requires the understanding that experience alone affords and they often say: "Yes, I see the difference in the colour, but I shan't be able to remember it."

It is virtually impossible to illustrate the difference between good and bad patination from a photograph, but a brave attempt has been made here. The George III crested table spoon (left) is developing a good patination, but the spoon of the same period (right) has a remarkably poor colour. This latter spoon was once considerably longer than the former and has also had its bowl reshaped, reducing its length by approximately .3cm.

If you rub an old patina with your thumb the surface after a moment or two will feel *slightly rougher or resistant* while a modern surface may feel quite slippery by comparison. Some experts consider that new surfaces have a pink appearance while old, unrestored surfaces have a steely blue look. When you have handled a hundred or more pieces of good and bad patina, you will be able to go about without your model for comparison. You will decide that on silver of thick construction the recognisable tinge on good patination is white-grey and on items of thinner construction the tinge is blue-grey.

You must go to a specialist dealer of long standing and of great knowledge, in whom you have complete confidence. Then, put yourself unreservedly in his hands. Ask for a small item of silver, something that will fit into your pocket, perhaps a Queen Anne table spoon, of glorious patina and impeccable quality throughout. Tell the dealer that you are just starting to collect and you require a piece as a model of excellence with which to compare all the other silver that you propose to inspect in the coming months.

With such an approach it would be a very mean character indeed who did not warm to the task of helping you, but he might keep you waiting some time for the right article.

Starting off on the right foot in this manner and keeping your small specimen piece always at hand wherever you go, the recognition of patina will represent an early break-through into the most important single aspect of expertise.

A word about silver gilt. Much silver throughout the ages was gilt or parcel (partly) gilt. The difference between antique and modern gilding is usually recognised at a glance, but the harshness of the latter is sometimes cleverly softened nowadays. With the exception of vessels or boxes used for containing corrosive substances in everyday use, it is wise to avoid all items with modern gilding for such pieces usually have something to conceal. As electro-gilding wears thin rather rapidly, glass liners may be considered more satisfactory than modern gilding for vessels such as salt cellars. Items with modern gilding may not be considered suitable for your cabinet.

CHAPTER 5

How quality affects value

Let me say at the outset that other considerations besides quality influence the value of a piece, but that does not alter the fact that quality is one of the principal factors which determine how much you will be asked to pay. Some members of the trade may object to the use of figures later in this chapter, and I accept that some of the sums may appear a trifle crude, but to condemn them is to miss the point. The figures are there to make you understand how to go about working out the importance of different factors. Once you understand what to look for and what weight to give to them you are well on the way to making a sensible judgement. That this approach is correct was proved to me by the comments made to me by a number of dealers. "Why wise up the mugs? Why make life harder for all of us? What are you trying to achieve?" Strangely, some of these men I would trust in any dealings they had with me, as a fellow dealer, yet their attitude to you the collector is quite different. There is only one answer: you have to have the knowledge. But to return to quality.

Some porringers, caudle cups, wine tasters, early boxes and many miniature items, for example, may lack quality in several respects, but they are often appealing to collectors for a variety of reasons and have plenty of charm and other endearing attributes. Let us consider miniature items of silver of the late seventeenth to early nineteenth centuries (see p. 94). We may derive interest from and delight in their collection, but they are usually flimsy and constructed as playthings for favoured nurseries, laying no claim to artistic merit. There are, of course, other miniature items that are of fine quality but these, unless they were made for the children of exceptionally influential parents, were probably either hawked around as samples by goldsmiths' travellers in order to solicit orders for full-sized articles of identical design or, perhaps, they were merely constructed by advanced apprentices whilst practising their art.

Quality is a word much used in the silver trade and it is usually misused. Novice collectors should be prepared for these irregularities. My first impression of the meaning of 'quality', when applied to silver by dealers, was that it was synonymous with thick or sturdy construction and the phrase 'better quality' implied, above all other considerations, a greater weight for size. Subsequently, after I had heard the word employed as an adjective ('it's a real quality piece') I decided that quality must express a general desirability and (usually) something well worth buying. But the word is frequently used in sales talk and I have even heard rarity (of an item) included amongst the attributes of quality. There are degrees of quality, the usual extremes of which are termed either superb or poor.

As we are discussing silver we might as well write about it in the vernacular of our trade and so, for the purposes of this chapter, my interpretation of quality — presented with profuse apologies to *The Oxford English Dictionary* — is a peculiar excellence (relating to any item of silver) caused by a number of favourable, valuable and diverse attributes, the most important of which, I think, is beauty.

Two handled cup and cover with a form of beading applied to the scroll handles and also to the cut-card work representing acanthus leafage. London, 1697, by John Boddington. Courtesy the Worshipful Company of Goldsmiths.

A simple tazza or paten on spreading foot. Exeter, 1712, by Pentecost Symonds, marked on face and foot, 13.5cm diameter, 7oz. 2dwt. Pentecost Symonds worked at Plymouth and has been called the 'Lamerie of the West'. Courtesy the Eagle Collection, Devon.

Realism compels us to include good marks amongst the attributes of quality, because if such marks are in a specimen state they are likely (but by no means necessarily) to reflect the general overall pristine state of the article; otherwise hallmarks have nothing whatsoever to do with quality. An unmarked item, if of superlative quality with an attractive and identifiable heraldic coat might be considerably more valuable and of far greater interest than many reasonably good fully-marked pieces. Hallmarks, providing they are genuine, may be considered as the reassuring bottom in the children's paddling pool before the toddlers grow up to enjoy themselves safely in deeper waters. An insistence by collectors for the presence of hallmarks indicates to me either an admission of their inexperience or that they are collecting for the wrong motives (i.e. that they are basically dealers anxious to cash in on the widest uninformed market). Contemporary heraldic arms (though they are not always genuine ones, see Chapter 12) can in themselves contribute to the beauty and therefore to the quality of an item, but very rubbed examples, in the same way as worn hallmarks, can be detrimental to quality.

The pleasantest understanding of quality might recall the craftsman's lingering inspection of his finished article, his reluctance to turn away, his compulsive return to admire again and finally his glow of happiness and pride from confirmation of his artistry.

Do our eyes deceive us? Is personal taste, born of long experience, an unreliable guide? If beauty lies in the eye of the beholder then the assembly of middle-aged hard-headed, elderly bald-headed, silver dealers — sometimes referred to as 'The Boys' — sitting round the table at Christie's must be consistently deceived or deceiving! The important point at issue is that all these dealers and many of the small ones too, the auctioneers, and their more senior porters, the better-educated members of the public who swarm to these important auctions all share a remarkable unanimity of opinion as to what constitutes beauty, and this unanimity is proven invariably by the high price a beautiful piece obtains.

Left, the earliest known tea pot with its spout set at an angle to the leather-covered handle. London, 1670, maker's mark TL, 33.8cm high. Right, the earliest known coffee pot. London, 1681, by George Garthorne (probably), 24.4cm high.

The tea pot would have been considered a coffee pot but for an inscription engraved upon it: 'This silver tea-Pott was presented to ye Committee of ye East India Company by ye Honourable George Lord Berkeley of Berkeley Castle. A member of that Honourable and worthy Society and A true Hearty Lover of them 1670'. Courtesy the Victoria and Albert Museum.

On the other hand, the general public as they buy their turn-of-the-century junk, their fussy Victoriana, their terribly ordinary, poor quality, Georgian milk jugs and their much-restored vinaigrettes seem to suffer a conception of beauty that the patrons of the big auctions would abhor.

In about 1950 when I returned home after a buying trip, frequently having been obliged to buy junk together with the better items, I used to climb the stairs to a window and throw items such as turn-of-the-century vesta boxes

Left, a superlative pair of Irish table spoons of Hanoverian pattern. Dublin, 1741, by William Williamson, only 20.25cm but weighing over 5oz. The marks are in specimen state but it is the unusually high ridge travelling only 6cm down the stem which makes them so attractive to the author.

Right, a pair of heavy Irish gravy spoons of the 'kitchen' type. Dublin, 1770, by John Craig, 30cm, 8oz. It is said that the spoons were hung by the turnover ends in the kitchen when not in service. Maybe this is so, but an alternative purpose must have been to prevent the spoon slipping over the edge of a dish into the gravy. Courtesy the James Aspin Collection, South Africa.

(then with a value of about five old pence for melting) down to the children assembled eagerly in the garden below. Children are, of course, magpies and all this trivia gave them pleasure. In retrospect, I realise that I was irresponsibly throwing away items which today would have been worth hundreds of pounds, but, then as now, I cannot find any interest or merit in mass-produced trinkets of the twentieth century. I do not, of course, refer to some novelty vesta boxes made from about 1844 for a few of these are ingenious, amusing and full of quality.

We cannot blame money for extreme contrasts of taste. Although a large part of the public's purchases would not be accepted for sale at a big auction, and the remainder, mostly lumped together in 'lots' of numerous items and sold for about a quarter of cost price, their actual outlay amounts to a tragic squandering of hard-earned money, viz., tiny Edwardian silver match boxes at £25 or more each, silver thimbles at £10, pairs of berry spoons at £60, forged caddy spoons at £20 and later embossed Georgian tankards and similar coffee pots at around £800.

The explanation, I think, is that those whose work involves the constant handling of beautiful things and even those who are shrewd enough to buy beautiful things, grow to love and understand them. Broadcasting has brought the appreciation of good music into millions of homes, but the appreciation of beauty in other forms of art requires effort. That is perhaps why one quite often hears people saying, for example: "We don't like silver particularly but my husband and I collect anything within our means."

In the auction rooms the quality of antique silver can be assessed in cash, but however high one's personal assessment of an outstanding piece may be, it is, from personal experience, inevitable that others assess the value even higher!

I will list the attributes of quality and place them, first in the order of preference that I think an experienced dealer considering purchasing for stock would rate them, and secondly for an experienced collector (or dealer) forming his personal collection.

Dealer

1. Beauty and outstanding design.
2. Brilliant marks.
3. Crispness of design (if applicable).
4. Unspoiled patina.
5. Good weight for size.
6. Balance.

Collector

1. Beauty and patination (synonymous where silver is concerned).
2. Brilliant marks.
3. Crispness of ornamentation (if applicable).
4. Good weight for size.
5. Balance.

The next useful step is to attempt to put a cash value on quality, though we will be working only on broad approximations. Let us assume that a George III coffee pot of 30oz. is worth £3,000 and that its quality is perfect in every respect. Below, I try to estimate how the figure of £3,000 is arrived at, supposing scrap silver to be worth £10 per ounce, this being a convenient rather than a realistic figure.

Melting value of the coffee pot	300
Beauty, design and craftsmanship	800
Superb patination	600
Brilliant marks	625
Very satisfactory weight for size	315
Fine contemporary coat of arms	210
Exceptional balance	150
	£3,000

Crispness of decoration (not applicable in this instance) must be considered in conjunction with beauty.

The reader may be confused when he glances at the table on the previous page for the first time and so the following comments may help to make the points clearer.

Q. How could anyone in their senses assess the melting value of a mid-Georgian coffee pot at only £300?

A. If the general condition was so poor that it was virtually beyond repair and therefore considered suitable only for the melting pot.

Q. But surely a price is fixed by the age of an article?

A. Age is certainly an important factor of price. A good Queen Anne coffee pot (rare) would certainly be worth very much more than a good George III pot (not so rare) but, on the other hand, a fine reproduction pot (costing about £600) might be worth more than a very poor antique example from which the reproduction was copied.

Q. Beauty is an intangible quality. How can it be valued?

A. By learning to appreciate it. Reread the first part of this chapter!

Q. What does good balance imply?

A. Handle a number of pieces of fine quality silver and you'll soon understand. Good balance is recognised by an instinctive approval of line and ornamentation. This approval appears to be common to all those who constantly handle antique silver. Bad examples of balance would include vessels with a lid or handle obviously of poor proportions, Victorian decoration encroaching upon plain Georgian lines and, normally, 'marriages' where two parts of different items have been joined to make a composite article.

Q. Do dealers really make valuations in this manner?

A. They work on similar lines, though they probably don't need to spell out the different factors in detail any more than an experienced cook needs to weigh out the ingredients she has used many times before to make the same dish. But that doesn't alter the fact that the recipe is the basis on which she works. Certainly, dealers would not guess values.

I will now deduct from the valuation of £3,000 for this coffee pot appropriate figures for lack of quality in others similar (i.e. in style, date and weight). After considerable experimentation, the resulting guides, if applied realistically, provide sensible final figures for the value of any similar coffee pot:

1. No combination of faults to exceed a total of £2,700.
2. Directly deductions have reached or passed a total of £1,500, all subsequent deductions to be at the rate of 20% of estimated reduction for a particular fault. Deductions must commence and continue with the biggest, single deduction outstanding.
3. When practising valuations on the lines outlined in the following list, you must consider carefully the meaning of the words 'up to' and 'about'. 'Up to' permits a wide discretionary variation from the maximum deduction recommended. 'About' does not, and should not, suggest much room for manoeuvre.
4. The reader is entitled to ask why we are bothering to discuss the valuation of items that, for example, have been electroplated, embossed and de-chased, when he has been warned against buying

them. It would be most encouraging for me if he were to take his question a stage further by asking: "If the buyer knows there are serious defects, he would not think of buying, surely?"

Some dealers have been trading in both poor and fine quality silver for decades and they know what they are doing even though the vast majority of their customers do not. Auction prices, in fact, are usually more accurately predictable on poor than on superb quality items. I feel it is important that students should find their way along all the paths of the 'jungle'. The recognition and understanding of bad silver helps you to appreciate the good.

5. It is, of course, pointless to practise valuations in this manner until you have acquired some general experience of prices on the lines suggested in Chapter 9.

List of deductions (from £3,000)
Visible repairs . . . . up to £2,500
A weak patch where, for example, a crest has been
    removed (this weakness could be patched over) . . . . up to £2,200
Rubbed hallmarks . . . . up to £1,500
Absence of all hallmarks, but with contemporary,
    identified coat of arms or crest . . . . about £1,300
Electroplated, concealing repairs . . . . about £2,000
Extensive later decoration or de-chasing of such
    decoration . . . . about £1,800
Indifferent design and craftsmanship . . . . up to £1,400
Poor patination . . . . up to £1,800
Marks missing from lid but lid not suspect (this
    consideration would not be deductible from pots made at
    provincial centres where it was not the practice to mark
    in the lids) . . . . about £500
Poor weight for size . . . . up to £1,500
Later initials, monogram or heraldic device . . . . up to £1,400
Poor balance . . . . up to £1,200
Later handle — this could be of silver and therefore
    inappropriate to style of pot (all later handles could
    be removed and replaced with a wooden handle
    in the correct style) . . . . about £250

Examples of comparing the price difference between the specimen coffee pot, valued at £3,000, with other similar coffee pots:

Example 1
Marks rubbed but decipherable . . . . deduct £1,400
Slight antique repair . . . . deduct £300
Later crest but in contemporary style — 20% of say £500 . . deduct £100
Later handle — 20% of £250 . . . . deduct £50

Total deductions £1,850

Value of coffee pot therefore £3,000 less £1,850 equals £1,150.

Example 2 (extremely poor condition)
Electro-plated, concealing repairs..................... deduct £2,000
Rubbed hallmarks — 20% of £1,000 .... deduct £200
Indifferent design — 20% of £900 .... deduct £180

Total deductions £2,380

Value of coffee pot therefore £3,000 less £2,380 equals £620.

I hope it is clear from this example that quality really is paramount and that one has to be very clear headed about factors such as quality of marks, quality of patination, quality of condition, quality of engraving and quality of design.

CHAPTER 6

The pitfalls: including forged marks, fake engraving, rigged prices

Just before Christmas one year an exciting parcel arrived for me containing four items of silver. They were not a present but it seemed that goods worth about £6,000 had been offered to me for considerably less than half their value by a reasonably experienced dealer of good repute.

I examined the two smaller pieces first. Both items were almost identical William IV snuff boxes, one by Mills and the other by Shaw, with superlative engravings on their lids, one of a college at Oxford and the other a scene of the river Cam at Cambridge. What a nice combination to possess, I thought, and then wondered if Mills and Shaw (both of Birmingham) had produced other engraved scenes from Oxbridge. I could not recall having seen any.

It was not until later, having already been bitterly disappointed by the two larger items in the parcel, that I was satisfied, after seeking the advice of an artist friend, that the engravings on both lids were by the same hand. There seemed nothing suspicious in this coincidence by itself, but the engravings were remarkably sharp and when inspected under a powerful glass did not seem to match indications of slight wear on other parts of the boxes. But for thinking that these engravings had been executed in modern times, thus making them unacceptable to me despite their commercial legality and outstanding quality, I would have bought them greedily.

The other two items of this Christmas box had already caused alarm. There was the largest shell snuff box that I had ever seen and its silver lid was gloriously engraved with a coat of arms in the taste of c.1730. It seemed to boast the mark of Peter and Jonathan Bateman (1790) but, blinded by the beauty of the engraving, I momentarily failed to note that the maker's mark lacked its normal precision and clarity. 'Kidding' myself that there could be some rational explanation for the disparity in periods between maker and style of engraving, I believed that the box before my excited eyes must be the only really important piece of silver created by the short partnership of the Bateman brothers. My short-lived ecstasy disappeared when I looked carefully at the supposed hallmarks. Under magnification, these marks were almost as crude as the pseudo-London and provincial marks of colonial silversmiths.

Finally, I inspected an imposing silver-gilt freedom box engraved with the arms of the City of London on its base and with a powerful coursing scene embossed on the lid. It was stamped with a genuine mark of Hester Bateman (probably on old stock without ornamentation and shelved after Hester's death), but with quite convincing pseudo-London marks for 1795. The lion passant, obviously disappointing the forger, had been partially erased and the whole box then fire-gilt recently. The purported recipient of the box, whose name was engraved beneath the coat of arms, became Lord Mayor in 1796, and was well known as an enthusiast of coursing.

The quality of the engraving together with the detailed research associated with the creation of three of the four boxes seemed such a far cry from the crudities of the forged marks that it seemed inconceivable to me that the engraver could also have been responsible for the illegalities. All members of the trade to whom I showed the boxes were agreed, rightly or wrongly, that there was only one man that they knew who could have produced such fine engraving. They confirmed my suspicions as to his domicile, but all preferred not to mention his name to me. However, learning that I was interested, an engraver was not only courteous enough to ring me and reveal his identity, but also called to see me. He explained that whereas he did engrave silver he certainly would not stoop to forgery. Moreover, what with his heavy commitments to important London dealers — the innocent touching up of heraldic arms, I presumed — he certainly had no time for any other involvement. Certainly, he is a young man of admirable good taste and it would be sad to think of his artistry being abused by one or more squalid silver dealers.

Modern engraving in a style contemporary with the period of manufacture of an item, which enhances its beauty and increases its value just slightly, will not be acceptable to the unrelenting purist; but it may not seem seriously detrimental to the vast majority of collectors even if they know about it. After all, all silver started life unadorned. However, when such engraving is calculated to increase the price of an article very considerably, even doubling its value and more — such engraving thereby transforming the ordinary into the exceptional (perhaps, like the two snuff boxes just described) or purporting to associate the article with an important historical event or person — then the retailer, by all personal standards of right or wrong, even although he is not breaking any of the regulations pertaining to hallmarks, must be guilty of cheating his customers. The actual engraver executing the crooked retailer's order is merely earning his living whilst exercising his art and he therefore escapes censure in such a jungle as our world.

The distinctions between forgeries and offending pieces are often academic, but conditions of silver listed under the latter and more charitable heading were frequently — especially in the last century — perpetrated in ignorance and without dishonest intent. The reader should refer to Jackson for detailed information of the regulations pertaining to hallmarks, but a useful précis of what does and what does not constitute a forgery, or an offending piece, can be contained in quite a few words.

Forgeries
1.   Any item with transposed, inserted or forged hallmarks.

Offending pieces
1.   Any item that, subsequent to being marked, has been altered in form and purpose (viz., spoons into forks, tea pots into tea caddies, pap boats into sauce or cream boats, tankards into jugs, etc). A piece which thus contravenes the regulations can be legalised with the co-operation of Goldsmiths' Hall by being restored to its original form and purpose, if possible, provided that all new pieces of silver used in the restoration are tested and, if acceptable, stamped with modern hallmarks. Even an

item with forged marks can be legalised if the article is found to be of standard, providing the false marks are obliterated and modern marks added.

This provides an explanation of, for example, a Charles II tankard bearing genuine antique marks normally positioned, and two modern marks (a lion and a date letter) where, say, a Victorian-added lip has been removed and the resulting space filled up to restore its original form and purpose (i.e. a jug back to a tankard).

2. Any item that, subsequent to being marked, has received a substantial addition (viz., a rim to a salver). If the original marks are not tampered with, the piece can be legalised if the addition is assayed and struck with modern hallmarks.

3. A marriage of two or more parts from articles of different origins, whether fully hallmarked or not.

Note: It is contrary to the Hallmarking Act for anyone to sell a piece of silver bearing marks that may be forged, altered, transposed etc., without consulting an assay office (which will 'legalise' the piece if necessary). A number of collectors have been pleasantly surprised by the advice given regarding items which they thought were worth little more than their scrap value.

This is an interesting forgery because the salt cellar seems attractive and of good craftsmanship. Although the author cannot recall for certain having seen genuine salt cellars in this exact style he would not be surprised if he did and he would assume that the date would be c.1800. It is said that this forgery was done c.1900 and the author wonders if the salt cellar was once a genuine unmarked item upon which spurious marks (see next illustration) were added. In 1900 unmarked pieces were neither understood nor appreciated commercially. Courtesy the Worshipful Company of Goldsmiths.

The spurious hallmarks on the salt cellar. Except for the shields, these are quite cleverly made, and try to represent the London marks for 1774.

Items which are neither forgeries nor offending pieces
1. Items with non-contemporary decoration where the purpose of the article and the weight of the silver have not been changed by the alterations (viz., Georgian tankards and coffee pots, etc., with decoration inflicted in the Victorian era).
2. Items of silver which have been electroplated in order to conceal repairs of a legitimate nature (see the jug on page 117).

Three spoons with their bowls reshaped from the Old English style into the fig shape of the sixteenth century, rat tails added (incorrect in form and period) apparently by chasing and embossing, cast terminals applied to stems and the original genuine marks (for London, 1780) left untouched. These alterations, probably of the late nineteenth century, display such an ignorance of antique silver styles that they would deceive scarcely anyone today. Courtesy the Worshipful Company of Goldsmiths.

Personally, I wish that both the items under this heading were classified as offending pieces.

Since the law specifically says that it is an offence to sell a piece that carries marks likely to be confused with genuine hallmarks no reputable dealer or silver collector would wish to be responsible for adding suspected or proven fakes or forgeries to a collection. Moreover it is an offence for a person to have custody of a piece he knows or suspects bears counterfeit marks.

The Wardens of the Goldsmiths' Company have, by reason of a number of charters granted to them since 1327, wide powers to control the goldsmiths' and silversmiths' craft. These powers represent such an anachronism in our modern state that although still exercising their right to search for, seize and destroy spurious plate, they do not themselves punish offenders. When they consider that a prosecution is necessary, suspects are passed to the comparative clemency of our legal system.

It must be some time since the Wardens have deported, imprisoned, or placed offenders in the pillory after slicing off an ear. On the debit side, we are confronted by the increase of the falsification of antique plate. In modern history the two most notorious periods for such activities are in the second half of the last century and today.

The Deputy Warden is the person charged by the Goldsmiths' Company with the application of the 1973 Hallmarking Act in all its facets. In this the Company works in association with the trading standards officers of local consumer protection departments as well as with the various police regional crime squads when they seek advice from the Company. On certain

The most important picture for novice collectors in the entire book! It should serve as an awful warning for those who, unappreciative of patination and careless in their source of purchase, buy repaired goods that have been electroplated to deceive the unwary. After some years of daily use, the plate wears off and reveals the previously concealed repairs. This item is neither a forgery nor an offending piece and it could be sold as a genuine George II cream jug.

There is now an acute shortage of three-prong forks, especially of the shield top style, to complete early sets of flatware, therefore one expects that this forgery is of modern date. It is a conversion from a bottom marked table spoon of London, 1776. The tines have been added at the bottom of the stem of the spoon, see the illustration below, and the top of the stem has been reshaped. Courtesy the Worshipful Company of Goldsmiths.

Detail of the three-prong fork in the illustration above, showing the marks of the junction of the tines with the bottom of the stem of the spoon.

occasions, the Arts and Antiques Squad at New Scotland Yard may also get involved.

However, police investigations are unlikely to start until the Assay Office of the Goldsmiths' Company has provided the confirmation that a piece of silver is a fake. Consequently, anyone who suspects he has acquired such an article will probably speed the investigative process if he first takes the piece to the Goldsmiths' Company.

I encountered the powers of Goldsmiths' Hall many years ago soon after I had started dealing in silver. There was a knock on my door and a Mr. Lindsey, the then Deputy Warden, announced his desire to inspect my silver. With a conscience as clear as crystal, I made him welcome and with the *naiveté* of most inexperienced dealers showed him my silver with pride and pleasure. Everything went well until he spotted a Queen Anne chamber candlestick — the very item for which, subsequently I was sure, he had expressly made the long journey from London to view — which I had bought at a big London auction earlier in the week at a price so cheap that an experienced dealer would have 'smelled a rat' immediately.

Unfortunately, I have forgotten all details as to why this piece was a suspected forgery, and Mr. Lindsey took it away saying that the chamberstick would be examined by the Antique Plate Committee at their next sitting in Goldsmiths' Hall and that I would be informed of its findings.

After the piece had been condemned by the Committee and destroyed, and I had been reimbursed by the auctioneers who sold it, I was left in credit from this incident by a greater awareness of the dangers and responsibilities of a reputable dealer.

In fact, the hallmarking laws applying at the time of this incident, were changed in 1975. Although the current Act gives the Goldsmiths' Company the power to break, i.e. to destroy, articles, the Company's practice since 1975 has been to remove any marks that could mislead a purchaser and give the owner the option of having the article assayed and marked as a new piece, or returned with a warning that without hallmarks it may not be sold as silver.

Almost all forgers of the past seemed totally ignorant of the subject and their efforts, which still turn up occasionally, are almost invariably, except with early spoons, unrepresentative of even an approximate period and style; so forgeries can be likened to hybrids. Even when the forger chose to superimpose a full set of marks, possibly cut from a Stuart piece, on the base of a genuine, unmarked tankard, the odds were about fifty to one on the forger selecting the wrong set of marks for the period.

Forgers display the same ignorance when putting a complete set of marks from one object to another as when they forge their own set of marks and strike such punches on unmarked or refashioned pieces. In the former case if you breathe on the hallmarks the insertion lines will normally, unless the item has been electroplated, become clearly visible. I have encountered antique hallmarks inserted into modern pieces and I have also found many such items plated in an attempt to conceal the insertion lines. Very recently I saw a pair of embossed Edwardian flower vases that had been soldered to the bowls of a pair of worn out circular salt cellars on ball and claw feet, with the Georgian marks on the bowls still quite clear.

I am convinced that the greatest compliment an expert is likely to pay to these types of forgeries is to reject them instantly and irrevocably without bothering to inspect the marks, thereby indicating no immediate recognition of fraud, but just an instinctive distaste for, and lack of interest in, antique silver that is so clearly below his desired standards.

Forged spoons of the sixteenth and seventeenth centuries have been cast from genuine spoons in considerable quantities. They are easy to recognise because of the 'woolliness' or lack of sharpness of the marks. Most of these forgeries are confined to seal top and apostle spoons, the two most popular types, and purport to be London spoons. I have heard of a number of provincial spoons with early, forged marks and these frauds are harder to detect owing to the poorness of the workmanship.

Far more dangerous than the cast spoons are some fine forgeries perpetrated, I suppose, towards the end of the last century. A talented rascal made excellent punch marks in close imitation of the small sized punches used by the London Assay Office on the slender shanks of seal top spoons which, when struck deep into the shanks and bowls, are extremely difficult to compare in detail with the genuine. I have handled such a spurious spoon and, but for the curious lateness and uncertainty of the date letter, which appeared to represent London 1673, on a spoon that I considered to be c.1640, I think I would have been fooled. The Victoria and Albert Museum considered this spoon to be the best forgery that they had ever seen, but this was no more than an opinion, and I handed it back to its owner with the recommendation that he should place it before the Antique Plate Committee for a ruling. Before this could be done, the suspected forgery was stolen by burglars. I wonder if the owner claimed compensation from his insurers and, if so, how the piece was described?

On another occasion, whilst waiting at the metalwork department of the Victoria and Albert Museum, a man seeking expert opinion came in with three seal top spoons. He thought one of them might be 'wrong', but that the other two should be 'right' because, he alleged, he had bought them at a big London auction. From a cursory glance, which I hope went unnoticed, they all looked 'probables' to me, but the Victoria and Albert Museum opined that all three were spurious. Therefore early spoons are particularly dangerous and should be bought only from the most reputable sources even when you have acquired very considerable experience.

Modern forgers and fakers know much more about their subject than the old timers, but even these rascals consistently make silly mistakes. Take for example a 'Death' or 'In Memoriam' spoon which was offered to me a few years back. It is certain that most genuine examples of this macabre design emanated from York although a few have been found which were made in Scotland. The first mistake the vendor made was to ask me £100 for it, making me suspect that it had been stolen from a museum, and the second error was the faker's choice of provenance. He had chosen a plain London trifid (maker's mark only) c.1665 which, with its wide top of shank was ideal for its subsequent reshaping into a skull. The engraving, as is usual with most of the modern forgeries and fakes that I have seen, was brilliantly realistic.

An interesting modern forgery which purported to be either a large so-called saffron pot or a very small bullet tea pot was dated London, 1725. The entire base, inclusive of genuine hallmarks within the foot and removed from another vessel, was soldered on to and right round the bowl at a point just above the foot. The lid and spout (the latter rather inexpertly soldered into the bowl) appeared to be of the George II period. The bowl itself could be modern for this forgery had been dark-plated in an attempt to conceal the alterations. The engraved coat of arms was certainly of very recent origin. In the summer of 1981 I heard of no less than fourteen other similar forgeries.

When the hallmarks, either spurious or inserted, are cancelled by scratching out after the article has been condemned by the Antique Plate Committee, a genuine or spurious stamp of a lion passant (normally), especially if concealed under the nut of a terminal bolt, is very occasionally overlooked and the owner, in certain circumstances, may opt to have the article returned to him without the addition of modern hallmarks. Should the article subsequently fall into unscrupulous hands, it is an easy matter to erase the not too deep scratches of the cancelled hallmarks before offering it for sale as a genuine unmarked period piece. The concealed lion passant could assist in this deception. In my early days, I do recall being puzzled when examining an ostensibly unmarked antique to find a solitary lion passant hidden away in a lid or appendage.

Some years ago, a number of forgeries from Italy, mostly candlesticks and salvers in the rocaille taste of the mid-eighteenth century, were smuggled into this country and hawked around the shops by Italian travellers. I have not seen any of these forgeries myself but understand that although their quality was extremely good the Italians made mistakes with their spurious London hallmarks. Some of these pieces may still be waiting for the unwary.

Whereas in England the majority of the forgeries and malpractices are of comparatively modern origin, many of those emanating from Ireland occurred in the eighteenth century and earlier. Admittedly, the penalties enacted for flouting the regulations of the Company of Goldsmiths, incorporated in Dublin in 1637, seem less severe than those enforced in London, and its supervision of the Dublin goldsmiths appeared slack, but this does not fully explain a suspected irrationality of the Irish silversmiths' practices, unless we accept that they enjoyed an inherent love of mischief for its own sake linked with an aversion to authority and discipline. If not so, why did such great goldsmiths as Charles Leslie (1735-57), with a thistle in his mark to recall his Scottish antecedents, Michael Keating, c.1775, and many

Duty dodgers were certainly not confined to Ireland alone. On the detachable, sliding bases of these otherwise unmarked caddies, the mark of John Newton of London is struck thrice alongside a genuine lion passant that is contemporary with the inscription dated 1740. Courtesy the Michael Graeme Macdonald Collection, U.S.A.

The inscription and markings on the caddies. The advanced collector will conjecture as to the reason why the form of the lion passant matches the year of the inscription while the style of the caddies suggests an earlier date.

others, most of whom were well patronised and most unlikely to be working under financial strain, so frequently choose to dodge paying duty on their products and, in addition, frequently fabricate slightly sub-standard silverwares? William Williamson, Master of the Company in 1737, who produced so much fine work, may be exonerated from these censures.

A majority of Irish silver was, of course, for obvious reasons, sent to be assayed in the proper manner, but many items were left either entirely unmarked or were struck thrice just with the maker's mark in a pattern resembling those of official assay marks. Few, if any, apart from the officials of the Goldsmiths' Company and its members, would have understood or recognised authentic markings.

Another common practice in Ireland was to transpose hallmarks of an earlier piece into a new eighteenth century production. The saving in duty by this forgery on a tea pot of sixteen ounces in weight, for example, would not have amounted to one pound and scarcely warranted, however frequently this crime was perpetrated, the risk of a term of imprisonment. The late Sir Charles Jackson wrote that 'the work of Charles Leslie was not inferior to that of Paul de Lamerie' and who could imagine the Huguenot master goldsmith jeopardising his liberty for a trifling sum?

I would not be averse to holding for my personal interest some of these eighteenth century Irish forgeries should they come my way and I am, reprehensibly, unable to regard them in the same murky light as articles forged in modern times. Moreover, such pieces were usually of great quality for, although they were intended to cheat authority, their beauty and craftsmanship were undoubtedly designed to delight their patrons. I believe that it is typical of the Irish nature to give of their best to friends and favoured customers whilst cocking a snook at their rulers.

Although, with the well-merited popularity of eighteenth century Irish silver today, there may be English silversmiths executing or contemplating the forgery of it, we know of only one, an Irishman I guess, who was a really productive forger in this century. He stamped his mark with initials IE surrounded by dots within an uneven oblong shield and I do recommend my readers to make a mental note of this mark. It is my personal conviction, formed from some examples of the IE mark which I have examined, that he started his operations by stamping unmarked Irish period pieces (perfectly genuine apart from the possibility that they were made from slightly sub-standard silver), graduated to stamping his mark on genuine but poorly hallmarked (therefore inexpensive) items where the real maker's mark had been erased by time or other processes and subsequently, only after exhausting the supplies of such silver available to him, did he fabricate his own productions of period Irish silver and apply his notorious spurious hallmarks which are so well known to both the Dublin and London authorities.

The best book to read upon the subject of Irish silver is, to my mind, Douglas Bennett's *Irish Georgian Silver*.

It is not recommended that collectors should invest their money in the inflated price league (henceforward referred to as the IPL), either of objects or makers, unless they are confident that the quality of such merchandise is worthy of their standards. Vinaigrettes, for there are many mediocre specimens, seem to head the IPL of objects, probably because they are so easily found and do not require much space to house. It is ridiculous to consider that an unusual Victorian example of these collectable little pieces can cost more than a fine small and rare article of the seventeenth century, especially if the latter is unmarked. If two or more big collections of vinaigrettes came on the market within a short space of time, and in a quantity which the market could not readily absorb, the values of all but the finest specimens would decrease noticeably for a considerable period of time. Mass-produced vesta boxes and similar trinkets of the turn of this century, although of too late a period to be considered as antique silver, must also be ridiculously overpriced.

Paul de Lamerie, the price of whose work averages some six times more than that of his contemporaries, including that of Pierre Platel to whom he was apprenticed, heads the IPL of makers with justification, but some of his work is quite ordinary and there are many makers whose creations are often as fine as those of the master craftsman. Silver from Peter and Jonathan Bateman's factory (1790), although generally reflecting nothing more than average competence, supplanted even Lamerie as head of the league in 1977/8, with ordinary table spoons made by these brothers fetching £200 each (about fourteen times the price of a spoon by most other makers of the period). However, people are coming to their senses and the brothers' silver seems to be losing second place in the IPL to Paul Storr (entered 1796), whose work is currently averaging some four and a half to five times the price of that of most of his contemporaries. The work of Hester Bateman, which often lacked fine craftsmanship, has eased a little in comparative values and may now be about twice the price of the work of her rivals. Frederick Kandler (entered 1735) a most worthy contemporary of Paul de Lamerie, may cost double the price of work by most others. The work of Nathaniel Mills, Senior (entered 1826), Matthew Boulton (entered Birmingham, 1773), Charles Fox (entered 1822) and members of the Garrard family of goldsmiths will command about half as much again as that of their contemporaries.

Prices, whether they be for specific makers or objects, are occasionally artificially boosted and the work of Peter and Jonathan Bateman is an example of this unsatisfactory situation. Although the partnership lasted

A well marked and fine fish slice. London 1790, pierced and engraved in the style of Hester Bateman (see also next illustration). Courtesy the Mr. and Dr. David Bayliss Collection, Hong Kong.

The mark of Peter and Jonathan Bateman on the reverse of the fish slice.

only a few months until Jonathan's death, its output was remarkably prolific and so, although uncommon today, the brothers' work is certainly not rare.

In order to boost their values should they be flagging, hoarders of considerable stocks of certain goods, possibly featuring in our IPL, sometimes resort to crafty manoeuvres to influence the market favourably; but these tricks are infrequent because prices generally are consistently rising and, in any case, present little threat to sensible buyers. However, I recently witnessed a farcical attempt at an auction to boost the price of Peter and Jonathan Bateman silver, which was doomed to failure from the outset. The auctioneer, with lunchtime approaching, refused to involve either himself or the assembly in a nonsensical waste of time. A toddy ladle with a rubbed maker's mark, yet probably expected by the auctioneer to obtain about £150 because it was discernible, had presumably had a silly reserve of £500 placed upon it, almost certainly at the last moment. It mattered not to the vendor if this item was sold or not, for all that he wished to achieve was the re-establishment of bygone price precedents.

Doubtless, the vendor hoped that the bidding would start at a more realistic figure which would persuade a few genuine buyers to participate in further bidding for a while. Thereafter, he would have hoped and expected that when and if genuine interest faded the auctioneer would carry on, by now plucking bids from the air, until a figure near the reserve price was reached. Instead of this, the auctioneer presented no vestige of reality to the proceedings: he opened the bidding at £500, glanced quickly round the assembly as if the ladle was causing a nasty smell under his nose and in well under five seconds brought his hammer down in favour of what most certainly seemed to be a fictitious name on the books of his clerk.

I have no proof to support this claim of attempted price-rigging by the vendor at that sale, but I'll bet that this account is accurate in substance. After an interval, to allow people to forget that farce, the hoarder of Peter and Jonathan silver may devise a cleverer technique; he might even be successful at his next attempt.

You are unlikely to learn much about prices at unimportant London sales or in smaller provincial auctions. At these latter venues, there is often insufficient expertise and financial backing to challenge the local 'ring' (a consortium of local dealers) who often co-operate with the London 'ring'. For many items, members of the 'ring', either for the purpose of diverting attention from their illegal activities or to prevent an outsider from getting a bargain, will bid, even amongst themselves, for the sake of creating a realistic facade, up to a fair price. But they will hope to buy some of the better items very cheaply, in the same manner as any individual such as myself. Two jealous housewives at daggers drawn or inexperienced over-excited dealers will often bid far above a realistic price. In such circumstances, I recall a late Georgian fiddle pattern pair of sugar tongs (worth about £11 at the time) reaching £80 before one of the contestants, fearful that the laughter rippling round the auction room was uncomplimentary, dropped out.

Prices, where the 'ring' is operating effectively, have no useful message for the student as they may be far below the final price obtained at the subsequent 'knock-out' (secondary auction) held in private by members of the 'ring'. Here, any surplus above the 'knock-down' price reached at the authentic auction is divided amongst the members of the consortium. Some small dealers may still scratch a tax-free living from these shareouts. Before legislation made auction 'rings' illegal — possibly the most farcical law ever introduced — the secondary auctions usually took place in full view of the public, often in a local hostelry and sometimes in the precincts of the sale. Nowadays, the 'ring' has to exercise some discretion and to make its presence less obvious.

Most of us make mutually agreeable arrangements with close friends or relatives if we are interested in the same items at an auction, but I have only acted with the wishes of a consortium on one occasion in my life. It was at a sale on the Welsh marches very many years ago. Having seen nothing to interest me at the preview in the morning, everything being too massive, dull and costly, I was leaving the auction room with the intention of returning straight home when I met the then leader of the London 'ring' just entering. "So, you're here," he said. Before I had time to explain that I was leaving and not returning, he added: "I'll give you ten pounds not to bid". I am still uncertain to this day as to whether his offer was a business or a charitable gesture.

To summarise the pitfalls in your paths, many of them far more sophisticated than booby traps, into which even the most experienced sometimes fall if rushed or feeling lazy; we appreciate that some are fraudulent, some offending, some with considerable interest and there are others which are insulting to our good taste. It is in this latter group, all of which are legal according to the regulations of the Hallmarking Act, that we find electroplated and later gilded silver, reshaped and remade (partly or wholly) bowls to spoons, and items which have been de-chased, patched and 'married'. Should you have the misfortune to discover examples of these undesirable conditions within your collection, you have no certain redress from the vendor. Forgeries present less of a hazard because, provided you make your purchases only from reputable sources, even if inexperienced ones, you should invariably get your money back.

This is because silver and gold enjoy a protection not available to other forms of antiques. For example, I sold a customer, before a proper inspection, an unimportant Irish basting spoon. The spoon's shank was great and untouched but the bowl had been remade in its original shape and then dull-plated to conceal the junction of old shank and new bowl. My customer took my mistake most sportingly for, with a rewarding smile, he averred that he would never have discovered our terrible error if he had not read my previous book.

If, instead, the item had been, say, a 'Sheraton' satinwood bureau bookcase which I had bought as 1790 and genuine, but it had turned out to be Edwards & Roberts 1890 (i.e. reproduction but with enough age to confuse the unknowledgeable) then, as far as I am concerned, without a twinge of conscience it would have gone to auction and the auctioneer could have described it as he wished. But it was silver, and *caveat emptor* does not apply to the sale of suspected forged silver items.

Had I sold the basting spoon after 1974, I, together with the auctioneer (assuming that he had gone along with my description), would have committed an offence for which the prescribed penalty on conviction is now a fine not exceeding £2,000. Nor would it have helped if the auctioneer had incorporated a disclaimer in the catalogue for, certainly as far as silver is concerned, this does not allow them to break the law.

Yet many auctioneers in their sale catalogues or elsewhere proclaim that they accept no responsibility (and therefore offer no redress) for defects, faults, etc., and errors of description, on the assumption that all items have been carefully inspected (sometimes in most difficult light) by intending purchasers, and it is a remarkable reflection on human gullibility that inexperienced punters are prepared to pay more, on average, at public auctions, than to purchase similar goods from reputable dealers who would co-operate faithfully, if requested, with their customers in the careful inspection of all items of their stock offered. Undue haste and over-excitement when considering antique silver should also be curbed.

But if you have made mistakes for which there is no redress, do not be down-hearted. We all have to buy our experience.

CHAPTER 7

Learning to interpret marks

Whilst the student remains unable to recognise the approximate date of an article at a glance, without recourse to hallmarks, he should make no purchases of silver except from a completely reliable concern. With this proviso, he should be encouraged to acquaint himself with the interpretation of marks.

This chapter is devised to make the student's task much easier, for it embraces and explains most of the inevitable problems that have beset a dealer of some forty years' experience.

For those who are willing and ready to learn, there are several reasonable comprehensive and portable guides to hallmarks on the market, one of the smallest (about half the size of a wallet), best and cheapest of these being *Bradbury's Book of Hallmarks.*

Any novice, if in possession of such a guide, and informed of the date and provenance of an article (if the marks are clear and complete), can check to see if the date suggested is correct, ambiguous or wrong. In this manner, the student will find a surprising number of errors in the catalogues of lesser provincial auctions and they will afford him a splendid opportunity to practise. At auctions where the actual vendor's descriptions of goods are accepted for inclusion in the catalogues of 'short-notice' sales, there may be intentional falsehoods concerning provenance, date and/or maker which, of course, are intended to increase the desirability of the merchandise. At most smaller auctions, such words as 'rare' and 'probably' prefixing a description, where marks are illegible or absent, may very often be wildly optimistic and sometimes hilarious to an experienced collector. Nevertheless, the student can usefully form his own conclusions.

For reference at home or at a library, Sir Charles Jackson's *English Goldsmiths and Their Marks* is essential. This embraces virtually all the hallmarks, etc., pertaining to English silver, together with a large number of makers' marks dating from 1479 to more modern times. [This work is currently being revised (by Ian Pickford for the Antique Collectors' Club) by the sensible expedient of using specialists in each of the provincial assay offices to correct the mistakes in the section which comes within their area. It is amazing that this has not been done years ago, for Jackson is most inaccurate in some sections, while in others his original work has withstood the test of time surprisingly well. (References to Jackson in this work are to the original edition.)]

Arthur Grimwade's *London Goldsmiths 1697-1837*, the product of many years of diligent research, is a remarkably comprehensive illustrated list of London makers' marks (mostly identified with names and addresses), including those of small-workers, dating from 1697. Before this date, we are usually unable to identify symbols and/or initials because the records of

An attractive West Country trifid spoon, the upper part of shank die-stamped with floral, foliate and scroll decoration, c.1695, 20cm long. As this good spoon is struck only with a maker's mark on reverse side, we have to consider several factors, such as the type of decoration, the shape of the stem and the bowl together with the overall proportion of the spoon, before deciding on its date and provenance. Courtesy Phillips.

these were destroyed, probably by fire, some time after 1677. On April 15th, 1697, a new register recording the names and addresses of London goldsmiths was opened.

[For Victorian London silver marks the key reference is John Culme's *The Dictionary of Victorian London Gold and Silversmiths 1838-1914*, a two-volume work to be published by the Antique Collectors' Club.]

The form of a goldsmith's mark can, even by itself, sometimes indicate the approximate date of stamping. Some mark of identification has been compulsory since 1363 but, as we know already, the relevant statute was frequently ignored. Up to the middle of the sixteenth century almost all makers identified themselves with a symbol by reason of the general illiteracy of the times, and thereafter even until 1696, whilst most punched initials, others continued with a symbol, and it was not unusual for both initials and symbols to be contained in one mark. From 1696 to 1720 it was compulsory for the first two letters of the surname to be used. Thereafter, and continuing until the present day, initials of individuals or companies have been employed. From about 1730 there seemed a general tendency to reduce the size of makers' marks. Most women goldsmiths of the first half of the eighteenth century contained their initials in a diamond shaped shield.

Apart from the marks on London silver dating from 1390, Jackson contains comprehensive details pertaining to all nine major assay offices and also attempts, sometimes tentatively, occasionally incorrectly but usually authoritatively, to group district and makers' marks with specific towns in about fifty instances all within the Kingdom of England (this, of course, embraces Scotland and all of Ireland) even at such towns where there exists no record of a guild of goldsmiths ever having been established. In all, I estimate that Jackson reproduces over two thousand date letters and nearly five thousand makers' and town marks, but it still remains far from complete.

How then, unless you have unlimited time at your disposal — and I think in terms of days rather than hours — are you going to identify marks on your English silver unless you already know its date and provenance to within ten or even twenty years? The thought of students failing to identify marks in Jackson and then turning in desperation to the tens of thousands of foreign marks is too dreadful to contemplate, but it happened to me in my early days. However, by the end of this chapter you will not only be able to decipher the marks on most items of silver, but you will be well advanced towards the necessary expertise needed to cope with some of the trickier problems. By recalling my own slow progress with silver I am confident that I can help you by anticipating, explaining and dispelling most of your early difficulties.

By referring to the illustrations in this book and from numerous other pictures in your library and scrap books you should be able to approximate your silver marks with the suitable date cycles in which to search; by recognising the town marks (viz., a leopard's head, anchor or crown for London, Birmingham and Sheffield respectively, representing three of the nine major assay offices), you can coincide the date cycle with the correct town. Do not, at such an early stage, start trying to identify silver from obscure minor guilds, etc., or anything with very rubbed or incomplete marks. Above all, do not seek inspiration for the approximate date-style by

A reasonably clear set of marks to read on a trifid spoon. London 1690, maker's mark IS with crescent above, 19cm long. Courtesy Phillips.

looking up the answers to the numerous pictures in the photographic quiz at the end of this book. These are intended to test your knowledge at the termination of your current reading (especially for those who have not completed the course of study in Chapter 9) to see whether you are reasonably safe to be let loose in the 'silver jungle' on your own.

When you can eventually recognise at a glance not only the approximate date of almost every item handled but also, because of its style and characteristics of craftsmanship (viz., London, West Country, North Country, Scottish or Irish), its likely provenance, you will then be laughing at the third form atmosphere of this chapter. It is not expected that you will attain such a degree of expertise within a few weeks!

I believe the most useful part I can play in familiarising you with the major assay offices is to concentrate on just one of them and to arrange in chronological order the most important developments that have occurred at the London Office. First of all, however, some general advice will help you with your inspection of marks:

1.   Acquire a powerful magnifying glass and a box of olive sticks. Many marks are clogged with dirt, so remove this (never using a hard material) by poking and scraping with the stick in order to decipher the marks when cleaned. The marks on bottom-marked spoons and forks, struck on the narrow part of the shank, may appear to have been very heavily punched for sometimes they disappear in distorted looking shields deep into the silver. Such marks are referred to as 'pinched' and are caused by the articles having been hallmarked before the final fashioning of the stem. Such marks when cleaned out are normally discernible.

2.   If, when comparing marks (be they makers' marks or hallmarks with their reproductions in Jackson), the student notes slight discrepancies while still confident that he is on the right line of research, it could be that the marks on the silver being examined have been subject either to the ravages of time, faulty punching, overstamping, laxity by the die-sinker or to a combination of two or more of these possibilities. Furthermore, I have no doubt that in many instances Sir Charles Jackson scrutinised several slight variations of the same mark and then instructed his penman to depict a mean average of these variations. Recently, I owned a silver and mother-of-pearl snuff box of Sheffield origin by James Law, assayed about 1790 but without a date letter. All marks were so distorted that I was obliged to seek guidance

Superlative sugar castor. London 1699, by Pierre Harache. Shown in two pieces in order to display the deep sleeve (the cover reaching down to the girdle on the body) and to show hallmarks. Courtesy the Worshipful Company of Goldsmiths.

from the appropriate assay office before I was convinced that the item was not colonial with pseudo-English marks.

3. If marks are difficult to decipher, study them carefully from all angles and in a good light. Sketch those parts of the date letter which are discernible and then try to fit these shapes to match a date letter in your reference book — i.e. the jig-saw puzzle technique.

4. If an item appears to be unmarked, search everywhere conscientiously to find some, but be warned against reading marks that don't exist. It is easy to be misled by wishful thinking and/or optical illusions into imagining marks. Once, I imagined that I saw a mermaid beckoning to me from the base of a rocaille candlestick. I dallied with her for several seconds before appreciating that I was inspecting a casting mark.

5. Items were frequently sent to be assayed before decoration. In consequence, such hallmarks were often damaged by piercing and embossed work and what remains to be seen of them may sometimes be identified only by the jig-saw puzzle technique.

6. Some sections of date letter cycles (London, 1787-95, and London, 1827-35, for example) are difficult to distinguish between, especially if the leopard's head is omitted or rubbed. The style of the article will normally indicate which of the two virtually identical date letters is relevant; and the maker's mark, if identifiable and recorded, may also provide firm evidence of the correct date.

7. Sometimes marks are omitted altogether. No silversmith of the nineteenth century, it seems, was more meticulous than the Nathaniel Mills (both father and son) in insisting that their work was fully marked; while Samuel Pemberton, also using the Birmingham Assay Office, was as indolent in this respect as he was industrious in production. But I once saw a nutmeg grater of superb quality made by the elder Mills and presumably sent to be assayed shortly after the death of George IV; the assay official had stamped the head of George IV on the lid and the head of William IV on the base and omitted a date letter on both sections. Had the official been celebrating and decided to puzzle posterity for a joke?

Up to the third quarter of the eighteenth century, the assay officials and goldsmiths of Dublin seemed consistently unpredictable in their use of marks. Thus, the beginner who is still unable to determine date by style is liable to become confused. As I write, I am looking at a Dublin helmet cream jug, c.1768, struck with one Hibernia mark, two crowned harp punches and lacking both a date letter and a maker's mark. On this item, the student by referring to Jackson (p. 613) would have expected one Hibernia punch, one crowned harp, a date letter and a maker's mark. Could it be that at the Dublin Assay Office, in olden times, the periods spent by officials in punching marks sometimes coincided with a very occasional glass of porter?

On Dublin silver, where there is no date letter, variations in the shape of the harp crowned will reveal the approximate date of the article.

8. The town mark at the York Assay was usually omitted, except on its early silver, and the same omission is often noted on other sets of provincial marks, notably at Newcastle and Exeter. About 1800 and later, and usually on smaller items, one frequently notices incomplete sets of marks assayed in London and in the provinces. The leopard's head is often missing, and date letters were also frequently omitted on small items. Sometimes we note just a

A caddy spoon formed as a right hand. London, 1805, by John Sanders, 6.5cm long. The leopard's head is missing from the set of marks and this omission often occurs on small objects of this period. It prevented the item being made into a larger piece. Courtesy Phillips.

maker's mark and a king's head. Very small items, for which no duty was requisite, are often completely unmarked (see Chapter 8 for other explanations of unmarked pieces) or sometimes they bear just a maker's mark, with or without a town mark.

9.   Frequently, we find Georgian silver, usually of the late eighteenth century, with one maker's mark overstamping that of another. There is nothing sinister about this. In order, perhaps, to fulfil a rush order, it was common practice for one goldsmith to buy from another and then to punch his own mark upon such purchases. Many of the items made by Hester Bateman were overstruck with the initials 'GG' (George Gray). I am amazed by the logic of the collectors of silver made by Hester Bateman who reject pieces made by this lady when her mark is the under-stamp and yet will buy silver made by someone else if she has overstamped the original maker's mark.

10.   When searching for makers in the alphabetical list of makers' initials, etc., in Jackson (Bradbury does not contain a list of makers), you will save time if you can first determine the approximate date and provenance of the item to be researched. Thus, for example, if you are searching for a London maker of about 1750 with initials 'IS', you should first turn to that section of Jackson which contains the marks and identity (if known) of all the makers listed. Next, turn to the index and, although there are some seventy options for 'IS' listed, there are only four options occurring in the relevant period. Try to identify the maker of the fish slice (p. 122) before reading the answer underneath it.

11.   Remember that when you are examining sets of marks they may be stamped in odd positions, some even upside down. Even in the later periods of silver, they are not always neatly arranged in orderly lines as in your books of reference.

And now to the chronological list of major events in the marking of silver at the London Assay Office.

Beginners should *refer conscientiously to each date letter cycle*, etc., detailed in the list below. All of these are to be found in Jackson. Although this may prove a tedious section of the book, make careful mental notes not only of the varying styles of symbols of every cycle but also of the shapes of the shield enclosing them. By studying the shapes of the shield, for just one example, it will be appreciated that the lion passant's shield between 1756 and 1895 is unlikely to be confused with a lion's shield of any earlier period.

1300.   Leopard's head established by statute (for details see Jackson). I recall that my first surprise when studying assay marks was to see the head of a lion described as that of a leopard. This irregularity originated because the ancient heraldic term 'leopart' means a 'lion passant guardant'.

1363.   Compulsory maker's mark.

1478.   First London date cycle, Lombardic lettering, A to U or V and probably omitting I or J.

1478.   Leopard's head is now crowned.

1498.   Second London date cycle, small Black Letter, A to U, omitting J.

1518.   Third London date cycle, Lombardic and Roman capitals, A to V, omitting J and U.

1538. Fourth London date cycle, Lombardic and Roman capitals, A to V, omitting J.

1558. Fifth London date cycle, small Black Letter, A to U, omitting J.

1578. Sixth London date cycle, Roman capitals, A to V, omitting J and U.

1598. Seventh London date cycle, Lombardic capitals, A to V, omitting J and U.

1618. Eighth London date cycle, small Roman and Italic letters, A to U, omitting J.

1638. Ninth London date cycle, Court-Hand, A to V, omitting J and U.

1658. Tenth London date cycle, capital Black Letter, A to U, omitting J.

1678. Eleventh London date cycle, small Black Letter, omitting J.

1696. The temporary departure from the sterling standard (18dwt. of alloy to 11oz.2dwt. of silver) in 1696, in order to prevent goldsmiths from melting the coinage — a cheaper and already refined source of silver — with which to fashion plate, and the establishment of the so-called Britannia standard (10dwt. of alloy to 11oz.10dwt. of silver) presents the student not only with marks of a new style (the figure of Britannia and the lion's head erased) but with a new style of maker's mark. London goldsmiths were required to stamp their personal mark with the first two letters of their surname. This regulation was not applicable to Dublin, Edinburgh and Glasgow Assay Offices for the London Goldsmiths' Company held no jurisdiction over them.

1716. Thirteenth London date cycle, Roman capitals, A to V, omitting J and U.

From the date cycle starting London, 1598, please determine the date of these marks. Courtesy Phillips.

From the date cycle starting London, 1618, please determine the date of these marks. Courtesy Phillips.

From the date cycle starting London, 1638, please determine the date of these marks. Courtesy Phillips.

From the date cycle starting London, 1678, please determine the date marked clearly in the bowl of the wine taster. Courtesy the Eagle Collection, Devon.

See p. 132 for the answers

1719. Return to sterling standard (leopard's head and lion passant) as an alternative to Britannia standard. After the restoration of the sterling standard, there was for some years a considerable variation in the form of the lion passant. This important fact is insufficiently stressed in Jackson and only three minor variations are drawn. I failed to realise for quite a time that the London date cycles, starting with 1716 and each cycle consisting of twenty letters, commenced therefore in the sixth year of a decade (viz., 1716, 1736, etc.). Furthermore, it follows that the date letters 'E' and 'P' must fall on the first year of a decade (viz., E for 1720 and 1740, P for 1730 and 1750, etc.). Therefore, it is possible to place a precise date for any clear London marks (from 1716 onwards) without reference to a guide to hallmarks.

1736. Fourteenth London date cycle, small Roman letters, A to U, omitting J.

1739. Different style of shields for leopard's head, lion passant and date letter.

1756. Fifteenth London date cycle, capital Black Letter, A to U, omitting J.

1776. Sixteenth London date cycle, small Roman letters, A to U, omitting I.

1784. Sovereign's head (duty mark) introduced. Head incuse, looking to left, for first two years. Please confirm date of marks in illustration below before reading the caption.

1796. Seventeenth London date cycle, Roman capital letters, A to U, omitting I.

1816. Eighteenth London date cycle, small Roman letters, A to C, omitting J.

1821. Leopard loses crown and, from 1825, sometimes lacks whiskers. The lion passant is no longer guardant, i.e. it is now in profile.

1836. Nineteenth London date cycle, capital Black Letter, A to U, omitting I.

1837. Queen's head replaces king's head at London. At provincial assay offices this replacement came later.

The marks on a salver (page 59) showing the maker's mark, date letter for 1785, lion passant, leopard's head, the king's head incuse and the drawback mark. The maker of this salver was James Young. Courtesy the Worshipful Company of Goldsmiths.

Currently, we are living in the twenty-sixth London date cycle; the sovereign's head omitted (apart from special occasions in the twentieth century) after 1890. The drawback mark is still unknown to most casual collectors and small dealers for it is not illustrated in Jackson. It is not unlike the Britannia mark at first glance, but it is shown quite clearly above. It was discontinued within eight months of its inception on December 1st, 1784, when an act gave relief from duty to manufacturing exporters of gold and silver articles by allowing them to draw back the duty they had already paid on goods destined for export. The mark was stamped at the assay office to indicate that duty had been repaid. It is possible that for the purpose of promoting export sales the concession of 1784 proved insufficiently attractive to goldsmiths so that virtually no silver was exported from this country. Certainly, this mark is quite rare. Another possible explanation for the scarcity of this mark is that its imposition, before goldsmiths had grown reconciled to the intrusion of the king's head mark (1784), led to such a storm of protest that authority bowed to it and discontinued its use. Throughout the history of our subject, there have always been indications that some goldsmiths resented the intrusion of large marks biting into the lines of their work and, where practicable, hallmarks were often positioned unobtrusively. An act of 1890 terminated the 'drawback' concession.

Before concluding this chapter I include two more illustrations for which you should try to determine dates. Their correct dates, together with those for the other undated illustrations in this chapter, are given at the foot of the page.

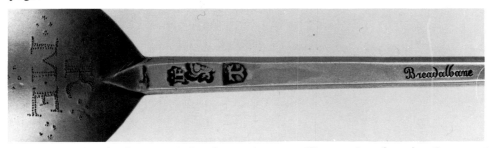

Please determine the date on this London-made spoon. The practice of carving the current owner's name on the stem (or anywhere else) at a later date is not to be encouraged, however famous the collection. Courtesy Phillips.

Please determine date of this bosun's call made in London by James Stamp (probably), about 11cm long. These were available some years ago but now they seem to have vanished into collections, Georgian examples are quite scarce. Courtesy Ward & Chowen (Tavistock).

Dates of the undated illustrations. Page 130, left hand column: top, 1606; centre, 1632; bottom, 1640. Page 130, right hand illustration, 1686. Page 132, spoon, 1616; bosun's call, 1798.

By now, I trust, you can identify London marks and so will note that provincial date cycles fall into similar patterns to those of the senior assay office. The style of their symbols and shields together with their distinctive town marks (viz., an anchor for Birmingham and a crown for Sheffield, etc.) will present few problems. Before passing on to the much more advanced Chapter 8, please spend some time — an hour should suffice — studying both major and minor town or district marks in your reference books. To start you off, I have included (pp. 133-143) tables of date letters and marks on plate from London, Birmingham, Chester, Exeter, Newcastle, York, Sheffield, Edinburgh, Glasgow and Dublin. These tables are taken from *A History of Hallmarks* by Wynyard R.T. Wilkinson, and are reproduced by kind permission of Queen Anne Press, London.

Throughout the tables the date letters have been printed black on white (not white on black as in the shields) for ease of identification.

TABLE OF MARKS ON LONDON PLATE

A	1678	1697	1716	1736	1756	1776	1796	1816	1836	1856
B	1679	1697	1717	1737	1757	1777	1797	1817	★37	1857
C	1680	1698	1718	1738	1758	1778	1798	1818	1838	1858
D	1681	1699	★19	★39	1759	1779	1799	1819	1839	1859
E	1682	1700	1720	1740	1760	1780	1800	1820	1840	1860
F	1683	1701	1721	1741	1761	1781	1801	★21	1841	1861
G	1684	1702	1722	1742	1762	1782	1802	1822	1842	1862
H	1685	1703	1723	1743	1763	1783	1803	1823	1843	1863
I	1686	1704	1724	1744	1764	★84	1804	1824	1844	1864
K	1687	1705	1725	1745	1765	1785	1805	1825	1845	1865
L	1688	1706	1726	1746	1766	★86	1806	1826	1846	1866
M	1689	1707	1727	1747	1767	1787	1807	1827	1847	1867
N	1690	1708	1728	1748	1768	1788	1808	1828	1848	1868
O	1691	1709	1729	1749	1769	1789	1809	1829	1849	1869
P	1692	1710	1730	1750	1770	1790	1810	1830	1850	1870
Q	1693	1711	1731	1751	1771	1791	1811	1831	1851	1871
R	1694	1712	1732	1752	1772	1792	1812	1832	1852	1872
S	1695	1713	1733	1753	1773	1793	1813	1833	1853	1873
T	1696	1714	1734	1754	1774	1794	1814	1834	1854	1874
U	——	1715	1735	1755	1775	1795	1815	1835	1855	1875

1719 Britannia Standard becomes voluntary and sterling marks are re-introduced.

1784—6 Octagonal intaglio King's Head duty mark used.

1786—1837 Oval King's Head duty mark used but in 1797 it can be found in silhouette.

1821 Leopard's Head becomes uncrowned.

1837—90 Queen's Head duty mark used.

London marks continued overleaf

A	1876	1896	1916	1936	1956	1975
B	1877	1897	1917	1937	1957	1976
C	1878	1898	1918	1938	1958	1977
D	1879	1899	1919	1939	1959	
E	1880	1900	1920	1940	1960	
F	1881	1901	1921	1941	1961	
G	1882	1902	1922	1942	1962	
H	1883	1903	1923	1943	1963	
I	1884	1904	1924	1944	1964	
K	1885	1905	1925	1945	1965	
L	1886	1906	1926	1946	1966	
M	1887	1907	1927	1947	1967	
N	1888	1908	1928	1948	1968	
O	1889	1909	1929	1949	1969	
P	1890	1910	1930	1950	1970	
Q	1891	1911	1931	1951	1971	
R	1892	1912	1932	1952	1972	
S	1893	1913	1933	1953	1973	
T	1894	1914	1934	1954	1974	
U	1895	1915	1935	1955	———	

1935 King and Queen's Head stamped to celebrate Silver Jubilee of George V.

TABLE OF MARKS ON BIRMINGHAM PLATE

A	1773	1798	1824	1849	1875	1900	1925	1950	1975
B	1774	1799	1825	1850	1876	1901	1926	1951	1976
C	1775	1880	1926	1851	1877	1902	1927	1952	1977
D	1766	1801	1827	1852	1878	1903	1928	1953	
E	1777	1802	1828	1853	1879	1904	1929	1954	
F	1778	1803	1829	1854	1880	1905	1930	1955	
G	1779	1804	1830	1855	1881	1906	1931	1956	
H	1780	1805	1831	1856	1882	1907	1932	1957	
I	1781	1806	1832	1857	1883	1908	——		
J	——	1807	——	1858	——	——	1933	1958	
K	1782	1808	1833	1859	1884	1909	1934	1959	
L	1783	1809	1834	1860	1885	1910	1935	1960	
M	★84	1810	1835	1861	1886	1911	1936	1961	
N	1785	1811	1836	1862	1887	1912	1937	1962	
O	★86	★12	1837	1863	1888	1913	1938	1963	
P	1787	1813	★38	1864	1899	1914	1939	1964	
Q	1788	1814	1839	1865	1890	1915	1940	1965	
R	1789	1815	1840	1866	1891	1916	1941	1966	
S	1790	1816	1841	1867	1892	1917	1942	1967	
T	1791	1817	1842	1868	1893	1918	1943	1968	
U	1792	1818	1843	1869	1894	1919	1944	1969	
V	1793	1819	1844	1870	1895	1920	1945	1970	
W	1794	1820	1845	1871	1896	1921	1946	1971	
X	1795	1821	1846	1872	1897	1922	1947	1972	
Y	1796	1822	1847	1873	1898	1923	1948	1973	
Z	1797†	1823	1848	1874	1899	1924	1949	1974	

1784—5 Octagonal intaglio King's Head duty mark used.
1785—97 Oval King's Head duty mark used.
1797 Double duty mark sometimes used.
1797—1833 Oval or silhouette King's Head duty mark used.
1833 William IV Head used in Oval.
1838 Queen Victoria's Head introduced until removal of duty in 1890.
1935 King and Queen's Head stamped to celebrate Silver Jubilee of George V.

TABLE OF MARKS ON CHESTER PLATE

A	1701	1726	1751	1776	1797	1818	1839	1864	1884	1901	1926	1951
B	1702	1727	1752	1777	1798	1819	1840	1865	1885	1902	1927	1952
C	1703	1728	1753	1778	1799	1820	1841	1866	1886	1903	1928	1953
D	1704	1729	1754	1779	1800	1821/2	1842	1867	1887	1904	1929	1954
E	1705	1730	1755	1780	★01	★23	1843	1868	1888	1905	1930	1955
F	1706	1731	1756	1781	1802	1824	1844	1869	1889	1906	1931	1956
G	1707	1732	G 57	1782	1803	1825	1845	1870	1890	1907	1932	1957
H	1708	1733	1758	1783	1804	1826	1846	1871	1891	1908	1933	1958
I	1709	1734	1759	★84	1805	1827	1847	1872	1892	1909	1934	——
J	——	——	——	——	——	——	——	——	——	——	——	1959
K	1710	1735	1760	1785	1806	1828	1848	1873	1893	1910	1935	1960
L	1711	1736	1761	★86	1807	1829	1849	1874	1894	1911	1936	1961
M	1712	1737	1762	1787	1808	1830	1850	1875	1895	1912	1937	1962
N	1713	1738	1763	1788	1809	1831	1851	1876	1896	1913	1938	
O	1714	1739	1764	1789	1810	1832	1852	1877	1897	1914	1939	
P	1715	1740	P 65	1790	1811	1833	1853	1878	1898	1915	1940	
Q	1716	1741	Q 66	1791	1812	1834	1854	1879	1899	1916	1941	
R	1717	1742	R 67	1792	1813	★35	1855	1880	1900	1917	1942	
S	1718	1743	1768	1793	1814	1836	1856	1881	——	1918	1943	
T	★19	1744	1769	1794	1815	1837	1857	1882	——	1919	1944	
U	1720	1745	U 70	1795	1816	1838	1858	1883	——	1920	1945	
V	1721	1746	V 71	1796	1817	——	1859	——	——	1921	1946	
W	1722	1747	W72	——	——	——	1860	——	——	1922	1947	
X	1723	1748	X 73	——	——	——	1861	——	——	1923	1948	
Y	1724	1749	Y 74	——	——	——	1862	——	——	1924	1949	
Z	1725	1750	(1775)	——	——	——	1863	——	——	1925	1950	

1719 Britannia Standard becomes voluntary and sterling marks are re-introduced.

1767—75 Date letter marks in serrated punch.

1779 New town mark introduced.

1784—6 Octagonal intaglio King's Head duty mark used.

1786—1835 Normally silhouette King's Head duty mark used although it is sometimes found in an oval.

1835—40 Either silhouette or oval King's Head duty mark used.

1840—90 Oval Queen's Head duty mark used.

TABLE OF MARKS ON EXETER PLATE

A	1701	1725	1749	1773	1797	1817	1837	1857	1877
B	1702	1726	1750	1774	1798	1818	1838	1858	1878
C	1703	1727	1751	1775	1799	1819	1839	1859	1879
D	1704	1728	1752	1776	1800	1820	1840	1860	1880
E	1705	1729	1753	1777	1801	1821	1841	1861	1881
F	1706	1730	1754	1778	1802	1822	1842	1862	1882
G	1707	1731	1755	1779	1803	1823	★43	1863	
H	1708	1732	1756	1780	1804	1824	1844	1864	
I	1709	1733	1757	1781/2	1805	1825	1845	1865	
K	1710	1734	1758	1783	1806	1826	1846	1866	
L	1711	1735	1759	★84	1807	1827	1847	1867	
M	1712	1736	1760	1785	1808	1828	1848	1868	
N	1713	1737	1761	★86	1809	1829	1849	1869	
O	1714	1738	1762	1787	1810	1830	1850	1870	
P	1715	1739	1763	1788	1811	1831	1851	1871	
Q	1716	1740	1764	q 89	1812	1832	1852	1872	
R	1717	1741	1765	r 90	1813	1833	1853	1873	
S	1718	1742	1766	f 91	1814	★34	1854	1874	
T	1719	1743	1767	t 92	1815	1835	1855	1875	
U	——	1744	1768	u 93	1816	1836	1856	1876	
V	1720	——							
W	★21	1745	1769	1794	——	——	——	——	
X	1722	1746	1770	1795	——	——	——	——	
Y	1723	1747	1771	1796	——	——	——	——	
Z	1724	1748	1772	——	——	——	——	——	

1721 Britannia Standard becomes voluntary and sterling marks are re-introduced.

1784—6 Octagonal intaglio King's Head duty mark used.

1886—97 Oval King's Head duty mark used.

1797—1816 Either oval or silhouette King's Head duty mark used.

1816—38 Oval King's Head duty mark used.

1833 William IV Head introduced.

1838—82 Oval Queen's Head duty mark used.

TABLE OF MARKS ON NEWCASTLE PLATE

A	1721	1740	1759	1791	1815	1839	1864
B	1722	1741	1760/8	1792	1816	1840	1865
C	1723	1742	1769	1793	1817	★41	1866
D	1724	1743	1770	1794	1818	1842	1867
E	1725	1744	1771	1795	1819	1843	1868
F	1726	1745	1772	1796	1820	1844	1869
G	★27	1746	1773	★97	★21	1845	1870
H	1728	1747	1774	1798	1822	★46	1871
I	1729	1748	1775	1799	1823	1847	1872
J	—	—	—	—	—	1848	—
K	1730	1749	1776	1800	1824	1849	1873
L	1731	1750	1777	1801	1825	1850	1874
M	1732	1751	1778	1802	1826	1851	1875
N	1733	1752	1779	1803	1827	1852	1876
O	1734	1753	1780	1804	1828	1853	1877
P	1735	1754	1781	1805	1829	1854	1878
Q	1736	1755	1782	1806	1830	1855	1879
R	1737	1756	1783	1807	1831	1856	1880
S	1738	★57	★84	1808	1832	1857	1881
T	1739	(1758)	1785	1809	1833	1858	1882
U	—	—	★86	1810	1834	1859	1883
W	—	—	1787	1811	1835	1860	
X	—	—	1788	1812	1836	1861	
Y	—	—	1789	1813	1837	1862	
Z	—	—	1790	1814	1838	1863	

1721—28 Sterling Standard mark sometimes faces to the right instead of the left.

*1733—90 Date letters are roman capitals and NOT italics.

1784—5 Octagonal intaglio King's Head duty mark used.

1786—96 Oval King's Head duty mark used.

1797—1820 Silhouette King's Head duty mark used.

1821—32 Oval King's Head duty mark used.

1832—42 Oval William IV King's Head duty mark used.

1840—84 Oval Queen's Head duty mark used.

TABLE OF MARKS ON YORK PLATE

A	1776	1787	1812	1837
B	1777	1788	1813	1838
C	1778	1789	1814	1839
D	1779	1790	1815	★40
E	1780	1791	1816	1841
F	1781	1792	1817	1842
G	1782	1793	1818	1843
H	1783	1794	1819	1844
I	——	1795	1820	1845
J	★84	1795	——	——
K	1785	1796	1821	1846
L	★86	1797	——	1847
M	——	1798	——	1848
N	——	1799	1824	1849
O	——	1800	1825	1850
P	——	1801	1826	1851
Q	——	1802	1827	1852
R	——	1803	1828	1853
S	——	1804	1829	1854
T	——	1805	1830	1855
U	——	1806	1831	——
V	——	1807	1832	1856
W	——	1808	1833	1857
X	——	1809	1834	1858
Y	——	1810	1835	
Z	——	1811	1836	

1784—5 Octagonal King's Head duty mark used.
1785—96 Oval King's Head duty mark used.
1796—1825 Silhouette King's Head duty mark used.
1825—39 Both oval and silhouette King's Head duty mark used.
From **1839** Queen's Head in oval.

TABLE OF MARKS ON SHEFFIELD PLATE

A	1779	1806	1824	1844	1868	1893	1918	1943	1968	1975
B	1783	1805	1825	1845	1869	1894	1919	1944	1969	1976
C	1780	1811	1826	1846	1870	1895	1920	1945	1970	1977
D	1781	1812	1827	1847	1871	1896	1921	1946	1971	
E	1773	1799	1828	1848	1872	1897	1922	1947	1972	
F	1774	1803	1829	1849	1873	1898	1923	1948	1973	
G	1782	1804	1830	1850	1874	1899	1924	1949	1974	
H	1777	1801	1831	1851	1875	1900	1925	1950		
I	★84	1818	——	1852	——	1901	1926	1951		
J	——	——	——	——	1876	——	——	——		
K	★86	1809	1832	1853	1877	1902	1927	1952		
L	1790	1810	1833	1854	1878	1903	1928	1953		
M	1789/94	1802	★34	1855	1879	1904	1929	1954		
N	1775	1800	——	1856	1880	1905	1930	1955		
O	1793	1815	——	1857	1881	1906	1931	1956		
P	1791	1808	1835	1858	1882	1907	1932	1957		
Q	1795	1820	1836	——	1883	1908	1933	1958		
R	1776	1813	1837	1859	1884	1909	1934	1959		
S	1778	1807	1838	1860	1885	1910	1935	1960		
T	1787	1816	1839	1861	1886	1911	1936	1961		
U	1792	1823	1840	1862	1887	1912	1937	1962		
V	1798	1819	1841	1863	1888	1913	1938	1963		
W	1788	1814	——	1864	1889	1914	1939	1964		
X	1797†	1817	1842	1865	1890	1915	1940	1965		
Y	1785	1821	——	1866	1891	1916	1941	1966		
Z	1796	1822	1843	1867	1892	1917	1942	1967		

From the opening in **1773** the town marks and date letter were amalgamated on small pieces of silver to prevent unnecessary damage.

1784—6 Octagonal intaglio King's Head duty mark used.

1786—96 Oval King's Head duty mark used.

1797 Double duty mark sometimes used.

1796—1824 Silhouette King's Head duty mark used.

1835 William IV Head introduced.

1824—40 Oval King's Head duty mark used.

TABLE OF MARKS ON EDINBURGH PLATE

A	1705	1730	1755	1780	1806	1832	1857	1882	1906	1931	1956	1975
B	1706	1731	1756	1781	1807	1833	1858	1883	1907	1932	1957	1976
C	★07	1732	1757	1782	1808	1834	1859	1884	1908	1933	1958	1977
D	1708	1733	1758	1783	1809	1835	1860	1885	1909	1934	1959	
E	1709	1734	★59	★84	1810	1836	1861	1886	1910	1935	1960	
F	1710	1735	1760	1785	1811	1837	1862	1887	1911	1936	1961	
G	1711	1736	1761	★86/7	1812	1838	1863	1888	1912	1937	1962	
H	1712	1737	1762	1788	1813	1839	1864	1889	1913	1938	1963	
I	1713	1738	1763	1789	1814	1840	1865	1890	1914	1939	1964	
J	——	——	——	1789	1815	——	——	——	——	——	——	
K	1714	1739	1764	1790	1816	★41	1866	1891	1915	1940	1965	
L	1715	★40	1765	1791	1817	1842	1867	1892	1916	1941	1966	
M	1716	1741	1766	1792	1818	1843	1868	1893	1917	1942	1967	
N	1717	★42	1767	1793	1819	1844	1869	1894	1918	1943	1968	
O	1718	1743	1768	1794	1820	1845	1870	1895	1919	1944	1969	
P	1719	★44	1769	1795	1821	1846	1871	1896	1920	1945	1970	
Q	1720	1745	1770	1796	1822	1847	1872	1897	1921	1946	1971	
R	1721	1746	1771	★97	★23	1848	1873	1898	1922	1947	1972	
S	1722	1747	1772	1798	★24	1849	1874	1899	1923	1948	1973	
T	1723	1748	1773	1799	1825	1850	1875	1900	1924	1949	1974	
U	1724	1749	1774	1800	1826	1851	1876	1901	1925	1950		
V	1725	1750	1775	1801	1827	1852	1877	1901	1926	1951		
W	1726	1751	——	1802	1828	1853	1878	1902	1927	1952		
X	1727	1752	1776	1803	1829	1854	1879	1903	1928	1953		
Y	1728	1753	1777	1804	1830	1855	1880	1904	1929	1954		
Z	1729	1754	1778	1805	1831	1856	1881	1905	1930	1955		
			1779									

1759 Thistle mark introduced.

1784—6 Octagonal intaglio King's Head duty mark used.

1786—96 Oval King's Head duty mark used.

1796—1823 Silhouette King's Head duty mark used.

1786—1826 Various forms of Castles used.

1823—40 Oval King's Head duty mark used.

1840—90 Oval Queen's Head duty mark used.

TABLE OF MARKS ON GLASGOW PLATE

	1	2	3	4	5	6
A	1819	1845	1871	1897	1923	1949
B	1820	1846	1872	1898	1924	1950
C	1821	1847	1873	1899	1925	1951
D	1822	1848	1874	1900	1926	1952
E	1823	1849	1875	1901	1927	1953
F	1824	1850	1876	1902	1928	1954
G	1825	1851	1877	1903	1929	1955
H	1826	1852	1878	1904	1930	1956
I	1827	1853	1879	1905	1931	1957
J	1828	1854	1880	1906	1932	——
K	1829	1855	1881	1907	1933	——
L	1830	1856	1882	1908	1934	1958
M	1831	1857	1883	1909	1935	1959
N	1832	1858	1884	1910	1936	1960
O	1833	1859	1885	1911	1937	1961
P	1834	1860	1886	1912	1938	1962
Q	1835	1861	1887	1913	1939	1963
R	1836	1862	1888	★14	1940	
S	1837	1863	1889	1915	1941	
T	1838	1864	1890	1916	1942	
U	1839	1865	1891	1917	1943	
V	★40	1866	1892	1918	1944	
W	1841	1867	1893	1919	1945	
X	1842	1868	1894	1920	1946	
Y	1843	1869	1895	1921	1947	
Z	1844	1870	1896	1922	1948	

1841—90   Oval Queen's Head duty mark used.

TABLE OF MARKS ON DUBLIN PLATE

A	1720	1747	1773	1797	1821	1846	1871	1896	1916
B	1721	1748	1774	1798	1822	1847	1872	1897	1917
C	1722	1749	1775	1799	1823	1848	1873	1898	1918
D	1723	1750	D 76	1800	1824	1849	1874	1899	1919
E	1724	1751	E 77	1801	1825	1850	1875	1900	1920
F	1725	1752	E 78	1802	1826	1851	1876	1901	1921
G	1726	1753	G 79	1803	1827	1852	1877	1902	1922
H	1727	1754	H 80	1804	1828	1853	1878	1903	
I	1728	1757	I 81	1805	1829	——	1879	1904	
J	——	——	——	——	——	1854			
K	1729	1758	K 72	1806	1830	1855	1880	1905	
L	1730/1†	1759	L 83	1807	1831	1856	1881	1906	
M	1732	1760	M 84	1808	1832	1857	1882	1907	
N	1733	1761	1785	★09	1833	1858	1883	1908	
O	1734	1762	1786	1810	1834	1859	1884	1909	
P	1735	1763	★87	1811	1835	1860	1885	1910	
Q	1736	1764	1788	1812	1836	1861	1886	1911	
R	1737	1765	1789	1813	1837	1862	1887	1912	
S	1738	1766	1790	1814	1838	1863	1888	1913	
T	1739	1767	1791	1815	1839	★64	1889	1914	
U	1740	1768	1792	1816	1840	1865	1890	1915	
V	——	——	——	——	1841	1866	1891	——	
W	1741/2	1769	1793	1817	1842	1867	1892	——	
X	1743/4	1770	★94	1818	1843	1868	1893	——	
Y	1745	1771	1795	1819	1844	1869	1894	——	
Y	1745	1771	1795	1819	1844	1869	1894	——	
Z	1746	1772	1796	1820	1845	1870	1895	——	

From **1730** Figure of Hibernia used as duty mark.
For details of various Harps and Hibernias used between **1730** and **1772** refer to
Hall-marks on Dublin Silver published by the National Museum of Ireland.
1807—9 Rectangular King's Head duty mark used.
1809—21 King's Head duty mark in shield used.
1821—46 Many different shields used for all symbols, but these can be
recognised by eliminating the other series first.
1838—90 Oval Queen's Head duty mark used.

CHAPTER 8

Rare and unusual marks

Beginners usually start their collections by buying fully hallmarked pieces. Considerably later, with the purpose of picking up bargains unrecognised by the vendor because of the obscurity of origins, beginners may start collecting uncommon marks regardless of the quality of the article bearing them. This is a dangerous stage, for there is a risk that they will forget their initial goal — pieces of fine quality silver, and they may develop instead into sleuth-hounds sniffing only through junk. Such collectors will seriously limit their experience and knowledge of our subject.

However, after a few weeks of scrabbling without the reward of aesthetic satisfaction from their finds, they may seek an explanation for the comparative rarity of some of the nineteenth century flatware of thin gauge produced, for example, at lesser known Scottish localities. Should they reach the logical conclusion that this scarcity is probably due to the scant patronage of second-rate silversmiths by the discerning customers of the day, by reason of the poor quality of the goods offered, then we see in embryo a real collector of silver.

I would be disappointed to think of readers of this book developing into scrabblers to the exclusion of all other considerations but, equally, I would not wish to deter collectors from seeking and appreciating unusual marks, especially on earlier silver, for this can prove an interesting side line of antique silver which sometimes helps us all with research and leads to a better understanding of our subject. What I have written in this chapter is designed to put obscure marks in a suitable perspective so that the collector may keep the search for quality as the prime objective.

Having deviated briefly from the true search whilst searching in the junk, collectors will normally return to more worthy pursuits and, with increased experience, will become aware of the many splendid unmarked pieces of great interest which, if fully marked, they might not be able to afford.

There are several reasons which I will suggest, why so much important plate went unmarked, even into the early part of the nineteenth century.

There is evidence to suggest that by the sixteenth century the nobility and gentry preferred to purchase silver with London hallmarks, but this, I think, was only because the London craftsmen enjoyed a reputation for a quality of work superior to that of their provincial rivals. If, on the other hand, the provincial customer had the confidence to bestow his patronage in support of a local silversmith, then the desirability of marks did not arise. Indeed, if the patron was in a hurry for his orders, he would not have wished them subjected to the two-way delays between silversmith and assay office.

Until 1696 it was legally only necessary to dispatch silver to be assayed when it was intended to put it into stock. So whereas almost all the 'bread and butter' goods of the early periods, such as spoons and drinking vessels,

Top, Aberdeen, c.1775, Alexander Thompson.
Below, Wick, c.1800, James Sinclair. Courtesy the
M. Gubbins Collection.

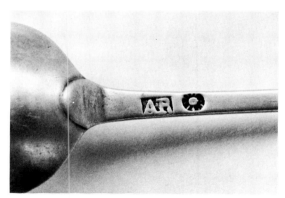

Dingwall, c.1800, Alexander Ross. Courtesy the
M. Gubbins Collection.

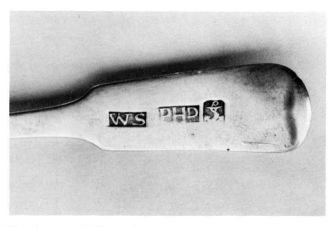

Peterhead, c.1815, maker's mark WS. Courtesy the M.
Gubbins Collection.

Top, Elgin, c.1800, Charles Fowler. Bottom, Banff, c.1820,
John McQueen. Courtesy the M. Gubbins Collection.

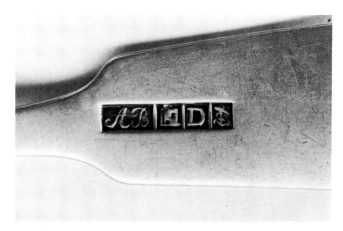

Dumfries, c.1820, Adam Burgess. Courtesy the M. Gubbins
Collection.

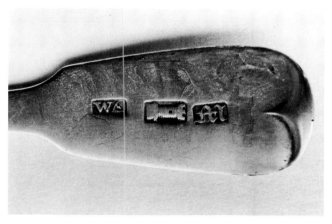

Forres, c.1810. Maker's mark WA. Courtesy the M. Gubbins
Collection.

made and retailed in considerable quantities, were fully marked, many of the more unusual pieces, for which there was only occasional demand, went unmarked. As it has never been required to mark silver for the royal household and because it is unlikely that goldsmiths fashioning something extra special for their own domestic use would bother to get such work assayed, it is understandable that these unmarked pieces are often of exceptional quality. However, these latter considerations would not fully account for the considerable amount of unmarked pieces found subsequent to 1696.

Many believe, rightly or wrongly, that, notwithstanding the legislation of 1696, the assay offices were either lax or impotent in its application, and that a gentlemen's agreement developed between the goldsmiths and the authorities, whereby the latter turned a blind eye on items unassayed if fashioned to special orders. It is more likely that the assay offices were virtually powerless to implement the regulations. It is certain that many goldsmiths felt so confident in their ability to dodge the law that they freely proffered evidence against themselves by stamping their wares with their registered marks of identity. From the evidence shown on p. 120 it seems probable that the maker had 'borrowed' two authentic lion passant punch marks stamped on other articles and by reshaping this silver adapted it to fit as sliding bases on a hitherto unmarked pair of tea caddies, probably of earlier date. For the further bamboozlement of the customer, this silversmith stamped his registered mark thrice, thus presenting a pattern and number of marks quite similar to authentic assay marks.

If an article consisted of several parts, such as a Queen Anne oil and vinegar cruet stand, with its two silver bottle tops and castor, it was not unusual for the set to be assayed as one unit on the underneath of the footed stand, with the total weight of all the silver components scratched nearby. I have seen very few of this type and period of cruet but they were all marked in the manner described. In the course of time, most of these early cruet frames have disappeared — probably they were melted and refashioned into other articles — but a number of their fine small castors, probably used for ginger, survive and some of these are without either assay or maker's mark.

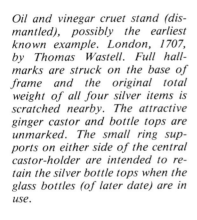

Oil and vinegar cruet stand (dismantled), possibly the earliest known example. London, 1707, by Thomas Wastell. Full hallmarks are struck on the base of frame and the original total weight of all four silver items is scratched nearby. The attractive ginger castor and bottle tops are unmarked. The small ring supports on either side of the central castor-holder are intended to retain the silver bottle tops when the glass bottles (of later date) are in use.

It could be argued that such totally unmarked pieces might have been made at a considerably later date to replace those damaged or stolen, but it is unlikely that replacements, unless made within a few years of their originals, would either conform precisely to the style of the original or bear a replica of the original heraldic devices. Finally, of course, there is the appearance of the patination to consider, for this, in due course, will indicate an approximate age.

The commercial reaction to a completely unmarked item of fine quality silver in the London auction rooms has changed. A perfect unmarked piece, if bearing a contemporary and identifiable heraldic device, virtually identical to a fully marked piece of equal quality, might now obtain half the price of the latter. Twenty years ago, it would have fetched less than one quarter of the price. This same unmarked piece today might realise very much more than a similar but fully marked item of mediocre quality.

Now that antique silver is understood by a significant minority of collectors, I do not think that the price gap between marked and unmarked pieces will narrow further and it would be unrealistic should it do so. There is no denying the fact that a bold set of hallmarks is a satisfying extra on fine silver. But in my case, I fear, this satisfaction is kindled by cupidity due to the marketable, additional interest that good marks convey to the majority, rather than from any aesthetic consideration.

Personal research into the origins of your silver may cost you money and time; and discoveries, if any, are likely to prove of greater commercial benefit to others, adept at exploiting new situations, than to the researcher who did all the work. Nevertheless, this fact of life should not deter you from the delights and excitements associated with your conscientious attempts to unravel for yourself the history of unusual pieces.

In *The Connoisseur* of August, 1975, I described my discovery of what might be the rarest of all the nineteenth century hallmarks. On a vinaigrette made by Thomas Shaw, with the normal Birmingham assay marks for 1823, there was an oval shield enclosing the figure of Britannia, denoting the higher standard of silver. (The Assay Master at Birmingham was unaware that such a mark had been struck in Georgian times but, during an unsuccessful search through the archives and vaults of the Assay Office for this very punch, another similar Britannia mark which had been used in the years 1844-6 was discovered.)

Proudly engraved within the lid of this vinaigrette and carefully unimpinged upon by the hallmarks, there were the words 'The Produce of Hudgill Burn Lead Mine' and with this as my clue I decided, if possible, to discover the history of my box, hoping that there was a romantic story attached to it.

In the south of England, no one had heard of Hudgill Burn for it is a very tiny stream, even in the spates of spring, but after a comprehensive search in a nineteenth century edition of 'Bartholomew's Citizens' Atlas' of those districts in which lead had been mined in the past, I spotted the name of a hamlet called Leadgate, situated a few miles south west of Alston in Cumbria. The location and history of the mine were well known to the Abbot Hall Museum, Kendal, for the opening and closing of the Hudgill Burn mine had made significant social impact over the surrounding countryside.

The full set of marks on the vinaigrette. Birmingham, 1823, by Thomas Shaw.

This previously unknown mark was discovered at the Birmingham Assay Office during the abortive hunt for the punch for the 1823 version of the Britannia mark. It was used in 1844-6. Courtesy the Master of the Birmingham Assay Office.

The outside of the Hudgill Burn vinaigrette.

This mark of Britannia, again indicating the higher standard of silver and also employed with the normal assay marks for sterling quality, was used at Birmingham for 1889/1890. Courtesy the Master of the Birmingham Assay Office.

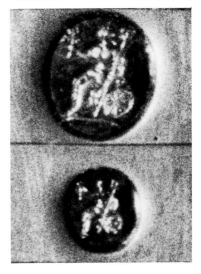

The Britannia mark was used again at Birmingham for 1894/1895. All these Britannia marks from Birmingham, even the later examples to a lesser degree, are well worth searching for. Courtesy the Master of the Birmingham Assay Office.

The locals seemed gratified to see and handle the little vinaigrette and I felt that by right it should have belonged to Alston. Everyone confirmed that the opening of the mine in 1814 was extremely fortuitous as the worthy brothers, John and Jacob Wilson, who were financing the project, had decided at long last that they could afford no further expenses in the search for lead and had reluctantly given notice to their workers. But these resolute men, the ancestors of some of the present inhabitants of the town and neighbouring district, had faith and they greatly respected the Wilson brothers, who lived at the Manor House (now the hospitable Hillcrest Hotel) situated almost at the foot of the hill. The men elected to work on without wages until their candles were exhausted. Literally at the last moment, on their thirteenth day underground without pay, they struck their massive vein of lead. The joyous workforce downed tools, and, descending the cobbled streets of Alston in high spirits, announced their find by hurling a brick of lead through the front window of the Wilsons' home.

In 1821, alone, some eight thousand pounds worth of silver was extracted from the lead and this was sent to be refined at Nenthill, some two miles from the mine.

About three months after the publicity attending the finding of the Britannia mark, my friend Peter Cameron, who has the sharpest eyes in the business coupled to a wide knowledge of silver, arrived with another vinaigrette of identical marks and inscription. He kindly offered it to me for less than I had obtained for the first vinaigrette, but as it was a 'tired' specimen I most foolishly turned it down. This latter vinaigrette together with a snuff box of the same date, maker and inscription, also a 'tired' specimen, appeared shortly afterwards at different auctions and both boxes realised amazingly high prices. Thus, 'The Produce of Hudgill Burn Lead Mine' is obviously worth looking for and there must almost certainly be other specimens waiting somewhere for you.

Another personal attempt at research was abortive but enjoyable. The nutmeg grater (or tobacco rasp) in the form of a mitre (see illustrations), by

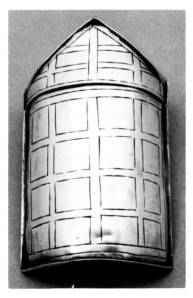

The only known nutmeg grater (or tobacco rasp) in the form of a mitre. Norwich, c.1690, with the maker's mark of the distinguished Thomas Havers. Courtesy the Michael Graeme Macdonald Collection, U.S.A.

The same box with the grater or rasp removed from its mitre-shaped box. Silver is really too soft a metal on which to grate a nutmeg.

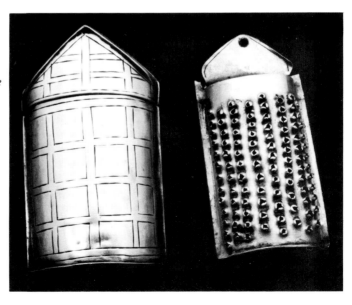

Thomas Havers of Norwich, is almost certainly a unique piece. I had hoped that the contemporary initials 'EP' on the back of the box would reveal the identity of its original owner, surely a bishop. The University Library at Cambridge was good enough to make available for my research the voluminous records of accounts kept meticulously by John Moore, Bishop of Norwich (1646-1714), and beautifully written in his own hand. Unfortunately, although I found an occasional reference to small silver boxes bought by the Bishop from Thomas Havers (1646-1732), who was a donor of plate to Norfolk churches, descriptions of these items were insufficient to identify either a nutmeg grater or a rasp.

The back of the nutmeg grater or tobacco rasp shaped as a mitre showing the contemporary initials discussed in the text, below the mark of Thomas Havers.

Regularly, about once a month, the bishop would travel to a hostelry still popular today at Barton Mills, situated almost exactly between the two cathedral cities of Norwich and Ely, where he would dine and stay overnight. From the accounts, it was clear that in strict alternate rotation he was either guest or host and so, chiefly because of the invariable location of the rendezvous, the friend whom he met so regularly in all seasons, probably to discuss problems or events in respective dioceses, was most likely to be Simon Patrick, Bishop of Ely (1626-1707). John Moore's bills at the hostelry ranged from less than two pounds, as a guest, to variable sums on occasion well in excess of twenty pounds when he was the host. Accordingly, it seems likely that John Moore sometimes had other guests besides Simon Patrick. Thomas Havers, the Norwich goldsmith, playing a full part in city affairs (he was one of the sheriffs of the city in 1701 and Mayor of Norwich in 1709), would have made a suitable companion to travel to Barton Mills and he might have made the silver box for Simon Patrick instead of for John Moore. I understand that Simon Patrick would not normally have been addressed as Episcopus Patrick (or EP for short), but who knows what irregularities might have been acceptable during the conviviality of dinners at Barton Mills? Alas, no trace of either the will or records of Simon Patrick can be found and, even if we found an entry for a grater or rasp, would we be satisfied? I think not.

All these conjectures are valueless and without hope of substantiation, but they may indicate that when, as usual, the research proves nothing, it does provide scope for thought and some fun as well.

Those of my readers who live in districts where silver was once mined or worked, and have both the time and inclination to study ancient records and legends will certainly, through research, introduce themselves to an enthralling but sometimes expensive hobby. Local smiths, whose marks were so often capricious rather than significant (and variable into the bargain) must surely have left some clues, legends or descendants which are worth pursuing if only for the enjoyment of the chase.

My friend and customer of the early fifties, J.W.Clark, L.D.S., R.C.S., of Newcastle upon Tyne, has spent much time researching the Newcastle goldsmiths and his investigations extend back to 1185. In about 1959 he discovered and identified the communion cup and cover at Ilderton, dated 1583, and made by Valentine Baker. This is seventy-three years earlier than any item of Newcastle plate known to Sir Charles Jackson. In the *Archaeologia Aeliana* Bill Clark's article 'The Copper Plate of the Goldsmiths of Newcastle upon Tyne' (the copper plate upon which all the Newcastle makers' marks are impressed from 1702) is invaluable to any student specialising in Newcastle silver of the eighteenth and nineteenth centuries.

I quote an extract from his letter to me of December 19th, 1951: "The mug is interesting. The maker's mark is an overstamp. The rest of the marks are undoubtedly 1757 (I have tankards of that year by John Langlands). Scott commenced his apprenticeship in 1760. Admitted 1781. Went into partnership with Pinkney. The partnership was dissolved in 1790. They were apprentices together. They worked for Langlands together. I'll bet this mug, somehow, stuck to them when they went into business together and their mark was struck over Langlands. Pinkney was a man of substance. He had married money in a big way — and retired at the age of 46. He died 1825 aged 73. Scott was the son of a blacksmith. His mother was a parson's daughter — and his son became a parson. He died 1793 and left very little. Dear, dear, dear, I rhyme on about these Newcastle 'smiths as though I knew them. They were a great set of lads and the wangles they got up to were nobody's business."

The mug referred to in this letter might have confused even an experienced collector, for it was dated 1757 and it bore the mark of makers who did not start operations until 1781!

Another extract from another letter from Bill Clark is well worth recording: "I like old Parsival. In my searches in the old minute books of the Associated Company I find: 'Jan. 6th, 1681. Parsival Soulsby fine againe for not paying ye former fine. 3s.4d. Paid in full.' And he is fined 'againe for grosse abuse to the company generally in getting upon the table with his foot and striking violently with his cane at Christopher Lodge endeavouring to beat out his brains and this not to be abated. Paid in full 3s.4d.' "

Considerable doubts exist regarding the marks attributed to Lincoln in Jackson. Only the 'I over M' is accepted as certainly of Lincoln origin. The device of the fleur-de-lis, the emblem of the Virgin Mary, to whom is dedicated the city's cathedral, is contained in the arms of Lincoln, but the same device is also incorporated in the arms of many other places.

The marks attributed by Jackson to Belfast (p. 712) have been proven incorrect by Victor F. Denaro. In his article entitled 'Maltese Silver and the Red Hand of Ulster', he explains that like Churchill's famous V sign, the open hand is regarded in Malta as a symbol of defiance and in the period 1780-1800 the island was either under threat or under occupation by the French. He states that the marks 'M and R' (in Jackson) represented two of the three standards of silver wrought in Malta during this period while unidentified makers' marks tentatively attributed by Jackson to Belfast have also been identified and named as Maltese silversmiths. Finally, the 'Red Hand of Ulster' incorporated in the royal arms of Ulster is a *right* hand. The symbol shown in Jackson is a *left* hand.

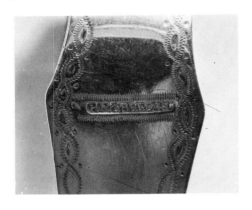

Section of a pair of sugar tongs made at Belfast, c.1788. The mark of H Mc Belfast is struck on both sides and in the bow of the tongs. In addition, H Mc only is repeated twice in the bow and must be the mark for Hugh McCulloch who registered this mark in Dublin in 1784 when working in Corn Market, Belfast, and again in 1785 when working in New Quay, Belfast. Although pleasing, this item is rather crude in comparison to contemporary Dublin-made tongs. Courtesy Mr. Brian R. Bolt.

At Newcastle, the goldsmiths were obliged to wait until 1702 before the establishment of their office. During the interval, 1700 to 1702, Newcastle silver was assayed at York.

Attention must be drawn to the curious antics of the lion passant at Newcastle both in the seventeenth century and in the years between 1722 and 1728, for sometimes he faced to the left and sometimes to the right. John Wilkinson, c.1660, and John Douthwaite, who worked between 1663 and 1673, both punched their wares with a lion facing to the left. Francis Batty, who was apprenticed to John Douthwaite and subsequently married his widow, probably inherited his late master's set of punches and he, in turn, may have passed them on to his successor, Francis Batty, junior, thus

Silver was never assayed at Liverpool. This rare provincial mug bears the maker's mark SH struck on either side of 'Ster/ling'. Liverpool, c.1710, 10.2cm., 6oz.15dwt. The Rev. Maurice Ridgway, in Some Chester Goldsmiths, *records this mark on p. 141 as probably that of Robert Shields. Courtesy Phillips.*

accounting for further lions facing to the left even into the eighteenth century.

Mr. Kent Karslake has been studying West Country silver for more years than he or I care to remember. I am very grateful to him for sending us this paper on Barnstaple silver:

The establishment of a tradition of silversmiths in Barnstaple was almost certainly due to the fact that it was the nearest town of any consequence to the silver mines at Combe Martin, on the North Devon coast, which are known to have been productive from the reign of Edward I probably until that of Elizabeth I. Thereafter the richer one at any rate seems to have been exhausted; but by the seventeenth century Devonshire was an important centre of the woollen industry and Barnstaple was specialising in the export of baize to Spain and the Low Countries. It is a commonplace of economic history that for at least two centuries after the discovery of America, Spain chronically ran what would nowadays be called an unfavourable balance of trade, paying for her imports with precious metals from the 'treasure of the Indies', and instead of silver reaching Barnstaple from nearby Combe Martin, it now came from Peru.

In the early days of this century, the Rev. J.F. Chanter, who devoted a considerable amount of study to the matter, compiled a list of over twenty goldsmiths registered at Barnstaple, from Hugh Holbrook in 1370 to Peter Arno who was working at the beginning of the eighteenth century. A fair amount of church plate by Barnstaple makers dating from the sixteenth century, notably by Thomas Matthew (1563-1611), whom Chanter considered 'perhaps the greatest of the Devonshire goldsmiths', and John Cotton (1576-1601) is still extant, chiefly in North Devon churches and in Chanter's opinion 'for workmanship and design will bear favourable comparison with (that) of any English goldsmith'. But apart from church plate, little Barnstaple silver seems to have survived apart from spoons. One or more spoons, after all, represented the sum total of most people's silver possessions, and those who could aspire to something more sophisticated, such as a tankard or a porringer, probably sent to London for it.

The problem of identifying Barnstaple silver has led to a widespread search for a Barnstaple town mark, which, however, seems likely to prove a will-o'-the-wisp. It seems highly unlikely, in view of the complicated technique of assaying silver either by cupellation or by 'the touch', that there was ever an assay office in Barnstaple — or even in Exeter before the passage of the Act of 1700. While, from medieval times, purchasers of silver marked by the Goldsmiths' Company in London had an assurance that they could reconvert it if they wished into sterling bullion, customers of provincial goldsmiths had no guarantee beyond the fact that the man who set his mark upon the piece staked his reputation on the fact that it was made of silver more or less. Modern collectors of provincial silver, however, need see in this little cause for loss of

Left, spoon with 'terminal figure', marked in bowl LS in monogram, possibly for Lawrence Stratford of Dorchester or unknown Barnstaple maker, c.1600. Right, spoon with so-called 'Krishna' knop, marked on back of stem RC or PC, for Richard Chandler of Plymouth, c.1620. Courtesy the Kent Karslake Collection.

A seal top spoon with the same LS in monogram in the bowl as in the illustration, on p. 153, with the small rudely formed incuse mullet of six points and a small saltire cross, all marks attributed to Dorchester (Jackson). Courtesy the Professor John Browning Collection, Canada.

Marks struck on the back of stem of the seal top illustrated left.

sleep — unless they expect its antique value to fall below its worth in bullion.

In the absence of an accepted town mark, most Barnstaple goldsmiths seem to have marked their products either with surname in full, e.g. Matthev for Thomas Matthew, or, more often, with their initials. In addition Matthew, and other makers at various periods, punched their pieces with a mark resembling a pomegranate or what has been called a 'fruit or acorn', and an attempt to identify this as a town mark was only stultified by the fact that other Barnstaple makers used such devices as a bird in a circle, which seems to represent the old arms of the borough. A reasonable explanation of these marks would seem to be that in former times innkeepers were not alone in using signs, and that a succession of silversmiths may have worked 'at the sign of the pomegranate' or the 'town arms'. It is perhaps more intriguing that a number of undoubtedly Barnstaple pieces bear as mark a lion rampant or a fleur-de-lis, or both; and it has been plausibly suggested that these marks may indicate that these pieces were made from Spanish coin (from the lion representing the arms of Leon on the reverse of a Spanish dollar) or from French écus, either of which would establish the standard of the silver. Finally, something of a puzzle has been set by pieces which bear the marks of recognised Barnstaple makers cojoined with marks which seem to belong to some other West Country towns, particularly Cornish ones; and it would seem that some Barnstaple silversmiths were itinerant, using a special mark in each place where they worked on their travels.

In the sixteenth and early seventeenth centuries the familiar terminals such as apostles, maidenheads, seal tops, and so on, were as commonly found on Barnstaple spoons as on those made in London and elsewhere. From the early years of the seventeenth century, however, these were sometimes replaced on Barnstaple spoons by a curious knop in which the earlier students of such things saw a real or fancied resemblance to Buddha, Krishna or

A spoon with an aggressively female figure terminal, struck in the fig-shaped bowl and thrice on the stem with a device mark attributed to John Quycke of Barnstaple, c.1639, 19.5cm long. Courtesy Phillips.

Left, a 'Krishna' knop, marked in bowl with fleur-de-lis and marked RC on back of stem for Richard Chandler, Plymouth. Pricked on back of bowl 1637. On the right, a maidenhead knop, marked in bowl with 'fruit or acorn' mark, Plymouth, c.1570. Courtesy the Kent Karslake Collection.

Two decorated Puritans, both probably West Country, c.1660, one marked with initials within a serrated edge, perhaps for Thomas Dare of Taunton (see Jackson), the other with a fleur-de-lis. Courtesy the Kent Karslake Collection.

Vishnu. While these are still generally referred to as 'Buddha knops', further study has suggested that they are in reality stylised versions of an earlier Barnstaple terminal, current around 1600, which may be described as aggressively female. It appears, in fact, to represent some sort of fertility goddess whose origin remains something of a mystery, since attempts to relate this primitive Venus to a German original do not seem very convincing. A 'Buddha knop' has also been found on a spoon by a Plymouth maker, but this could of course have been quite easily supplied to him from Barnstaple, and careful measurement of a number of these knops, which were still being used in the second half of the century, suggests that all of them may have been cast in the same mould, the difference in their detailed appearance being due to the vagaries of tooling.

By the time the last of them were made such separate terminals were going out of fashion in favour of the square-ended stem known as the Puritan design, of which the only special feature, as far as Barnstaple makers were concerned, was that, in common with other West Country makers, they favoured a broader end than was usual in London. This Puritan design, after a relatively short life, at least in London, was replaced by the trifid end, which is generally supposed to have arrived in this country in its fully developed form from France. It is therefore something of a curiosity that some Barnstaple spoons have survived which look very much like an intermediate form, in that the end, instead of being split vertically in order to form a trifid, remains more or less straight, with the vertical divisions merely engraved on its surface. If this is not in fact an intermediate form the explanation of it may be that some Barnstaple makers had heard of the new fashion current in London and, without having seen an example of it, tried to follow it without fully understanding it.

Left, trifid, marked 'IP' for John Peard and castle flanked by 'I' and 'P' with 'BAR' above for Barnstaple, c.1680. Right, Puritan trifid marked four times on the back of stem with a device, Barnstaple, c.1660. Courtesy the Kent Karslake Collection.

The back of a Puritan spoon, c.1655, pitted by reason of burial, thought to be by a William Trewin of Launceston. Members of the Trewin family still live in Launceston. Courtesy the Professor John Browning Collection, Canada.

By the act of 1700 all provincial silversmiths were obliged to send their products to one of the appointed offices for hall-marking, and from that date onwards, therefore, such silver as was still made in Barnstaple usually carries an Exeter mark together with that of the Barnstaple maker.

The introduction of the Britannia standard marks in 1696 certainly occasioned dismay, hardship and a few rare marks at all major provincial centres. Such offices were not allowed to conduct their business, using the new standard marks in conjunction with their town mark, until 1700. In this interval goldsmiths had no option but to confine their activities to special orders, presumably in secret. On such wares of this period, 1696-1700, if there were any marks at all, we normally find only a maker's mark and, very occasionally, the words either 'Sterling' or 'Britannia'. What a feather in the cap for a beginner if he should find an example of these marks! If subsequently it should emerge that his prize did not originate from the provinces between 1696 and 1700 but from say Chester, 1609-95, or Cork, c.1710, he would not experience great financial disappointment.

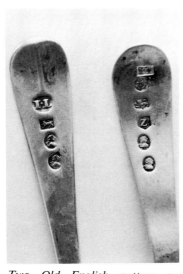

Two Old English pattern tea spoons with the 'double duty' marks. Left, Newcastle, c.1797, by John Langlands. Right, the double duty receipt for Birmingham, 1797.

We have already noted the vagaries of hallmarking c.1800, when incomplete sets of marks were so frequently stamped on small articles (see p. 128), and the illustrations of the marks on the two spoons seen left may seem even more irregular to you. In 1797 the imposition of doubling the duty payable on silver wares was met with such a storm of protest from the goldsmiths that the tax was rescinded. Whilst it was still in force, the Birmingham and Sheffield Assay Offices stamped their wares twice with the duty mark (the king's head) as a form of receipt for the double charge inflicted. It is presumed that in London the indentation in the shield of the duty mark during the year of 1797 served the same purpose.

At Newcastle, from whence come the marks illustrated to the left of the picture, we are left with an insoluble conundrum. There is no record of receipts for double duty paid being acknowledged by stamping the duty mark twice and yet there seems no reason why this office should not have experimented in this manner and then, finding it unpopular with the tough Newcastle goldsmiths, abandoned the practice immediately. As the date letter, town mark and leopard's head are all missing from this set of stamps, we do not even know the precise date of the spoon illustrated. These marks might be interesting or they could represent nothing more than a silly human mistake.

From the end of the seventeenth century into the first half of the nineteenth (Jackson) a considerable quantity of silver was wrought at Guernsey and Jersey in the Channel Islands. Although frugality seemed to be a major consideration with many of the articles fashioned, probably because customers were generally not as affluent as those on the mainland, some praiseworthy silver was produced. Their small two-handled christening cups, never varying in style, are particularly attractive. A strange feature of Channel Islands silver, which the less experienced collector should note, is that all styles appear to have originated, though at a rather later date, from the English or French mainlands. Hence a collector is likely to be deluded into thinking that a trifid spoon from the Channel Islands, possibly as late as

A typical Channel Islands christening cup with beaded scroll handles, Guernsey, c.1750, by JH, 6.7cm high, 3oz.15dwt. On this example the initials seem to relate to an engagement and not a christening. Courtesy the Captain and Mrs. John Milner Collection.

the second half of the eighteenth century judging from mainland styles, had been fashioned some sixty years earlier. Richard Mayne's *Old Channel Island Silver,* covers the subject.

Wherever there was a considerable number of prosperous British emigrants we find silversmiths, often emigrants themselves, who catered for them. Thus, silver was made in the late Georgian period in Calcutta, Canton, the West Indies and Bermuda, and even earlier, in Canada and South Africa. In the middle of the nineteenth century much silver was wrought in Australia.

Presumably in order to make their customers feel at home many of the colonial silversmiths made crude imitations of the London and English provincial marks and punched them on their wares. In style these craftsmen tended to conform, more or less, with those in vogue within the mother country. Because there are avid collectors for silver made in Canada and Australia and at Cape Town, these colonial products, of otherwise no exceptional merit, are sought after and prices are high. If the marks on a piece of genuine-looking antique plate are so crude as to do injustice even to a local forger, they are likely to be of colonial origin. Many small dealers are still both ignorant and suspicious of colonial marked pieces and occasionally they can be acquired very cheaply indeed.

It is not within the scope of this book to discuss colonial silver in considerable detail. The imitation English marks (viz., a lion passant, king's head, anchor or crown) punched on many colonial pieces are regarded as spurious in this country, but they can be valuable forgeries and, if antique (i.e. at least one hundred years old), are tolerated by the Goldsmiths' Company and are therefore not impounded. Auctioneers and dealers infringe the current regulations only when selling colonial silver that does not qualify as antique; but items wrought in the colonies just before or after the turn of this century are often considered to be antique by less experienced traders and are sometimes sold as such in error. Collectors are advised to tread warily.

Silver made at Calcutta and Madras is usually of fine quality. The work of Hamilton & Co., to mention just one of the colonial silversmiths, and established c.1805 in Calcutta, is well worth collecting and must be under-priced because there are no British residents left in India to collect it. Doubtless Sir Charles Jackson had valid reasons for his obvious conviction that Hamilton emigrated to India from Inverness, a source of several good Scottish provincial makers, and if Sir Charles is correct then this maker must be one of the finest Scottish craftsmen.

Silver made in the Cape of Good Hope is covered by David Heller's *A History of Cape Silver 1700-1870* and by Stephan Welz's *Cape Silver and Silver Plate*.

Collectors will sometimes find Cape Silver, especially in the early nineteenth century, stamped by two makers' marks in conjunction, probably, with one or more typical colonial imitations of English marks.

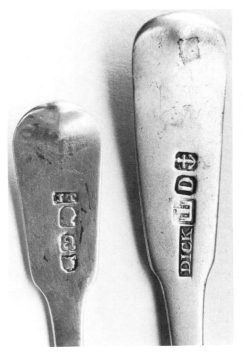

Left, pseudo-London hall-marks on a spoon by John Townsend of Cape Town, South Africa, c.1830. Right, marks of Alexander Dick of Sydney, Australia, mid-nineteenth century. Dick was a native of Edinburgh, Scotland. Courtesy the M. Gubbins Collection.

Sugar box by John Anton Bunning (arrived at Cape Town from Bremen as a soldier in 1758 and died in 1793), Cape Town, c.1780. Courtesy the James Aspin Collection, South Africa.

There was much intermarriage within the families of silversmiths resident in Cape Town and it was customary for a young silversmith to use the mark of his father-in-law in addition to his own, which seemed to indicate a tactful filial respect.

Australian silver, 1800-1900, is mentioned only because it seems to be valuable and popular 'down under'. The subject is covered by J.B. Hawkins' *Australian Silver 1800-1900* and by Kurt Albrecht's *Nineteenth Century Australian Gold and Silversmiths*. The work of the makers J.M. Wendt and H. Steiner is much sought after. The former often stamped his name in full in conjunction with 'Adelaide' or with permutations of marks depicting kangaroos, lions passant and/or an anchor. H. Steiner punched his name in full or with his initials, 'HS' or 'H.ST', sometimes punching 'Adelaide', with or without a crown, lion passant, kangaroo or emu. There is some uniformity, if only because of their whimsicality, on the markings of Australian silver which may be recognised by collectors especially when the place of manufacture, one of the then growing Australian towns, is punched as well. Many of the more formidable items of Australian silver, if not copying the typical over-decorated styles of Victorian silver, depict aborigines, elaborate silver-mounted emus and ostrich eggs and an extensive use of the fern-leaf motif. Complete palm trees, contributing to the decoration, often make these items uncomfortable both to handle and to behold. Australian silver arrived too late on the scene to reflect the fine designs of the eighteenth century in England and elsewhere.

Although I cannot recommend Australian silver to collectors of fine antique English silver, I have little doubt that Australian silver products are more valuable than comparable English items.

In England an act in 1830 substituted transportation for the death penalty for those craftsmen who trangressed the law and forged the assay office marks. It may be mischievously amusing, although unfair, to suggest that criminal silversmiths deported from England probably contributed to the fraudulence rife amongst Australian jewellers and silversmiths in the boom days of the Australian gold rush in the middle of the nineteenth century. From the end of the nineteenth century there was prolonged lobbying by influential members of the very many honest Australian silversmiths to induce authority to control the industry by legislation, but, up to the time of writing, nothing concrete has resulted — despite continuing palaver — from such laudable efforts. Perhaps, in the continued absence of legislation, a highly unsatisfactory situation has been resolved by enlightened common sense.

CHAPTER 9

Course of study

After an introductory first month, the remaining months are split into five quite distinct periods of antique silver: the Britannia standard era (1697-1719) in the second month; the rocaille vogue up to 1750 in the third month; the degeneration of the rococo decoration and the emergence of the styles inspired by the excavations at Pompeii in the fourth month; the first sixty years of the nineteenth century in the fifth; we conclude with a study of very early silver. For each of these periods of study a list of museums, etc., is appended where a comprehensive selection of silver of the period under review may be studied.

It is my personal opinion that the order of study starts (second and third months) and ends (sixth month) with the very best that antique silver has to offer its students, but all periods, not excluding the once despised Victorian era, have much to interest and appeal to the connoisseur. Another purpose for starting specialised study with the Britannia standard era is that the simplicity of design (after the first few years), the higher quality of silver and the above average robustness of most items of this period are all factors that tend to facilitate the recognition of good or bad patina.

This course must be a visual and palpable experience and I think you will enjoy it. The written word also helps, and a bibliography appears at the end of the book. If you can acquire Charles Oman's *English Domestic Silver* and Michael Clayton's *Collectors' Dictionary of the Silver and Gold of Great Britain and North America,** please do so.

You can and should obtain from your bookseller Jackson, and Frederick Bradbury's *British and Irish Silver Assay Marks* (your pocket guide to hallmarks). From the Victoria and Albert Museum obtain the nine titles dealing with English silver in their inexpensive *Small Picture Books* series. Above all, I recommend Eric Delieb's *Investing in Silver* and his *Silver Boxes*. A more recent and important book is Peter Waldron's *Price Guide to Antique Silver*. It will help you with prices and give you a good insight into styles and fakes. It is also well worth enquiring at the library of the Worshipful Company of Goldsmiths to ascertain if they have any left-over catalogues from some of their exhibitions at Goldsmiths' Hall. The Westminster Reference Art Library of Orange Street, London, behind the National Portrait Gallery, has copies of all out of print works concerning art.

Those of my readers who live within easy reach of London and can find time to conduct their studies in the manner recommended should reach a stage of reasonable proficiency in our subject within the six months. Those living in remoter districts or overseas may be severely handicapped in finding sufficient specimens to handle. In such circumstances, the problems may be resolved by each reader's individual initiative. One sound scheme is to suggest yourself as an unpaid assistant, whenever time permits, in a big shop specialising in silver.

* The Antique Collectors' Club revised edition is now in preparation.

Another recommended policy is to join as many collectors' clubs or circles as is convenient. However, whilst enjoying the friendships, enthusiasms and information exchanged at these gatherings, one should retain a critical outlook of opinions voiced in the certain knowledge that most members and even many of the guest lecturers are either amateurs like yourself or, at a probable best, specialists only in one area of our subject. This stricture, less important than the benefits you will reap, is especially pertinent to those circles of collectors who concentrate exclusively on numerous and interesting variations of just one type of silver article, thereby drastically limiting their general knowledge.

Moreover, a considerable group of would-be specialists meeting together to discuss and display their treasures, although beneficial to trade, is certain to accelerate a rise in prices. The collector is therefore recommended to concentrate his pecuniary investments on those numerous types of articles that have not yet inspired a significant collectors' club with their inflated prices.

At the meetings of some specialised enthusiasts, it is common practice for members to buy, sell or exchange specimens. Regrettably, a member with a rare and complete set of picture back tea spoons or wine labels, for example, may dispose of it in singles or pairs, probably retaining just one example for his personal collection. This is the prime reason why interesting sets of small collectables have become so scarce in recent years. Although this development is easily understandable, because it provides an opportunity for members to acquire an example of a rare type without the financial outlay of buying a set, the practice does not assist the preservation of our national heritage and even smacks of vandalism.

An even worse abuse perpetrated by an otherwise highly estimable club is its custom of displaying exhibits in a desperately over-cleaned state, even to the degree of removing patination. I know of one member of this club who uses a buffing-wheel and of another who dipped a small fire-gilt article into some chemical cleaning fluid and stripped it of much of its gilt!

Lack of sufficient important museum collections to inspect is not such a handicap, for an even greater activity with the scrapbook (see C1 of this section) could be even more helpful if not as exciting.

First month

A1.   Go to a thoroughly reliable dealer, or take expert advice from Sotheby's, Christie's or Phillips, and acquire one or more items of impeccable quality. Carry one such piece around with you in your pocket, taking care not to get it scratched or damaged. Acquire perfection and don't worry about the price! You may have to wait for what you want.

B1.   Purchase large scrapbooks, a magnifying glass and the recommended books.

C1.   Acquire as many illustrations of antique silver as you can find — illustrated sales catalogues from leading auctioneers and new and second-hand art magazines are good sources of supply — and paste them into your scrapbook, together with a brief description of each. All periods and as many styles as possible should be represented. Do not arrange your illustrations in any sequence of periods. *Keep them well mixed up.*

D1.   If you have not already done so in Chapter 7, make yourself familiar with the identification of assay and makers' marks in your Jackson.

E1. Visit as many collections, exhibitions and auctions of antique silver as time will permit. Try to date every item you see before checking with your descriptive catalogue.

F1. Handle as many items as possible and check them all with the routine inspection recommended in Chapter 10 (Part 2, p. 169).

G1. As you learn to recognise the numerous conditions of patina by comparing all silver with your specimen example (A1), keep a watch for silver which has been electroplated (there is much of it about) and for items which have been dull-polished after recent repairs. The former condition sometimes affords a reasonable looking patina at first glance, but mellowness and depth of colour are missing and the touch seems sticky, with the impression of finger marks being noticeably more pronounced than on untreated surfaces. Silver which has been dull-polished is distinctly dull in appearance.

The comparison between antique and very recent gilding is so obvious (usually) that you will not encounter initial difficulty in this respect. Modern gilding is harsh in appearance but, recently, modern platers have learned to modify the colour so that it no longer looks out of place on items of use such as in the interior of salt cellars. Modern fire-gilding, producing a soft and attractive colour, is rare and costly and the process can nowadays be undertaken only by special licence (it is damaging to the health of craftsmen performing it).

As recent gilding so frequently conceals repairs, it is good training to try and discover the exact purpose of the gilding.

Second month

A2. Continue schedules C1, E1, F1, G1.

B2. Inspect collections at the Victoria and Albert Museum, Ashmolean, Oxford, Hampton Court and auction rooms. Silver is on view at the big London auctions for at least two clear days before the sales and these galleries do not close during luncheon hours. Concentrate studies on 1690-1719 period.

C2. Begin taking a keen interest in auction sales, they are your only criterion of prices. At the outset they will be unintelligible and even when you are competent to appreciate fully the items under consideration, you will still have to exercise your cunning and imagination.

Paradoxically, an expert on antique silver is not necessarily an expert at valuation, but there are a number of dealers, not necessarily experts on our subject, experienced in valuations who are in constant attendance at the big London auction rooms. You will soon get to know them by name because of their numerous purchases. These gentlemen will assist you tremendously, albeit unwittingly.

Some tips for inexperienced students attending sales may not be out of place, for important business is being conducted there at a high speed. Nothing should be risked that could distract the auctioneer and make his task more difficult. Gossiping, even in whispers, and fidgeting can be distracting. It is, of course, the auctioneer's job to accept as many bids as he can contrive and thus obtain the best price for his vendor and the maximum commission for his firm. With well-practised eyes and ears he attains a remarkable perception, scouring his domain below the rostrum.

Auctioneers are usually nice people and few of them could have experienced their job and remained rational without either developing or enhancing a keen sense of humour together with a sympathy for human errors. If a mistake should occur and you find yourself somehow laden with a lot that you didn't intend to buy or, if intending to buy it, you consider that the price stated to be in excess of your last bid, you must have the courage to shout your objection clearly, authoritatively and *immediately*, without caring a damn what others may think of you: "Not my bid, just scratching", or "Sorry, I understood that you were selling the next lot", or "Sorry, I bid only up to x pounds". Should your courage fail you and you leave your objection until after the sale, you will almost certainly have to pay up unless you pretend to be an undischarged bankrupt without visible means of support.

The best advice that I can offer to the student of prices is to note the last bid (preferably an unsuccessful one) by a very experienced dealer. Record such bids together with your personal assessment of the lots concerned and when such notes are reasonably comprehensive use them to assist in your inspection prior to sales. Your notes must be constantly revised. Continual comparison between your estimates and the actual price obtained is your quickest route to efficiency. But please remember that enquiry into the reasons for wide discrepancies will teach you far more than the satisfaction gained from your accurate prognostications. All this requires resolution and I wish that I had practised at the outset what I now preach.

If, after inspecting items at auction, you are unable to attend the sale, ask the auctioneers to send you a list of prices obtained. At Christie's, Sotheby's and Phillips catalogues and price lists can be sent to you for the entire season for a reasonable inclusive fee.

If you have inspected silver at a sale some days before an auction commences, it is wise to reinspect, if possible, any items in which you are interested, immediately before the auctioneer mounts the rostrum. Some people are heavy-handed and inconsiderate in their handling of silver and terrible wounds such as broken hinges, finials and handles and other damage inflicted by clumsiness (or intent) may have occurred since your first inspection. It is possible, too, that a removable part such as a nozzle for a candlestick or even a glass liner for a salt cellar, has been subsequently pocketed by a rogue.

D2. Try and spot items in salerooms which have received later decoration. It is essential that all beginners and all others who lack confidence in the understanding of contemporary and later decoration should study the illustrations on p. 164. Even as late as the mid-'sixties of this century many experienced collectors lacked the confidence to acquire items decorated in most late rococo styles because they feared that this embellishment had been applied, or had at least been added to, by the Victorians. It was the late-rococo decoration that attracted mid-Victorian customers to satisfy their craving for ostentation, thus tempting the 'smiths of the day to create a travesty of Georgian silver with numerous and deplorably *unbalanced* imitations of mid-eighteenth century embossed work.

Those collectors in the recent past who lacked confidence in recognising authentic rococo decoration had little or no help from books about antique

A mug of the George I period. On the assumption that the chasing is Victorian, as it almost certainly is, since this type of decoration never occurred in the George I period, it is surprising that about one third of the mug has been left undecorated. The Victorians were wont to cram decoration into every available space.

The item is clearly unbalanced in appearance. The severely plain scroll handle, for example, is a most unsuitable companion for the heavy chased work. The stiffness of Victorian decoration is well illustrated by this example. Courtesy the Worshipful Company of Goldsmiths.

Baluster tankard of typical George III form. London, 1780, by Hester Bateman. Chased c.1850. The chasing is of quite a high order (though the general effect is atrocious) and certainly not by Hester Bateman, who never chased her work in this manner.

The beaded girdle (original decoration) is incongruous in these later-chased conditions, and the handle, with heart-shaped terminal and open work thumb piece, would never have been made in such a simple form if the rest of the article had been so heavily chased in the first place. It being impossible to hammer decoration from the inside of a handle, decoration should have been applied on the handle to balance such a heavily chased body. Courtesy Sotheby's.

A large porringer with hollow scroll handles, the cartouche surmounted by a flower head, the lower part of the bowl with wrythen flutes. London, 1709, by John Wisdome, 12cm high, 14oz.10dwt. The decoration and initials are certainly contemporary and typical of the period, with only about fifty per cent of the surface worked. The item is quite well balanced, the somewhat robust handles being necessary because of the weight and size of the porringer. Courtesy Sotheby, King & Chasemore.

Milk jug, Edinburgh, 1760, and cream jug, London, 1761. In both cases typical contemporary crest and decoration in the late rocaille style. The chasing is limited, and the items are well balanced by the scroll handles, leaf-capped in the case of the milk jug. The cast shell feet with mask heads on the cream jug would seem to indicate further decoration on the body to maintain balance.

Some thirty years ago, so little was known about period styles for silver that both would have been condemned by many as later chased. Courtesy Sotheby's.

silver; and if a very few works did make an attempt to help readers with illustrations of Victorian decoration on Georgian silver they were likely to prove misleading. Indeed, one senses from the inconsistencies in the advice of some writers that they were trying to skirt round a difficult subject. When we remember that up to the beginning of the last war most authentic late-rocaille decoration was believed to be subsequent Victorian enrichment of plain Georgian styles, we appreciate a valid excuse for all this palpable evasion.

For the purpose of comparing the Victorian conception of rococo decoration with its Georgian counterpart it is a good idea to pretend that a central motif, common to both periods — in all probability it would be a cartouche embracing a coat of arms — be represented for our experiment by a country house in a rural setting and then, in our imaginations, to take two flights above this house and observe how it is sited firstly by the Victorians and then by the Georgians: our first aerial photograph would normally reveal a house built in the middle of a forest and partially obscured by a mass of impenetrable tree tops stretching as far as the eye can see; our second picture would be likely to show a well defined and more gracious residence nestling amongst formal lawns and flower beds at the end of a well-grown but carefully spaced avenue with the whole scene set in a pleasant pastoral countryside. From this apparently far-fetched simile you are given the basic elements to enable you to differentiate between Victorian and Georgian tastes.

There may be two questions that the reader wishes to ask and the less embarrassing one will be tackled first:

Question 1. Was it only the Victorians who added decoration to earlier silver?

Question 2. Does the author ever experience doubt as to whether embellishment is contemporary or not?

Answer 1. Yes and no because there is insufficient evidence to form a firm conclusion. I have seen an isolated instance of a seal top spoon of the early seventeenth century with its bowl flat chased in the rococo manner of the eighteenth century and I was confident that this was not a Victorian addition. I have seen also several eighteenth century pieces of the late 'thirties, especially cream jugs, embossed in the late rococo taste (c.1745-75). As such decoration is still virtually contemporary, this issue need not worry us too greatly. It is possible also that silver assayed c.1738, but unsold and then shelved by its retailer, was subsequently embellished and re-offered to purchasers.

Answer 2. Yes! If, as very occasionally happens, I find myself deliberating for some seconds as to whether decoration is contemporary I decide that it is undesirable, uncertain of the truth. There is also very occasional confusion arising from Irish silver. A few Irish Victorian 'smiths seem to have enjoyed a greatly superior appreciation of balance than most of their English counterparts and in consequence an error of judgement can occur. Conversely, a few Georgian Irish 'smiths may have had less conception of balance than most of their English counterparts. Such warnings are added only to emphasise that no one writing about silver is infallible, even if he or she believes otherwise. As you master the differences between contemporary and later decoration very quickly, you will find yourself confident with about 99.9 per cent of your inspections. Please, *do not forget our flights of fancy* over the Victorian and Georgian houses.

E2.   Examine the form of hinges of boxes.

Third month

A3.   Carry on with schedules C1, E1, G1, C2, D2, E2.

B3.   Visits to Victoria and Albert Museum and Ashmolean, Oxford, and auction rooms. Concentrate on the 1719-50 period.

C3.   Start trying to assess values of items inspected in accordance with suggestions outlined in Chapter 5.

Fourth month

A4.   Carry on with schedules C1, E1, F1, G1, C2, E2, C3.

B4.   Visits to Victoria and Albert Museum, Ashmolean, Oxford, British Museum and auction rooms. Concentrate on 1751-1800 period.

C4.   Make a careful study of the styles in vogue (viz., bead and feather edges, bright-cut engraving, pierced sides, etc.) so that you will recognise Victorian embellishments, in imitation of these late eighteenth century styles, on the many plain designs created in this and earlier periods.

D4.   When handling silver, start routine check as detailed in Chapter 10, (Part 1, p. 168).

Fifth month

A5.   Carry on with schedules C1, E1, G1, D2, E2, D4.

B5.   Visits to Ashmolean, Oxford, Windsor Castle, Apsley House, London, and auction rooms. Concentrate on 1800-60 period.

C5.   Try and spot items in shops and auctions that have been de-chased.

Sixth month

A6.   Carry on with schedules C1, E1, G1, C2, D2, E2, D4.

B6.   Visits to British Museum, Knole Park, Windsor Castle, colleges at Oxford and Cambridge and important auctions. Concentrate on pre-1690 period.

Before setting out on any expedition, check times and all other arrangements which may be necessary for viewing silver. Special arrangements may be made for students to visit the city livery companies. All places recommended for your visits are within some fifty miles of London but there are, of course, a number of other places well worth visiting including the Manchester City Art Gallery, the 'Royal Scottish' at Edinburgh and the National Museum of Wales at Cathays Park, Cardiff, which is strongly recommended. Here there is on view the collection of silver formed by Sir Charles Jackson which forms the basis of his *An Illustrated History of English Plate*. Sir Charles' main interests lay in English seventeenth and eighteenth century silver, but at this museum you can also inspect the distinguished spoon specimens and see a small collection of Welsh church plate drawn from parishes all over the principality.

It should be added that courses of study are run by the Adult Education Departments of the Universities of London and Surrey, and various local education authorities. Weekend and mid-week short courses are conducted at such places as the Earnley Concourse (near Chichester). Museums also have individual lectures at regular intervals. Do investigate; you may well be pleasantly surprised by what is available locally.

CHAPTER 10

Routine inspection of silver

A conscientious dealer is certainly more distressed by inadvertently selling a faulty item than his customer is in purchasing it. The dealer would urgently wish to have the item returned to him, and to reimburse his customer without quibble rather than that the customer should suffer in silence, thus retaining the offending article but with confidence unjustifiably lost in the dealer. Obviously, the offending piece should be returned immediately or the dealer is entitled to wonder if the fault developed subsequent to the sale. Customer's children, if not disciplined, can wreak havoc with antiques of every description, whilst heavy-handed cleaning of fragile articles is yet another of several typical risks, for none of which the dealer can be expected to take responsibility.

Thus, if a reputable dealer has told you that an item under consideration is in perfect condition, it should not be necessary to spend a very long time inspecting it minutely at the time of purchase, for this can be done at leisure directly you get home. But it is undiluted folly to purchase from unknown sources, from whence you will probably have no redress, without checking and rechecking and spending a long time, if necessary, as you implement all the rules laid down in this section of the book. No advice could be more important to a collector of antique silver.

A pap boat recently purchased represented a serious mistake on my part. At first glance it appeared to be a highly desirable item created by good makers: the moose's head at one end of the cast and applied rim would have thrilled any serious collector of these vessels and, in all probability, it gave constant delight to the unknown child or invalid who took nourishment from it. The gauge appeared to be thick all over, the hallmarks in specimen condition, the design and balance good and I should imagine that it sold originally for quite a lot of money, it being considered then, as today, an attractive novelty.

I bought it in the Portobello Road one Saturday from an active young dealer, who brought it down to show me, most probably in all innocence of its fault. I placed it in a pocket with satisfaction for it seemed a bargain. After a while, I began to play with the pap boat with my fingers, enjoying the feel of its quality, until I discovered a small but very thin area on its base where a late owner's crest, initials or other emblem had been removed. With dismay, I withdrew the vessel from my pocket and then, apart from the visible concavity of the erasure, I noticed also that the patination skin was lost in this small area. Further inspection revealed very faint traces of lettering which had been incompletely removed.

My spirits were not at a low ebb for long because I soon realised that this very item would prove of value to my readers in demonstrating to them the importance of their routine inspection. It was also a sharp reminder to myself that I was drifting into slackness. In these circumstances, I did not bother to remonstrate with the vendor, whom I scarcely knew, for I was truly delighted with a purchase so useful to my purposes.

I showed the pap boat without comment to several dealers passing by and, after their customary examination, all expressed their admiration of it. I then adopted a different approach and, in seizing upon every experienced dealer and collector whom I saw, must have made myself a tiresome bore for the rest of the day.

"There's something wrong with this piece," I announced, "can you spot the fault?"

All these judges gave the vessel a most searching examination without discovering anything but general excellence. One or two, less experienced, but not wishing to appear so, made the silliest guesses as to the cause of my concern. The only man who pin-pointed the fault without even being asked to, grabbed the vessel and moving his thumb instantly to the weak spot gave it a ping, glancing up at me with mischievous satisfaction. "I believe you owned that pap boat, earlier this morning," I ventured. He grinned but did not reply. Pieces of silver move around rapidly in the Portobello Road on Saturdays.

It is true to say that a majority of pap boats, unless presented as christening presents, have never had an emblem of ownership engraved upon them. This is probably because, being used either by invalids or children, there can rarely have been any personal pride of ownership associated with them. Where emblems of ownership do appear upon pap boats, they have invariably (in my experience) been engraved either on the sides or within the bowl of the vessel. However, merely because I was not expecting an erasure on the base of the vessel does not excuse my laziness in disregarding the rules of inspection when buying from immature dealers, virtually unknown to me. Neither is the rush and bustle of the Portobello Road on Saturdays a valid excuse. Remember, please, that an item of antique silver is only as satisfactory to the connoisseur as its worst feature and that *every tiny bit of every item* must be painstakingly examined.

Routine inspection: Part 1

This routine of selectivity is obviously unsuitable for those dealers catering for inexperienced customers and wishing to 'turn an honest penny' on all opportunities offered; and some of it is too advanced for those of my readers who have not yet completed the course of study.

1. Satisfy yourself concerning the patina and condition of item.
2. Estimate date of item.
3. Satisfy yourself regarding design and craftsmanship.
4. Satisfy yourself regarding weight for size and apply gentle pressure all over to ascertain if there is any thinness of metal or weak patches.

At this stage, you will have rejected the vast majority of antique plate inspected (if you are a perfectionist), but if you remain satisfied:

5. Check hallmarks, if any, with your conclusion (see 2). If there is a discrepancy of more than ten years from either extremity of your estimated period, you will decide that the item is one of three things:

(a) A pioneer style — which is both interesting and suspicious.

(b) A reproduction or replacement item — which is not so interesting.

(c) A forgery. This, in view of your reasonable satisfaction after the implementation of the first four rules, is extremely unlikely. If a very clever forgery is suspected, recheck the first three rules and examine for transposed, inserted or imitation hallmarks. If the item is not a forgery:

6. Satisfy yourself about condition of marks and see that all movable or attached parts are marked (this does not apply to the lids of many *provincial* vessels) and that all sets of marks coincide in every detail. If one or more of such parts be unmarked, check its patina very carefully with the rest of the item. If there is a discrepancy of patina and no evidence of a repair, consider if the unmarked section could be a replacement. If it should be a replacement, I expect you will reject it unless it be of exceptional antiquity, historical importance and/or rarity.

7. Satisfy yourself that coats of arms, crests, initials and monograms are contemporary. During the six-month course (Chapter 9) and your preliminary study of Chapter 12 you will have instinctively absorbed a reasonably sound knowledge of the heraldic designs, etc., in vogue at all periods. If there are no devices engraved, or occasionally applied, one must conclude that they have been removed unless the patination is satisfactory. Recheck on 4 above.

If from your past experiences you suspect that a surface has been subjected to an erasure, a closer inspection may discover a very slight concavity. However, should an erasure be discovered, which leaves neither a thinness of metal nor a loss of patination (for such an erasure probably occurred within a few years of the item's manufacture) then it is a mistake to denigrate an otherwise fine piece merely because of this one minor misfortune. Of course, a very few items of antique silver were never engraved with any device.

Never allow yourself to be rushed or bullied during your inspection and treat aggressive salesmanship either as deceitful camouflage or as pathetic ignorance. A good dealer does not need to foist his stock on anyone.

If in a market you are handling an item from which some symbol has been crudely erased, you may be inspecting stolen property. If the thief was caught, he would probably be persuaded under interrogation to reveal the name of the fence who bought the stolen property from him. The item is then tracked along the list of its subsequent purchasers, often rather dubious characters, and finally it is returned to its rightful owner. Someone is certainly going to lose money in these circumstances, and that unfortunate person could be you.

Routine inspection: Part 2

In this second section we will consider a number of items and demonstrate a routine search for faults. This is a highly important part of the book and it has two purposes:

In the first place, though much of the content has already been used extensively in the course of study, in the years ahead it can serve as a refresher course should one feel that one is getting slack and making mistakes through over-confidence. For example, it is commonplace for even experienced collectors to miss a small repair on some attachment to an article — such as foot or handle — for it may be virtually insulated, so far as the repairer's processes are concerned, and the patination is destroyed on so small a proportion of the surface that it is well nigh impossible to spot in some lights. Such repairs, too, may have been stuck with Araldite, or something similar, or neatly soldered with lead and neither repair would have necessitated the application of intense heat and the ruination of the patina.

Secondly, this section should provide considerable assistance to those readers who were unable to complete the course of study. It must be assumed that such readers can at least recognise extremes of patina by now and, if still unable to differentiate between subsequent and contemporary decoration, have decided to concentrate on items of simple, well-known designs.

1. Apply gentle pressure over *entire* surface as you check for weak spots.
2. Breathe over surface to detect repairs and insertions.
3. Examine all areas of open-work silver with the utmost care.
4. Check the junctions of appendages to main body very carefully and make sure that the appendages are not damaged.
5. Examine all parts (especially the rims and border ridges of salvers, trays and the embossed areas of vessels, etc.), examine against the light to spot small, unrepaired holes. Obviously, it is at high spots and not recesses where, because of constant cleaning and handling over many decades, heavy wear will have certainly occurred. Unless the gauge at such high spots was very thick originally, pin-point holes or repaired pin-point holes are likely to be discovered. If even one such hole is discovered others will develop with use. Vessels should be *filled with boiling water* before the finalisation of a purchase to double-check upon this hazard and although the request for boiling water in a shop may cause surprise, a good dealer will not take umbrage and, if he assures you that this test has already been done, you may be satisfied.
6. Reject: later decoration; electroplated items; items with poor patina; items with recent gilding.

Beginners should be assisted in the early stages of their routine inspection by studying the risks pin-pointed by the illustration on p. 171.
a. Check if handle of tea pot or coffee pot is original. The Victorians sometimes replaced wooden handles with silver substitutes. Moderns have replaced wooden handles with plastic substitutes. With the latter alteration, it would be nicer to have a wooden one made in the old style.
b. A lid will often break away from its hinge. It is then usual to repair by adding a piece of silver on a hidden surface beneath to support the junction of lid and hinge. Such an addition, which is usually a rather untidy reinforcement, should not be confused with the neat applied section (added for the purpose of strengthening this potential weak spot) which was sometimes embraced in the original construction of pots.
c. Silver leafage (if any) at the foot of an ivory knop might be snapped in places.
d. Look for mark(s) on the lid of tea pot (it may be only a lion passant) and see that such mark(s) check with duplicate(s) on body (with this style of pot the full set of marks would be found on the base). However, marks on lids are frequently omitted on items of provincial manufacture. The absence of marks on the lid of a London pot, even although the lid is certainly contemporary, does detract somewhat from the value of the article.
e. Junctions on the tea pot of spout with body and handle with body have often suffered repairs.
f. On a tea pot stand legs (if any) may have been broken off the body and

A late eighteenth century tea-set. The arrows indicate the areas which should be examined. Courtesy Sotheby's.

replaced; legs may have been broken as well.

g. Look for signs of repairs (both inside and out) at junctions of base and body of tea pot and milk jug.

h. Look for splits (hold against light) or repairs on rim of tea pot stand, especially where the rim joins the flat surface of the body.

i. All protuberances (such as flutes and edges) are subject to more wear than are other parts and should be inspected with extreme care.

j. Frequently, the end of the spout has been buckled or split. The spout may have been cut right down, even as far as an inch, and such a repair ruins the lines of a pot.

k. Rims of jugs, baskets, sauce boats and tumbler cups, etc., are liable to splits.

l. Junctions of body to handle of a milk jug have often been repaired.

m. Frequently, an oval or circular patch has been inserted or applied to strengthen the junction. But many makers anticipated this weakness and applied a strengthening plaque at time of manufacture.

n. The handle of a jug may have snapped and been repaired.

o. Swing handles are normally marked with a lion passant and/or a maker's mark. The absence of such marks, providing the handle is clearly contemporary to the bowl, will not deter the connoisseur, but he may expect to pay a little less for the vessel.

p. and q. Other danger spots. There may be weak patches on one or all of the items where heraldic devices or initials have been removed. Alternatively, there may be a patch applied over a weak spot to strengthen it or, even worse, a patch inserted into the body for the same reason. Remember, too, that if the gauge of silver is too thin for satisfactory erasures, the symbols may have been flushed with silver to obliterate them and the entire item then electroplated in an attempt to conceal the flushing. In these latter circumstances, the outline of the original symbols may still be just visible on the inside of the vessel. However, by now the reader may be too advanced to be caught with an item of silver which has been electroplated.

Let us now consider the tankard below.

a. It may seem simple enough to hammer out a dent or twist on this type of foot on mugs, castors, coffee pots, etc., but in doing so there is a risk of the foot splitting and thus requiring a major repair. Sometimes, the repairer has thought it best to replace the original foot with a new one. It is usually simple to distinguish between old and new solder.

b. Rims, with items of thin gauge, are liable to splits.

c. Junctions of handles with body need careful inspection.

d. Occasionally the handle has been removed from its original position and replaced on another part of the tankard to protect or conceal a weak patch. Do not forget to check this point.

e. The Victorians may have cut a triangle at this point and, by adding a spout, turned the tankard into a jug. In modern times, the spout is likely to have been removed and the jug turned back into a tankard. If the replacement patch of silver is assayed with modern hallmarks, the new tankard is not an offending piece, but I trust that none of my readers would entertain such an atrocious piece.

f. A false base with clear antique hallmarks may have been soldered over an unmarked or reproduction piece. If one cannot see a faint outline of the

An eighteenth century tankard. The arrows indicate the areas which should be examined. Courtesy Sotheby's.

marks from the inside of the mug (unless the gauge of silver is unusually thick) check very carefully for this type of forgery.

g. Occasionally, we find thin areas, about the size of a man's middle finger, at points on or around 'g' on the illustration. It is my theory that some hard drinkers had the habit throughout their lives to position their fingers on the same spot whenever they lifted their tankard, thus gradually wearing the silver thin. The popular belief that these thin patches so low on the bowl and within finger-reach of the handle (either to the right or left of it) were occasioned by the erasure of emblems must, because of their unbalanced position and odd siting, be discounted. The important point to remember is that the collector must search for these rather rare weak patches in this unusual area.

The next illustration, below, illustrates a fault sometimes found on the rims of feet. Where there is deep engraving adjacent to the edge of the foot of a small jug of light gauge, probably of the 1765-85 period, we sometimes find a small or large section of the edge broken away because of the fragility caused by the deep engraving. This fault is usually very difficult to spot and quite recently, having disposed of such a faulty vessel at an auction, I almost bought the same jug back again in a shop a few months later. It was a pretty jug with much to commend it.

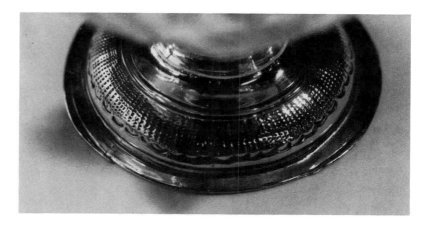

Deep engraving near the edge of a foot on a flimsy article is a hazard. On this George III cream jug a piece of the edge has broken off. Such a fault may be difficult to spot.

Having examined some of the general risks which can be encountered when examining articles, let us now look at some of the points to be borne in mind when inspecting specific items. Containers of most types are very popular with collectors. As many, such as counter boxes, nutmeg graters, patch boxes, pomanders, snuff boxes and vinaigrettes, were often carried in daily use throughout the lives of their owners, jangling around in pockets or suspended from chains, we find comparatively few boxes that have escaped damage or hard wear. Obviously, we expect to find damage to hinges, corners and edges on oblong or similar forms of boxes, and much wear to engraving (if any) on circular designs, that spent most of their time rolling about.

Some **vinaigrettes** have lost their delicate grilles and have either had replacements fitted, or the grille hinge fixtures have been removed and the erstwhile vinaigrettes are sold now as snuff or patch boxes. These alterations, together with repairs to box hinges and corners, etc., are usually concealed by gilding. Unless the grille is very delicate, almost a filigree, it should normally bear a mark of some sort. However, the grilles of vinaigrettes that are fully marked just once on the rim of the body (not as is more usual on lid and inside base) are almost invariably unmarked. The presence or absence of marks on the grille, providing it is obviously the original one, is not of much consequence.

Many of the earlier **snuff boxes** are either unmarked or bear only a maker's mark. Modern restorers are active in acquiring broken boxes, beyond repair, and converting the debris into complete, saleable units. Often these creations are attractive and it is an interesting game trying to determine the origins and periods of the several components. One might spot a fine Stuart lid, complete with contemporary coat, inserted into the lid frame of a mid-Georgian box with a French mother-of-pearl or tortoiseshell body. The possible permutations of these 'marriages' are too numerous to think about.

The demand for vinaigrettes and snuff boxes of the 'castle top' and kindred varieties with repoussé plaques inserted into lids with raised edges produced one faker of some skill and knowledge. He cut out a scene from Windsor Castle, for example, from a hitherto unsaleable visiting card case, and inserted it on a flat-lidded box with raised edges of the appropriate period and made by one of the well-known makers of these repoussé tops. The faker's craftsmanship is far below that of the contemporary smiths, for the plaques invariably seem to be inserted a trifle out of true. When repoussé visiting card cases attracted the attention of collectors, sending their prices rocketing, the faker could no longer find a cheap source of 'castle tops' and, whereas I would have expected him to have switched to casting his own tops, probably from an example by Nathaniel Mills, Senior, he appears instead to have retired with his ill-gotten gains. These offending pieces are still to be seen around, sometimes even in big auction rooms, and many private collections of 'castle tops' must abound with them.

Loaded candlesticks (i.e. with stems and bases hollow but filled with a glue-like substance) are often constructed from a thin gauge of silver. There is some danger of serious damage when attempting to straighten a stem. Those with embossed decoration, if of thin gauge, almost invariably have breaks or lead fillings of breaks on some of the 'high spots'. Such defects are progressive with cleaning.

Some of the handles on **cups and porringers** are replacements and all must be carefully inspected for they were never marked. Many of these vessels have lost their lids, but may be none the less attractive for this.

Because **marrow spoons** have always been rated as rarer and more desirable than marrow scoops, and far more valuable than ordinary bottom-marked table spoons, it has been common practice for several decades to convert table spoons into marrow spoons. The earlier forgeries are easy to detect because of the lack of rigidity (due to thinness of the reshaped shank) of the scoop section. Today, a working silversmith has managed to overcome this weakness of the scoop section and the only traces of his conversions are seen in slight signs of tool marks at the junction of scoop and stem. Shell, scroll or 'picture back' bottom-marked table spoons are selected for these conversions as decorated backs are more popular than plain examples. Again, these conversions are on the decrease and although I have seen many genuine marrow spoons with decorated backs lately, I have not seen a conversion for over six months.

Some **meat skewers** have been mutilated either by being shaped into letter openers or by being shortened to tidy up the point of the skewer. All original surfaces of skewers must naturally carry scratches inflicted by carving knives.

Because little **cream boats** are in great demand, many pap boats, not invariably the quickest of sellers, have had three legs and a scroll handle

Loaded candlestick. London, c.1795. Courtesy Sotheby's.

added. These 'marriages of convenience' do not look right: whereas the eighteenth century cream boat usually has an undulating rim rising to the spout, the pap boat normally has an even rim of the same elevation at both ends of its bowl, which is shallower and proportionately longer than that of the cream boat. If missing their turned-wood handles, the heavier types of punch ladle have been converted to pap boats by the removal of the mounts. These will be smaller than the genuine pap boat.

Salt cellars are frequently paper thin in the base due to frequent cleaning to remove corrosion after the original protective gilding has worn away. Pulled legs (legs pushed inwards into the bowls) on the circular compressed type of cellar are unsightly without glass liners to conceal them and the indentations cannot normally be hammered out again satisfactorily.

All types of **plates** need skilled selection. Some plates when badly but honestly scratched have been flushed and electroplated. Others have had their rims and/or borders reshaped or decorated to conform to a new fashion or purpose. The position of the hallmarks may afford obvious proof positive if a plate has been reshaped or altered.

Spoons and forks. Spoons become worn in the bowls; sometimes the shank snaps or cracks. Of the two repairs, the reshaping of the bowls must be the more serious. The altered bowl is no longer representative of its period and, as an antique, the spoon becomes as ridiculous as a berry spoon. I have seen many early spoons (prior to the eighteenth century) with half or more of a new bowl, in the correct shape, replacing the original worn out part. It is wiser to leave a worn bowl as it is. Early spoons with knops, such as apostle or seal tops, retain traces of gilding in the recesses of these designs. Knops are liable both to damage and to loss of parts such as a nimbus or emblem from an apostle. Sometimes the knop has been broken from the stem and then soldered back again. Almost all London spoons have their knops joined to the stem by a V insertion while, if the stem is thick enough, most provincial spoons are connected by a slatted junction in the shape of an L. Collectors are urged to make a special study of early spoons, after the completion of their present course, before risking any considerable financial outlay on them.

The bowls of tea spoons of all ages, especially when sold in sets, have frequently been reshaped because they have worn thin at the ends. Students who have studied the shapes of tea spoon bowls will not be deceived by this but, if just a small number in an otherwise perfect set have been treated in this manner and providing that the reshaping is of a minor unobtrusive nature, then we should tolerate them. Trifid spoons with lace decoration at the back of the bowls and usually at the top of the front of the stems must be treated with caution. A dealer was active for some two years in buying all the plain trifid spoons which he could lay his hands on, but he avoided fully marked specimens because of their high price. These spoons reappeared, after a visit to a brilliant engraver, with lace decoration duly executed. Again, like the boxes, the engraving seems just too sharp for its purported age and does not quite agree with slight wear on other parts of the item.

A pair of trifid spoons. London, 1690, Francis Garthorne. The difference in their length, due to tidying up the bowl and destroying the original shape of the spoon on the left, is clearly discernible. The damaged spoon on the left was offered at auction where it realised more than the specimen with the undamaged bowl. Spoon on right courtesy of Captain and Mrs. John Milner.

Left, although there is clear evidence of honest wear on this bowl of a shield top spoon, it has mercifully been left untouched and therefore remains an interesting piece in an important collection of West Country silver. Assayed at Exeter, 1707, marked SE for H. Servante of Barnstaple.

Right, seal top, marked in bowl and three times on back of stem with fruit or acorn mark. Barnstaple, c.1600. Courtesy the Kent Karslake Collection.

Recently a young dealer produced an early spoon with which, together with others similar, he hoped to get rich quickly whilst keeping within the law. "What do you think of this?" he asked. On this rare occasion, I was able to reach a conclusion even before the spoon was in my hand. "Not for me," I replied.

I had spotted that the terminal had been regilt even before deciding that the patina was poor. However the bowl was good, there were no solder lines and no indication of electroplating to conceal repairs.

The young dealer noticed that I was very puzzled and he took me into his confidence. "A few weeks back this spoon scarcely had a bowl at all," he said, "but my repairer has invented a process — all very hush hush — which enables him to add new parts to a silver item without leaving a solder line." If this is so, then the ability to recognise a good or bad patina is an essential prerequisite before straying into the silver jungle. I have already warned collectors — and this applies even to amateur collectors of a lifetime's experience — never to purchase early spoons from anywhere but the most impeccable and experienced sources.

The tines of forks start deteriorating noticeably after about fifty years of constant use. In consequence, Georgian dessert forks, being more fragile than table forks, have become very scarce. Dessert spoons have been reshaped into dessert forks very extensively and these forgeries can be identified by the flatness and lack of normal rigidity of the tines. As Old English pattern tableware is more popular (or used to be) than the plain, Fiddle pattern, the shortage of Old English forks has been eased by reshaping dessert forks of the latter style. Such alterations provide an obviously unsatisfactory version of the Old English design. The position has been reached when it is difficult to obtain a genuine set of eighteenth century dessert forks and, personally, I would opt instead for a strong set of

Edwardian reproductions (see also Table services, p. 178).

Caddy spoons suffer the same troubles as larger spoons. The shovel types, probably used more often for sugar than for tea leaves, often appear with strange substitute handles to replace the original ivory or turned wood handles. Care should be taken when buying caddy spoons of the expensive jockey cap variety. Large specimens bearing Hester Bateman's mark inside the crown are highly suspect. It is believed in authoritative quarters that these crowns were originally watch cases of the mid-1770-80s, with modern peaks added and mock bright-cutting enrichment. I have never seen a watch case by Hester Bateman and so I cannot comment. Careful research has revealed that the smaller spoons marked inside their crowns, usually in a 'cross formation', and normally by Joseph Taylor of Birmingham are perfectly genuine. Similarly, jockey cap caddy spoons originating in London with marks in a straight line along the front or underside of the peak can also be genuine. At one time, all jockey cap caddy spoons unless marked on the side of the crown were considered suspect.

Sugar tongs and nips. Here the centre of the U-turn is a danger spot for tongs. Pierced tongs, constructed in three sections with two cast arms, usually have repairs or cracks on their pierced arms. Nippers are also fragile articles. See that the tendrils on later examples, facing each other on the edges of both the two circular thumb and finger grips, have not been broken off. Examine the fragile arms above the pans and throughout all the cast areas for cracks and repairs. If you notice casting faults (such as bubbles) proceed very cautiously for it is here that the metal is at its weakest and where a break may have occurred. With soldered repairs, more bubbles are frequently evident due to air locks escaping from the solder. Thus, for these two different reasons, several bubbles may be found at the point of repair. Casting faults, unassociated with a break, like flaking, are not normally detrimental to value. Flaking, which occurs on so many examples of antique silver of every description, is caused by an excessive amount of alloy remaining in a very small area (whilst being mixed into the pure silver) and by particles of dirt left unremoved from the sheet metal at the time of manufacture. These factors may cause crumbling on the surface of any item of antique silver in a tiny area. Only extreme examples of such blemishes need cause concern to the connoisseur.

Strawberry dishes are attractive items. If they are small and early they are almost always genuine. Unfortunately some (not the majority) of the larger examples were refashioned from plates, etc., c.1825, when such vessels became very popular and were in considerable demand. Few, if any, can invariably decide with certainty about the authenticity of a strawberry dish. However, crests or coats of arms, agreeing with the hallmarked date, and not much later than the styles of c.1800, must be taken as a strong indication of authenticity. Such emblems usually appeared in the centre of the strawberry dish, but crests were sometimes neatly engraved between the flutes on the rim. Emblems on plates were scarcely ever engraved on their centres (they would have become scratched in this position) and, if engraved on the rims (as was the custom) would be most unlikely to fit in neatly after subsequent

Detail of an interesting pair of sugar tongs (U-turn showing). Limerick, c.1800. The engraved plume of three feathers device, which appears on almost all table plate with engraved decoration from this centre between 1780 and 1820, is remarkably similar to the trefoil-like stamped mark seen on most items of Limerick plate during the same period. The plume of feathers or trefoil-like devices were possibly used as a town mark. Courtesy the James Aspin Collection, South Africa.

refashioning. The opinion of an expert differentiating between the patination of an item made, say, in 1770, and another item refashioned or made in 1825 would, I fear, be speculative, but he could or should be able to differentiate between patinations of 1825 and, say, 1730, providing that neither of the items under comparison had experienced vicissitudes. Perhaps, it is wiser to avoid large strawberry dishes without a contemporary emblem engraved thereon.

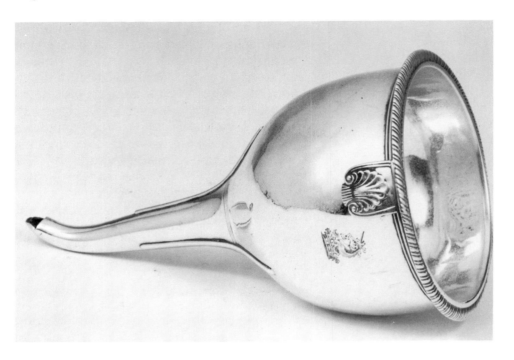

Wine funnel. London, 1812, by Crespin Fuller. Courtesy the Eagle Collection, Devon.

This **wine funnel** has survived unscathed but, subsequent to c.1785, *most* 'kettle-spout' ends to these items have been cut down to tidy up damage to this vulnerable point. Earlier funnels, being of tapering cylindrical form without the 'kettle-spout' terminal are not quite so liable to damage.

Wine labels. These popular little items have sometimes been re-engraved with less interesting but more popular titles, such as 'whiskey'. Traces of former titles can usually be discerned. Pieces of borders on fragile irregular designs have sometimes been broken and these defects are usually difficult to spot.

Table services. It is a great mistake, for example, to try and build a set of place settings around a nice dozen, bottom-marked, feather-edged table spoons (still in fairly plentiful supply) or forks in the Old English form. A collector would be extremely unlikely to find a contemporary set of dessert forks to match (dessert spoons would also be difficult) and if he should do so their cost would be prohibitive. Very properly, after acquiring such a set he will be afraid to wear them out in everyday use. In all probability, in order to match his nice set of bottom-marked table spoons or forks, he will be forced, knowingly or uninformedly (until some tactless guest arrives at his table and tells him), to acquire top-marked nineteenth century fiddle pattern components which have been reshaped into the Old English form and then embellished with feathering during the last few years. A set of such a nature looks ridiculous to the experienced eye.

If a collector should wish to acquire a genuine nineteenth century set, he has a great variety of patterns to choose from but, unless he wants a very expensive straight set (all components of one date and maker), it is virtually imperative that he should first acquire the dessert forks before buying other components. There is one exception to this rule: in the fiddle and thread pattern (popular from about 1790 until well into the nineteenth century), the dessert spoons are even harder to find than the dessert forks (it took me three years to find a suitable and not overpriced set of just half a dozen of these spoons to complete a customer's part-service). There can be little to interest connoisseurs of antique silver in nineteenth century flatware and I believe it is a sounder policy to invest in second-hand sets made around the turn of this century and not much used subsequently. Such silver is usually of good quality and it can be expected to withstand the rough and tumble of everyday use for much longer than late Georgian productions. It is also considerably cheaper, at the time of writing.

Customers' dogged insistence in buying place settings in multiples of six confirms my long-held views that customers are usually wrong and sometimes ridiculous. Why should a set of six cost almost double that of a set of five? Nevertheless, the customer exercises most considerable influence with the majority of traders, and merely by impolite gestures with his cheque book, he could alter all these absurdities in a short time. A place setting for one (eminently suitable for a recluse) should cost precisely one fifth of the cost of a setting for five, while a set of ten should cost no more than double the price of the latter or ten times the cost of the former.

Footed salvers. Sometimes a damaged foot has been replaced with a modern one; the replacement piece would then be unmarked. However, some feet have never been marked and are perfectly genuine and so you must rely on your judgement of patina. Occasionally we find that the foot has been removed and the item turned into a conventional waiter by the addition of three small feet, often of the wrong style for the period.

We have already remarked the results of wear on the highspots of chased decoration, but the problems do not end there. All angular edges on the bodies of articles, such as those of octagonal forms, and various types of rims, if hollow, are likely to have received more than their fair share of rubbing due to thoughtless cleaning.

For example, most of the items mentioned in this chapter, if manufactured during the last quarter of the eighteenth century, are applied with the attractive bead motif on their rims, legs or handles (p. 59). As every bead can be likened to a hollow, circular shell, prolonged rubbing may have fractured the highspot of either one or of very many of the beads in any design. Just one fractured bead could indicate that all the others had been worn almost equally thin on their highspots and that these also are ready to collapse at any moment. Broken beads, usually clogged with the cleaning powders of many generations, may be difficult to spot even when all are broken. If an item containing a number of broken beads is dirty, the fractures may be felt with the fingers. Although a number of broken beads (costly to repair) may not be detrimental to the beauty of an item, they would certainly impair its value very considerably.

It may not be out of place at this juncture to stress that in the interests of posterity the cleaning of silver should be a gentle, loving process. Beads, like all vulnerable sections of decoration, should never be worn thin by a clumsily applied cloth which necessarily rubs only the highspots effectively. They should be treated with a *very soft* brush which spreads itself evenly into the recesses of the decoration.

Conversely, some items have been neglected for many decades and rather than allow them to be buffed on the wheel, which will certainly destroy the skin of patination completely, many hours of patient and sensitive work may be necessary to restore them to their rightful beauty. In such cases, if an item is corroded or seriously tarnished, it is sometimes necessary to use drastic methods of cleaning, even to the unwelcome limit of wrapping a very mildly abrasive material around the end of a very soft wooden spike, such as an olive stick. Eventually, when you have at last got this decoration clean, it will be unnecessary in the future to use anything other than very soft brushes in conjunction, if expedient, with soap and water. Unrestored silver of good patination requires remarkably little cleaning.

CHAPTER 11

Sheffield plate

The town of Sheffield developed from a few scattered villages sheltering in the forests of Hallamshire, a district rich in coal and iron. The township of two thousand souls was famous for the making of cutlery in Elizabethan days and by 1743, the year in which the process of plating silver was discovered, the population of Sheffield was less than ten thousand and the cutlery industry was possibly experiencing some difficulty.

Legend has it that Thomas Boulsover was repairing the handle of a knife composed of copper and silver when he had the good fortune accidentally to fuse the two metals. From this unusual clumsiness he realised it was possible to coat copper with silver and, appreciating some of the commercial possibilities of his discovery, he began to manufacture a number of small items. The main significance of his discovery was the fact that once the two metals were fused together they would elongate in complete unison if rolled out in a sheet. Not all metals if fused like this would behave similarly.

Boulsover did not grow rich from his invention. He had too many other mechanical interests to concentrate his thoughts on just one of them and he failed to realise that, whereas the majority of his potential customers might still prefer and could afford a solid silver button to a plated one, the profitable future for his invention lay in the reproduction of imposing items which, because of their high cost when wrought from solid silver, were suitable only for those of high rank and considerable wealth.

Undoubtedly Boulsover was a brilliant mechanic and if he had perfected his invention before trying to market his immature product, thus revealing his secret, he might have reaped the early rewards. Eventually he made money by making saws.

Joseph Hancock saw Boulsover's invention, he improved upon it and then began the manufacture of imposing items of good design. He was shrewd enough to realise that he had two types of potential customers from all parts of Europe: some he would please by enabling them to stock their silver boards, and thus ape their betters, and to others he could offer the more worthy joy of acquiring beautiful possessions within their means. Hancock prospered, new companies began manufacture, and craftsmen from afar flooded to the flourishing industry. Sheffield opened her arms to receive them.

Sheffield plate originated as a reasonably priced substitute for silver and in consequence was not always cherished or respected, but I have now seen examples of it as sensuous of line as any contemporary silver, as original in conception as anything created by Paul de Lamerie, and although most styles ran behind in slightly later imitation of designs in vogue with goldsmiths, and very occasionally of the Leeds potters as well, there were increasing instances as the process developed when the precedence was reversed and silversmiths were not too proud to imitate the platers. Above all other considerations in the appraisal of our current subject, I can assure my readers that the beauty

Sheffield plate bread basket, c.1770, of outstandingly fine craftsmanship. Courtesy Harvey & Gore.

Superlative example of a Sheffield plate tea caddy, c.1775-80, with chased decoration. Courtesy Harvey & Gore.

Pair of Sheffield plate spoons from a set of eleven. Made from plated wire, chased by hand, bowls die-struck and soldered separately; this pattern is dated 1777 and made by Thomas Law according to the late Mr. F. Bradbury. To give a date and maker to unmarked items suggests Mr. Bradbury had access to Law's work book. Courtesy the Dr. Graham Hulley Collection, Canada.

A delightful cruet frame in Sheffield plate, c.1775-85, standing on four ball and claw feet. The form of the feet indicates that this item is unlikely to be even a few years later.

of the patination on some fine old plate is unsurpassed even by the best Elizabethan examples in silver. The unfortunate but inevitable tragedy of Sheffield plate is that the thin layer of silver covering the copper is sadly vulnerable to wear and damage and thus comparatively few examples survive in pristine state. If we are fortunate enough to find worthy specimens within our means we should never consider them as antique silver's poor relations. Sheffield plate must be highly prized and most *carefully preserved*. It should never be employed in household use, and at the fine museum at Sheffield no one is allowed to take specimens out of their airtight showcases unless wearing gloves.

Sheffield plate argyll, c.1790, a vessel designed by the 3rd Duke of Argyll for retaining the heat of gravy during the course of a meal. In this example, the gravy circulates round a central container filled with hot water. This is an outstanding specimen of Sheffield plate for it displays a beauty of line and decoration superior to the work of most goldsmiths. Sheffield plate was difficult to fashion and, for its finest examples, the platers were obliged — obviously with much enjoyment and artistry — to exercise a greater care and skill than contemporary goldsmiths. In this rare instance, there is no need to be worried by the vacant cartouche for there is no question of a possible erasure. Courtesy Harvey & Gore

One of a set of four Sheffield plate salt cellars, c.1790. Courtesy Sheffield Museums.

Old Sheffield plated globe-shaped inkstand, c.1795. Courtesy the Michael Graeme Macdonald Collection, U.S.A.

The globe inkstand with sliding lid opened revealing glass containers for sand, quill and ink.

A very rare Sheffield plate soup tureen in the form of a turtle, c.1800, approx. 56cm long, 17.7cm high. Courtesy Sheffield Museums.

A rare Sheffield plate 'bull's eye' lamp for spirit, with a lens on either side of the wick to intensify the light. Subsequent to 1821, unmarked. Courtesy the Michael Graeme Macdonald Collection, U.S.A.

However, there were craftsmen, usually unskilled with anything but their hands, who stinted and saved and then set up in business on their own account. Whilst admiring their enterprise one wonders if they were responsible for most of the very thinly plated examples of this industry. Evidence pointing to malpractices is to be found in the concern expressed by London goldsmiths regarding the marks punched by platers on their wares. The public had no pocket guide to assay office hallmarks in those days and in all likelihood accepted any set of symbols or initials as denoting sterling silver. Advantage was taken of this ignorance. The goldsmiths' agitation was probably as justified as it was certainly prolonged. It was not until 1773, when an Act of Parliament established an assay office at Sheffield, that platers were forbidden to punch their wares with marks. But an act of 1784 permitted the resumption of marks on Sheffield plate and indeed it tried to control the industry by requiring (even if optimistically) each maker of plate working within a hundred miles of Sheffield to register his mark at the Sheffield Assay Office.

Readers who wish for detailed information concerning the processes involved in the manufacture of Sheffield plate or who wish to make a more advanced study of the industry as a whole, are advised to read Thomas Bradbury's *History of Old Sheffield Plate*.

The base metal used in the production of Sheffield plate was predominantly copper but combined small quantities of zinc and lead. The silver employed was of the sterling standard. This combination produced a temper that was neither too soft nor too brittle for fashioning. From about 1830 German silver (an alloy of nickel and copper) was sometimes used as a base metal and this had the advantage of not showing through so obviously when the silver became worn.

Boulsover made his ingots (prior to rolling them into sheets from which he fashioned his wares) by fusing just one layer of silver to one bar of copper. This process left one side of his plated sheet devoid of copper.

The methods employed for finishing off the interiors of the early and interesting Sheffield plated boxes varied considerably and, after the passage of time, none of them proved to be entirely satisfactory despite the charm of their exteriors. Some boxes were left with the copper interiors uncovered, some were gilt and others were tinned.

An attractive Sheffield plate box, embossed and chased in the rocaille taste, unmarked, c.1755. Courtesy Sheffield Museums.

In the early days of the industry, if it was required to have a silver coating on both sides of an object then two sheets of Sheffield plate, plated on one side only, were used. From about 1770, ingots made from single bars of base metal, plated on both sides, seem to have been in production and the method of manufacture did not vary. One bar of base metal was sandwiched between two sheets of silver and these were of equal breadth and length and were thoroughly filed, planed and cleaned. Two outer copper sheets were then positioned to protect the two silver surfaces when the ingot was heated and a coating of chalk prevented them from fusing to the ingot. Thus, before fusing there were five bars or sheets and these were tightly bound together: a protective sheet of copper (prevented from fusing to the ingot); a sheet of silver; a bar of copper; a sheet of silver; a protective sheet of copper. The resulting ingot was from 3.8cm to 14cm deep by 6.4cm wide, and its length was made suitable to the particular projects in view. The ingot's content of silver, if of good quality, represented about five to eight per cent of the whole, but much Sheffield plate was made with a smaller proportion of the precious metal. Finally, the ingot was drawn out by rollers or forge hammers into a sheet of the requisite size and thickness. The rollers were at first pulled by hand, but once the industry was established they were replaced by water power.

Hollow-plated wire was used for edges in the 1760s, and from 1768 solid plated wire was used. In 1789 Roberts & Cadman began soldering silver wire and silver borders upon lips, edges and bases, areas exposed to heavy wear and early exposure of copper, and so it became possible to ornament plate successfully with beaded borders and other attractive decorations of that time. Various other refinements were introduced by individual platers (the firm of Roberts & Cadman continuing to be responsible for new ideas) until the advent of electroplating, in 1837, soon terminated the manufacture of Sheffield plate. The *early examples* of electroplated wares are of very fine quality.

Towards the end of the nineteenth century, some fifty years after the manufacture of true Sheffield plate had ceased, collectors began buying examples of the 'dead' industry and by the turn of the twentieth century it had become more valuable than contemporary sterling silver and this fact, of course, led to the mass production of imitation Sheffield plate. Copper articles fashioned in an approximation of antique styles were electroplated and some manufacturers stamped the words 'Sheffield Plate' upon their products. Dealers were within their rights in selling spurious reproductions so long as they did not describe them as antique in their sales patter.

But the public had much cleverer forgeries to contend with then and the position is still dangerous today. I am told that there is one dealer who *boasts* that much of the Sheffield plate currently passing through the salerooms was made by his father — employing the original, authentic processes — at the beginning of this century. But this claim is considerably exaggerated. Reproductions of Sheffield plate are almost invariably heavier for size than genuine examples of the craft.

Although these reproductions are confined to commercial rather than collectors' items (such as trays, candlesticks, chambersticks and wine coasters), the ability to recognise antique patination seems the first essential before a collector embarks on purchases without expert assistance.

Provided that antique plated ware has been cherished by all of its several owners, most of it that was fashioned from sheets with thick silver plate is usually, apart from a few inevitable scratches, more beautiful today than when it was made because of its delightful patination easily recognisable by its blue-grey tint. Sheffield plate is grossly undervalued by reason of a general ignorance of this subject. I recommend you to collect it and never be discouraged by gleams of copper peeping like a shrouded sun through the 'highspots' of the decoration.

Another abuse of Sheffield plate still flourishing openly today and which ruins much genuine old plate, is the electroplating with garish buffing of items that by reason of honest but unfortunate hard wear revealed too much copper for the public's taste. Antique plate after being electroplated — a very different process of silvering copper — automatically ceases to be Sheffield plate. Unless you are purposely making a collection of silverware that has been ruined by restoration (an interesting hobby, perhaps, but generally unrewarding as an investment) it is much wiser to spurn all replated items.

Often, items of erstwhile Sheffield plate have been electroplated more than once and so please do not fall into the trap of believing that any item with copper showing through the silvered exterior, often with beguiling innocence, is necessarily genuine plate.

After the boom of the late Victorian and Edwardian eras in both genuine and spurious plate, most erstwhile customers eventually considered that they had been duped, and the bottom fell out of this market, to the delight of a few fully experienced collectors. Today, I suppose, after a partial revival of interest, genuine collectors' pieces of Sheffield plate average about a third of the cost of their antique silver counterpart.

I am certain that less than ten per cent of the plate sold as Sheffield plate today is genuine. This deplorable situation springs both from the usual sources of ignorance and wishful thinking, and also because Sheffield plate has become a trade term for any item of silvered copper even if made in Mecca.

A Sheffield plated soup tureen made in France, c.1810. French craftsmen adopted the process of fused plate in about 1770, often stamping 'DOU' over 'BLE' (for double) on these wares. Plate had been produced in France at a much earlier date by a laborious process of burnishing leaf silver on to brass objects. Courtesy Harvey & Gore.

There are good and interesting examples of genuine, Continental pieces made in the eighteenth and nineteenth centuries. Such pieces often copy English styles and unless the item under review is a samovar, for example, it is often very difficult to determine the country of origin.

The question of recognising genuine examples of Sheffield plate is the most important part of this chapter and in order that readers may refer to it quickly when occasion demands, it seems best to list the characteristics of Sheffield plate concisely:

1. Patination: the blue-grey tinge on unrestored surfaces (so similar to good patination on antique silver) is very conspicuous when compared with surfaces that have been electroplated or otherwise ruined. If you can visit the City of Sheffield Museum at Weston Park, you will be able to recognise the difference between good and very bad patination with just one glance. Turn left immediately on entering the main hall of exhibits. In the first case by the door and against the wall and on the second shelf from the top of the show-case there is a tankard mug that has been electroplated, but the handle was shielded from this process and remains unimpaired. Presumably, the piece is retained in this superlative collection because of some special point of interest. I am told that the damage on the body which necessitated the replating was a large dent. It must, I fear, have had a hole as well. I cannot understand why the hammering out of a dent would have damaged the original surface. The contrast between the colour of this mug and the exquisite blue-grey tones of all the other pieces on the same shelf is so marked that it will be spotted by everyone. This restored mug was the first item that caught my eye as I entered the hall and is a splendid example of bad colour. Should this case have been rearranged by the time you get there, the number of the exhibit concerned is L.1943.142, and the curator will point it out on request.

It may be a chemical action produced by the copper or it may be the latter's obscure presence beneath the gradually thinning silver surface that provides Sheffield plate with a patination rather more pronounced than on contemporary silver items.

2. Seams: Sheffield plate has to be joined for the fashioning of almost all articles of depth. This junction is called a seam and it is clearly visible. If the seam has been covered recently by replating, it may not be visible or it may be visible only in places. Look also for seams on knops, feet and handles.

3. Applied rims, etc.: hollow-plated wire was used on edges in the 1760s. From about 1768 further experiments were made by applying solid plated wire to edges. From about 1789 silver borders were introduced. The eye can usually see and the thumbnail usually feel the junction of these various borders with the body of the item.

4. Bright-cut engraving: this was possible on items made from ingots with thicker silver sheets. Sometimes we find solid silver bands, with bright cut enrichment, soldered round the bodies of tea pots and so forth.

5. Hollow-ware: the interior of tea pots and coffee pots, or any receptacle into which a guest's eyes were unlikely to pry are tinned.

6. Shields: unless the plate was unusually thick it was necessary for crests and monograms, etc., to be engraved on a silver shield, which was either inlaid (soldered in a hole cut right through the body wall), rubbed in or soldered on. The inlaid shields date from about 1789 and rubbed in shields

from about 1810.

7. Decoration in relief: in the nineteenth century, when elaborate floral, vine and shell edges were in vogue, these were die-stamped from thin silver sheets and then filled with lead.

8. Tinned bases: in the nineteenth century it was usual for platers to economise by producing large articles such as trays with tinned bases.

As with antique silver, the collector should inspect as many pieces of Sheffield plate as possible, visit museums and exhibitions, and carry a small, carefully protected item — e.g. wine label — around with him for comparison.

CHAPTER 12

Armorial engraving

by Michael Ingham

There is no doubt that one of the most pleasing and appropriate forms of decoration on a piece of antique silver is an authentic coat of arms or crest engraved to the order of the original owner. But, in addition to their decorative effect, these emblems may also be a means of identifying the owner. Knowing whether the first owner was a nobleman, a politician, a country squire, or a London merchant, can add to the interest and pleasure of ownership. This identification of the original owner, when it is possible, does need some grasp of at least the elements of two branches of heraldry: armory, that part which deals with coats of arms, and then genealogy. Both of these are considerable subjects on which many books have been written, so within this chapter it is only possible to give an outline of how the puzzle of identification can be tackled and to indicate some of the books which can help. Quite deliberately, the scope of this chapter has been restricted to printed books which are likely to be found in the larger public reference libraries.

At the start, it is necessary to emphasise the importance of the authenticity of the engraving, and there are two aspects of this as far as armorial engraving is concerned. First, a later coat or crest often not only looks wrong in style but also can indicate a weak area of silver if an earlier engraving has been erased to make way for re-engraving. Nevertheless, such a later engraving may be completely authentic from the heraldic point of view, the piece having been sold or bequeathed to some other family at some time. The second aspect is the heraldic authenticity of the engraving, and it is an unfortunate fact that a fair amount of eighteenth and nineteenth century heraldry is bogus. This means that the engraving is quite genuinely contemporary but the person or family had no real right to use the arms shown. From the silver collector's point of view there can be no objection since the engraving is contemporary, but identification can be impossible simply because the arms are not recorded in any reference book. The collector must also beware of pieces originally plain, which have been embellished in modern times with coats of arms in a very close imitation of the correct contemporary style to increase their attractiveness and selling price; these fakes, for they are nothing better, can be very deceiving though one does see some heraldic impossibilities owing more to the imagination of a dealer or engraver than to the College of Arms.

Heraldry is generally thought to have its beginnings in the second quarter of the twelfth century; the growing popularity of tournaments and the introduction of the closed helm led to the adoption of distinctive personal devices painted on the shield as a means of identification in the lists or in battle. Quite rapidly the practice grew of including the same device on the seal which a man used on documents, so that the distinctive shield pattern was in effect a signature. Both sentiment and the convenience of recognising a lordship or fief by a particular design probably led to the practice of a son continuing to use his father's insignia on inheriting his father's lands and responsibilities. By the end of the century, the system had become firmly established; shield devices were distinctive and hereditary, and could therefore be used to identify the owner when displayed on furniture, silver, etc.

The practical military use of heraldry came to an end in the sixteenth century but it had become so established as a means of displaying family identity that it continued as a decorative art. However, once heraldry was divorced from the restraints imposed by its original use for recognition in battle, armory grew more elaborate, complicated and fantastical. In the period which is of interest to the silver collector, the achievement of arms, that is the complete display of armorial bearings, might consist of the following:

1. The shield,* also called the escutcheon or coat of arms. This is the essential centrepiece of the entire display and may be the whole of the bearings. Particularly in the eighteenth century, the shape of the shield was often distinctly non-military.
2. The helm, whose type and position shows the rank of the bearer.
3. The crest, a device displayed on the helm.
4. The wreath, a twist of coloured silks hiding the join between helm and crest.
5. The mantling or lambrequin, originally a cloth to protect the back of the head and the neck from the sun, conventionalised into a decorative background. On silver the style in which it is engraved is often a useful guide to dating.
6. The insignia of an order of knighthood.
7. The coronet of rank for a peer or peeress.
8. The supporters for the arms of peers and some other dignitaries.
9. The compartment, the ground or surface on which the supporters stand.
10. The motto, generally shown at the base of the achievement in England and Ireland; if shown above the crest it is most probable that the arms are Scottish.
11. Insignia of office.
12. Robe of estate of peer, sometimes used as a background to the entire achievement.

Naturally not even someone entitled to an achievement as elaborate as to include all these elements would necessarily have the complete thing engraved on a piece of silver. It would only be appropriate on a large tray or salver for example. There is also the point that the armorial engraving was part of the decorative embellishment of the article and, throughout the period which is of interest to the silver collector, it was usual to engrave armorial bearings in a decorative cartouche. The main styles of this decorative surround and a rough indication of the main periods of use are:
1. Plumes crossing and often tied with a ribbon below the shield (pp. 46, 47, 107); mainly used 1650-85.

---

*A lady used a lozenge-shaped shield but neither the helm nor the crest (p. 51, bottom right).

A transitional architectural/rococo cartouche, c.1730. Courtesy Sotheby's.

An asymmetric cartouche of floral sprays, c.1750. Courtesy Victoria and Albert Museum.

A cartouche built up of a combination of swags, leafy sprays, and a motto, c.1775.

An ornate cartouche, with an outer design of swags and gadrooning. London, 1788, by Hannam & Crouch.

A plain spade-shaped shield, c.1800.

2. The mantling subdivided into elaborate feathery scrolls (p. 98); about 1675-1700.

3. An architectural cartouche of scrolls or columns, often with shells or masks above and below the shield and with the space between the outer framework and the shield filled with engraved scales or brickwork (top left and p. 51 bottom left); used in the baroque period about 1700-40.

4. An asymmetric cartouche of scrolls, shells and/or floral sprays surrounding an asymmetric shield (top right); 1735-70.

5. A cartouche built up of a combination of swags, acanthus leaves, masks, etc., as shown here (above left and right), characteristic of the Adam or neo-classical style; about 1770-85.

6. A bright-cut oval or rectangle (p. 59); about 1780-85.

An ornate cartouche of the early nineteenth century, c.1815.

A cartouche of elaborate scrolls of mantling. London, 1808, by William Bennett.

7. No cartouche at all, a plain spade-shaped shield, sometimes with the crest above (bottom left on facing page and p. 42); about 1785-1820; in early examples the sides and top of the shield are usually curved, later the sides of the shield are straight and the top squared off.

8. Elaborate scrolls of the mantling similar to the late seventeenth century style but much more stiffly and accurately engraved as shown above; from about 1805 onwards.

After about 1830 a degeneracy similar to that which descended on design in general, affected heraldic engraving and one finds a mixture of styles but all cut in an unmistakable nineteenth century fashion.

The important point to remember is that the cartouche is not part of the armorial bearings. It is in many cases a very artistic decorative surround but it is just decoration, and is irrelevant to identification.

As in solving any puzzle, identifying the original owner from the armorial bearings engraved on a piece of silver is easier when full information is available, that is when the achievement has been engraved in full. It is also easier the higher the rank of the person concerned, quite simply because the number of possibilities is reduced and it is more certain that the arms and the person have been recorded in relatively accessible works of reference. For example, it is scarcely necessary to have much knowledge of armory if confronted with a salver dating from the mid-eighteenth century engraved with an achievement in which the shield is surmounted by a coronet with five strawberry leaves showing. All one really needs to know is that this coronet is that of a duke: the number of possible owners is so small that it is easier and quicker to compare the arms with engraved plates in a contemporary peerage book rather than decipher them. In most cases considerably more knowledge and effort is needed and the chances of success in identification reduce as you move down the scale from the arms of peers and baronets to those of commoners.

Barred helm of the sovereign and princes of the blood royal.

Barred helm of peer.

Vizored helm of baronet or knight.

Helm of esquire or gentleman.

If the engraved achievement includes the helm, its type and position gives a quick indication of rank:

1. A barred helm of gold affronté (facing the viewer) is used by the sovereign and princes of the blood royal.

2. A barred helm of silver placed sideways with five bars showing indicates a peer.

3. A vizored steel helm affronté with the vizor raised indicates a baronet or knight; a baronet can be distinguished by the insignia of the order on an escutcheon (a small shield placed on the main shield, usually top centre or mid centre) or on a canton (small rectangle at the top left of the shield as viewed from the front). At the time which interests the silver collector, these insignia could be: a. a left hand cut at the wrist shown upright and the palm showing for a baronet of England or a baronet of the United Kingdom; b. a saltire (St. Andrew's Cross) over which is placed a further escutcheon of the royal arms of Scotland for a baronet of Nova Scotia—Scottish creations, 1625-1707; c. a harp for a baronet of Ireland — Irish creations, 1619-1800.

4. A steel closed helm or vizored helm, with the vizor down, placed sideways indicates an esquire or a gentleman; corporate bodies also use this type of helm.

The coronet of rank of a peer is placed directly above the shield and, if the helm is present, this is placed above the coronet. The different types of coronet are engraved as follows, the cap which lines an actual coronet is sometimes also engraved:

1. A chased circlet with five strawberry leaves for a duke.
2. A chased circlet with three strawberry leaves and two silver balls for a marquess.
3. A chased circlet with five tall rays each topped with a silver ball and a small strawberry leaf between each pair of rays for an earl.
4. A chased circlet set with nine silver balls touching each other for a viscount.
5. A plain circlet set with four silver balls for a baron.

These are quite distinct from crest coronets which are coronets around the base of a crest and can be of several different patterns, the most misleading of which is the so-called 'ducal' coronet with three strawberry leaves showing. These are simply part of the crest and do not indicate rank. If only the crest of a peer was engraved, the coronet of rank was shown above the crest not round its base.

Duke's coronet.

Marquess' coronet.

Earl's coronet.

Viscount's coronet.

Baron's coronet.

A 'ducal' or crest coronet.

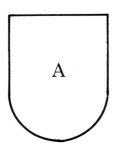

Single coat shield.

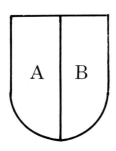

Impaled shield.

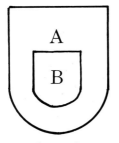

An escutcheon of pretence.

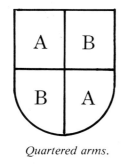

Quartered arms.

The main point about the insignia of rank is quite simply that, when they are present, identifying the original owner is relatively straightforward since the peerage is very thoroughly documented, even for families and titles that are now extinct. Tracing baronets may be a little less easy if the line is now extinct, but is still pretty certain of success. However, most engraved pieces will have the arms of commoners and how close we can get to identification depends on whether the arms have been recorded in a readily accessible book and on the amount of information the engraving gives us.

If the shield shows a single coat all that we can find is the name of a family. It is a fair assumption if the arms are Scottish that the original owner was the head of a family at the date of engraving because the Laws of Arms in Scotland after 1672 laid down that cadet branches of the family should use arms suitably differenced to indicate that they were those of separate branches. In England, although there was a system of indicating cadency by adding small marks to the arms, the system was ambiguous and, in practice, often ignored, especially in engraving on silver where the marks would have been tiny.

However, if the shield is divided down the centre with a different coat in each half, called impalement, then there is a better chance of identifying the original owner. Such a shield — or more rarely two shields side by side — are generally the arms of a husband and wife, a man from family 'A' married to a lady from family 'B'; hence if we can identify the two families and find the right family trees, the owner can be identified. The rare exceptions to impaled arms being those of a married couple come from certain official positions. Archbishops and bishops can impale the arms of their province or see, heads of colleges the arms of the college, deans of cathedrals, regius professors at Cambridge and kings of arms the arms of their office with their personal arms. In these cases, the official arms go in position A and the personal arms in B; it is rare to find this impalement of official and personal arms on silver.

The arms of a husband and wife can also be shown with the arms of the wife's family on a small shield placed over the centre of her husband's arms. This is done when the lady is an heiress or co-heiress (but not necessarily of estates or fortune, the inheritance may be only her paternal arms). There are no male representatives of the line, that is her father is dead and her brothers, if any, have died without leaving descendants; in order that the arms of her family will not disappear, she carried them to her husband who places them on an escutcheon of pretence. Identification is then exactly the same as for impaled arms. After her death, her children and their descendants represent both families and show this by quartering the arms of the two families.

This is the origin of most quartered coats seen engraved on silver and, since the paternal arms appear in the first quarter, top left as engraved, this is the first item to identify. A slight degree of caution is needed in the early stages of identification as some arms were granted divided quarterly.

In the course of time a family may have become the representatives of a number of families through marriages in different generations to a number of heiresses, some of whom may themselves have had quartered arms. This could lead to further sub-divisions of the shield, still called quarters no matter how many there are, though there was no obligation to display all the quarterings to which one was entitled. In periods of heraldic ostentation elaborate quarterings sometimes produced triumphs of engraving skill if not of the owner's taste or genealogical exactitude. The starting point for identification though is always the arms at top left as engraved.

Heraldry is a colourful affair and it can be essential for identification to know in what colours the various parts of the achievement were supposed to be. The tinctures, as the colours on a shield, crest, etc., are called, are few and simple but are grouped into three classes: metals, colours and furs. A system for showing the different tinctures in an engraving in a printed book, on a seal or on silver was devised in Italy towards the middle of the sixteenth century and gradually became standardised. The tinctures are:

Metals	**Painted as**	**Engraved as**
Or	Yellow or gold	Dots
Argent	White or silver	Surface left plain
Colours	**Painted as**	**Engraved as**
Gules	Red	Perpendicular lines
Azure	Blue	Horizontal lines
Sable	Black	Cross-hatch of horizontal and perpendicular lines
Vert	Green	Diagonal lines running down from left to right
Purpure (unusual)	Purple	Diagonal lines running down from right to left

Diagram showing how the metals and colours are indicated when engraved.

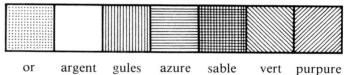

or   argent   gules   azure   sable   vert   purpure

Furs	**Painted as**	**Engraved as**
Ermine	White with black spots	Blank background with pattern of cross-hatched dots and tails
Ermines	Black with white spots	Cross-hatched background with pattern of blank dots and tails
Erminois	Yellow with black spots	Dotted background with pattern of cross-hatched dots and tails
Vair	Rows of interlocking shield shapes alternately blue and white	Shapes alternately blank and shaded with horizontal lines
Pean	Black with yellow spots	Cross-hatched background with pattern of dotted dots and tails
Potent	Rows of interlocking 'T' shapes alternately blue and white	Shapes alternately blank and shaded with horizontal lines

There are variations on vair and potent depending on whether the shapes

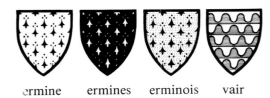

Diagram showing how the furs are indicated when engraved.

ermine   ermines   erminois   vair

are point-to-point or base to base; other combinations of colour and metal can be used when the colouring is described as, for example, vairy or and gules.

The use of this system of cross-hatching spread quite gradually and did not come into general use on English silver until about 1705-10. The identification of earlier arms is often impossible as the 'charges', the shapes and objects making up the design on the shield, are shown in outline or arbitrarily shaded and the field, the background tincture, is simply blank. Identification may be possible only if the design is very unusual or if additional clues are available from a crest or motto.

Even after 1710 it is best to keep a slightly open mind as to whether all the charges are coloured as indicated by the cross-hatching; artistic licence or ignorance may have led the engraver to shade some features differently. There is also the technical difficulty of shading a very small area; for example, making a distinction between ermines and pean in engraving on silver is almost impossible and the slightest trace of wear may have erased any try the engraver made. Real objects, human, animal, vegetable or inanimate, can be shown in natural colours, described as 'proper' in heraldry, and the engraver would then use his own taste in using any shading.

At this stage, it should be possible to pick out the various sections of the shield that are of interest, whether it is a simple coat, and to identify, at least tentatively, the colours of each part or object. Given the necessary artistic skill, the arms could be redrawn in colour, but to get any further the picture has to be turned into words; to use the correct term the arms must now be 'blazoned'. As might be expected, heraldry, over the years, has evolved its own language or jargon in which arms are described. This may look antiquated and cumbersome at first sight but it is a compact and unambiguous way of writing down what can be a complicated graphic design. In something like eight hundred years the heralds have probably invented less jargon than the computer industry has in thirty, but reference to a book on the subject is necessary. There is a fair choice of modern manuals of heraldry and the best thing is to find one whose author's style is found attractive. A few suggested titles:*

Boutell's Heraldry, ed. J.P. Brock-Little, Norroy and Ulster King of Arms; *Scots Heraldry,* Sir Thomas Innes of Learney, Lord Lyon King of Arms; *Simple Heraldry,* Sir Iain Moncreiffe; *The Pageant of Heraldry,* Col. H.C.B. Rogers; *Shield and Crest,* Julian Franklyn.

* Heraldic and genealogical books are usually most easily obtained from specialist bookshops such as Heraldry Today, 10 Beauchamp Place, London S.W.3.

Dictionaries of arms can clearly be arranged in two ways, either an alphabet list of families with a description of the arms of each, or a collection of coats of arms with the family name attached to each coat; this latter is called an Ordinary of Arms and is the one we now want. The standard, indeed the only, book covering British arms is *An Alphabetical Dictionary of Coats of Arms belonging to Families in Great Britain and Ireland* by J.W. Papworth and A.W. Morant. The full title is even longer so not surprisingly is it usually referred to as Papworth's 'Ordinary' or just 'Papworth'. It is a long way from being either one hundred per cent complete or accurate because the main source used by Papworth, *Burke's Armory,* is itself unreliable, but in the words of a leading modern authority, Sir Anthony Wagner, Garter King of Arms 1961-78, it is indispensable because there is nothing better which covers the ground.

Certainly Papworth's method of classification is a remarkable achievement and reasonably easy to use with a little practice. The coats are arranged under the main charge on the shield and then further sub-divided by the other features in a logical and consistent way. In the most favourable cases Papworth will give us not only a family name but also a seat, a place, or at least a county. Obviously further research is much easier if these are known, particularly if a common surname is involved; just knowing that the family was Smith does not get us very far but 'Smith of XYZ Hall co. Somerset' holds out hope that something more can be found.

If it is certain or at least highly probable that the arms being investigated are Scottish, there is an alternative to Papworth arranged in much the same way but more compact because of the smaller range: *An Ordinary of Arms contained in the Public Register of all Arms and Bearings in Scotland* by Sir James Balfour Paul, Lord Lyon King of Arms. This is a much more authoritative work as it is based on the register kept in accordance with the Act regulating arms passed by the Scottish Parliament in 1672 and, in suitable cases, it is much quicker to use than Papworth.

Another work, which can be very useful in tracing Irish arms including quite a number not to be found in Papworth, is *Kennedy's Book of Arms, Sketches collected chiefly from the Records in Ulster's Office and other authentic documents* by Patrick Kennedy. This is a photo-reproduction of a notebook which contains sketches of shields with, in many cases, crests and mottoes. There is an index of names but using it in the reverse direction, to attach a name to unidentified arms, takes time and there is no systematic arrangement at all. One has to run through more than two hundred pages, mostly with twelve arms to a page, looking for a match. This can be lengthy but often solves otherwise intractable problems. The Ulster's Office in the sub-title is the Office in Dublin of Ulster King of Arms, the then heraldic authority for all Ireland and the date of compilation, 1816, is near ideal for the silver collector.

A useful intermediate next stage is to crosscheck the name now tentatively attached to the arms in *The General Armory* by Sir Bernard Burke. All modern heraldic authorities rightly warn that care is needed in using Burke, the great standby of heraldic stationers, but their main concern is that many of the coats of arms are borne without authority — bogus heraldry in fact. Our main cause for complaint as collectors is of the errors in blazoning and attribution of a proportion of the sixty thousand or so coats it contains, errors that were carried over into Papworth and land us up a blind alley from time to time. In many cases the reference to Burke will enable a check to be made on the crest or quarterings which can supply pointers that we are on the right lines.

Additions and corrections to Burke's *General Armory* compiled by Alfred Morant, who completed Papworth, have been published in *General Armory Two* edited by C.R. Humphrey-Smith. A fairly high percentage of the entries concern arms of the medieval period which seldom concern silver collectors, but the book also contains an index of names in the 1895 and 1925/30 editions of *Armorial Families* by A.D. Fox-Davies which occasionally can be useful.

If our luck has held, we will be able to say at this stage with moderate certainty that our piece of silver is engraved with the arms of family A of place W in the county X. When a coronet of rank or the insignia of a baronet is present it is possible to identify an individual owner, even when no wife's arms are present, if it is reasonably certain that the engraving is of the same date as the piece of silver. Baronets present no difficulty as they are listed in works of reference by family name but peers are generally listed by titles not family names. Both, however, can be most quickly traced through Burke's *Family Index* which gives references to the most recent appearance of a family in one of their publications on the peerage or landed gentry.

Further details of the lives and careers of peers and baronets can be sought in: *The Complete Peerage,* and *The Complete Baronetage* by G.E.Cokayne, as well as in other reference works such as the *Dictionary of National Biography* and *Who's Who in History.*

For peers and baronets, the arms of the wife's family impaled or in pretence are only needed to confirm that our identification is correct, but in other cases positive identification usually depends on their presence. Sometimes, a quartering or quarterings will enable us to distinguish a particular branch of a family but in England, where arms are inherited by the lineal male descendants of the original grantee, one cannot be certain that marks of cadency were always used by junior branches. All one can say is that the piece of silver is engraved with the arms of such and such a family, without being able to identify a particular owner. When a wife's arms are present, either impaled or on an escutcheon of pretence, the process of identification has to be repeated so that we can say that the arms are those of Mr. A of W, county X married to a lady of family B of Y, county Z.

This will often be the end of the search, but if we want to know more about the family the initial line of research is to try and find the relevant family trees. Burke's *Family Index* also contains references to families who have appeared at some time in one or other of their publications (including *A Genealogical and Heraldic History of the Landed Gentry*), and since families may only appear in a few of these, or perhaps only in one edition of the *Landed Gentry,* one does need to have access to a library which holds a near complete collection of the different publications and the various editions. Naturally, looking for a Mr. Brown who married a Miss Jones in or before 1780 is hopeless without some identification of place — and that is not much help if the arms are Brown of London and Jones of London. A rare surname as well as landed possessions make searching a lot easier.

When neither the husband's nor the wife's families have appeared in one or other of Burke's publications, then a very much wider range of publications may have to be searched. Fortunately, indices to a very large number of printed pedigrees have been published: *A Genealogist's Guide* by G.W. Marshall; *A Genealogical Guide* by J.B. Whitmore; *A Genealogist's Guide* by G.B. Barrow. Each of the last two is a continuation of its predecessor so all three should be consulted. For Scottish families, references should be made to: *Scottish Family History* by M. Stuart.

It is as well to be aware, though, that following up all the references in these works can demand considerable patience and a great deal of time with no guarantee of success; it certainly will require access to a very large library or series of libraries. Full details of all publications are given in the bibliography at the end of this book.

If all the trails prove blank, it is likely that the task of identifying the Mr. A who married a Miss B is impossible or at least beyond the abilities of someone with a limited knowledge of genealogical research. Either the services of a professional are needed, which might be worth while for a highly important piece, or you will have to set to and acquire some of the knowledge yourself. The scope of the subject and how it fits into building up history made up of human lives, not only those of the rich and famous, has been splendidly described in *English Genealogy* by Sir Anthony Wagner.

Nothing has so far been said about identifying the owners of pieces engraved with a crest or crest and motto. It must be admitted from the start that the chances are not very good unless the crest or motto is very unusual. The main reason for this is that crest designs are very much less individual than those of arms, so that often one ends up with a list of ten or more possible families. There is also the point that as late as the 1780s it was the opinion of some heraldic authorities that the crest was an accessory which could be varied at will, though there would be a tendency to continue using an established design. It is, though, worth looking into the standard Ordinary of Crests: *Fairbairn's Book of Crests of the Families of Great Britain and Ireland*. A.C. Fox-Davies (who edited the 1905 edition) at least grouped most of the crests into some sort of order but excluded crests from earlier editions which he considered were used without due authority. The early editions are a complete jumble, and extremely tedious to use.

A crest of very common design (used by more than 130 families).

To this day, mottoes do not form part of an official grant of arms in England and can be varied at will, though again a long established motto would tend to continue in use. Once again the situation is different in Scotland where the motto is part of the matriculated arms and cannot be varied at the whim of the user. The main weakness of mottoes as aids to identification is that one is likely to find either that the motto being looked up is unrecorded or that it is ascribed to an uncomfortably large number of families. However, in some lucky instances the motto can be a short cut to identification, even when the shield is present, so it is worth checking the lists of mottoes in Burke's 'Armory' and Fairbairn's 'Crests' as well as consulting *Elvin's Mottoes Revised*.

To summarise, the process of identification involves the following steps:
1. Blazon the arms.
2. Look them up in Papworth's 'Ordinary' and cross-check in Burke's

'Armory'; if the arms are definitely Scottish consult Paul's 'Ordinary' and if Irish *Kennedy's Book of Arms*.

3. If the arms are those of a peer or a baronet, Burke's *Family Index* will lead to an appropriate edition of Burke's *Peerage*. If the arms are of a commoner and no wife's arms are present, the arms are of such and such a family but usually no closer identification can be made.

4. If a wife's arms are present, repeat the blazoning and identification in Papworth.

5. Try and find a married pair of right families, using initially Burke's *Landed Gentry* and if that fails, the references in Marshall, Whitmore or Barrow.

In conclusion don't become disheartened by the times that you draw a blank. Deciphering the arms on silver can at times seem like trying to solve a three-dimensional crossword puzzle with some clues missing and some misprinted. At times one is going to be beaten by the accident that arms have not been recorded in a readily accessible place or that they have been misrecorded or misascribed. On other occasions one is going to suffer the results of some eighteenth or nineteenth century goldsmith who assured a prospective customer that, because his surname was such and such, these were the arms or crest he should have engraved on his plate. These will be more than offset by the times when one can, for example, definitely ascribe the ownership to, for example, a naval officer and trace his complete career from a thirteen-year-old midshipman to admiral's rank. Or, perhaps, the trail of clues will lead to an eighteenth century county history where one finds not only details of the family but also a contemporary engraving of the country house where your silver was first used. These will be uncommon high spots but the search will always be interesting and will add a new dimension to the pleasure of collecting antique silver.

CHAPTER 13

So you think you've learnt something?

A picture quiz

Please do not embark on this chapter until you have followed the course of study (Chapter 9), unless you consider yourself knowledgeable, in which case you will no doubt score highly.

Sub-titling this chapter 'A picture quiz' echoes of the schoolroom, but, basically, we cannot get away from the hard fact that this quiz does represent an exam, and it will, of course, prove useless to you if the answers to the problems set are inspected before or during it!

What you are asked to do is to give the approximate date (and sometimes maker and district of origin) of every item illustrated on pp. 204-15. This you should be able to do by recognising period styles. Then enter your decision relating to each numbered plate on a piece of paper. When you have completed all the questions, *and not before,* turn to the answers on pp. 216-18 and from these, through comparison with your own estimate of dates, you will be able to total the number of points which you have earned and to determine whether you have 'graduated' or whether you must revise and resit your exam.

Don't hurry in your deliberations, and try not to make wild guesses but, from what you have learnt from previous chapters in the book, work out the answers carefully.

Start the exam at once, and if you 'fail' don't look back at either the questions or answers for two months — an interval of time which should ensure you forget them. Each time you 'sit' the exam pencil in your score and the date in the spaces provided on p. 218, and in this manner you can check your progress.

If you think you are weak in one period, yet strong in others, you may decide to concentrate much of your subsequent reading on this weakest period before sitting for your next examination.

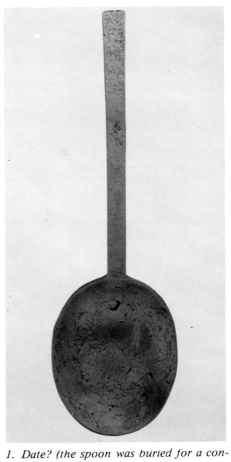

*1. Date? (the spoon was buried for a con-
siderable period).*
*Courtesy the Professor John Browning
Collection.*

2. Date and maker?
Courtesy the Worshipful Company of Goldsmiths.

3. Date?
*Courtesy the Worshipful Com
pany of Goldsmiths.*

4. Date?
Courtesy Sotheby's.

6. Date?
Courtesy the Kent Karslake Collection.

5. Date?
Courtesy Sotheby's.

7. Date and maker?
Courtesy Sotheby's.

205

9. Date?
Courtesy Sotheby's.

8. Date?
Is the coat of arms contemporary?
Courtesy Christie's.

10. Date?
Courtesy the Michael Graeme Macdonald
Collection.

11. Date?
Courtesy the Kent Karslake Collection.

12. Date?
Courtesy the Worshipful Company of Goldsmiths.

13. Date and district of origin?
Courtesy the James Aspin Collection.

14. Date?
Courtesy the Worshipful Company of Goldsmiths.

15. Date?
Courtesy Sotheby's.

16. Date?
Courtesy the Victoria and Albert Museum.

17. Date?
Courtesy Sotheby's.

18. Date?
Courtesy Sotheby's.

19. Date?
Courtesy Sotheby's.

20. Date?
Courtesy the Worshipful Company of Goldsmiths.

21. Date?
Courtesy Sotheby's.

22. Date?
Courtesy the Kent Karslake Collection.

23. Date and district of origin?
Courtesy Sotheby's.

24. Date?
Courtesy the Worshipful Company of Goldsmiths.

25. Date?
Courtesy Sotheby's.

26. Date?
Courtesy Sotheby's.

27. Date?
Courtesy Sotheby's.

28. Date and district of origin?
Courtesy the James Aspin Collection.

29. Date and district of origin?
Courtesy the Worshipful Company of Goldsmiths.

31. Dates of all articles?
Courtesy Sotheby's.

30. Date?
Courtesy Sotheby's.

32. Dates of all articles?
Courtesy Sotheby's.

33. Date?
Courtesy Sotheby's.

34. Date?
Courtesy the James Aspin Collection.

35. Date?
Courtesy Sotheby's.

36. Date?
Courtesy Sotheby's.

37. Date?
Courtesy the Michael Graeme Macdonald Collection.

38. Date?
Courtesy the James Aspin Collection.

39. Date?
Courtesy Sotheby's.

40. Date?
Courtesy Sotheby's.

41. Date?
Courtesy Sotheby's.

214

45. Date? Is the crest contemporary?
Courtesy Sotheby's.

46. Dates of all articles? District of origin of the two-handled cup?
Courtesy Sotheby's.

47. Date and district of origin?
Courtesy Dr. D.L. Serventy Collection.

215

Answers

1. Puritan spoon: 10 points for date within ten years of 1660.
2. Wine cooler: 10 points for date within ten years of 1810; deduct 2 for each year outside the stipulated period; add 5 extra for recognising the work of Paul Storr.
3. Tureen: 10 points for date within five years of 1795; deduct 1 for each year outside the stipulated period.
4. Tankard: 10 points for date within ten years of 1690; deduct 2 for each year outside the stipulated period.
5. Coffee pot: 10 points for date within ten years of 1770; deduct 2 for each year outside the stipulated period.
6. Cup and cover: 10 points for date within five years of 1785; deduct 2 for each year outside the stipulated period.
7. Mustard pot: 10 points for date within six years of 1784; deduct 1 for each year outside the stipulated period; add 5 extra for recognising the work of Hester Bateman.
8. Coffee pot: 10 points for date within ten years of 1710; deduct 2 for every year outside the stipulated period; add 5 extra for recognising later coat of arms.
9. Epergne: 10 points for date within ten years of 1770; deduct 2 points for each year outside stipulated period.
10. Castor: 10 points for date within ten years of 1690; deduct 2 for each year outside stipulated period.
11. Porringer: 10 points for date within eight years of 1698; deduct 1 for each year outside the stipulated period.
12. Cup and cover: 10 points for date within ten years of 1710; deduct 1 for each year outside the stipulated period.
13. Coffee pot: 10 points for date within ten years of 1760; deduct 2 for each year outside stipulated period; add 5 extra for stating Ireland as district of origin.
14. Tureen: 10 points for date within six years of 1755; deduct 1 point for each year outside the stipulated period.
15. Coffee pot: 10 points for date within eight years of 1755; deduct 1 for each year outside the stipulated period.
16. Teapot: 10 points for date within five years of 1785; deduct 5 for each year outside stipulated period.
17. Skean-dhu: 10 points for date within thirty years of 1850; deduct 1 for every five years outside the stipulated period.
18. Sugar box: 10 points for date within ten years of 1680; deduct 2 for each year outside the stipulated period.
19. Castors: 10 points for date within ten years of 1710; deduct 1 for each year outside the stipulated period.
20. Taperstick: 10 points for date within ten years of 1715; deduct 2 for each year outside stipulated period.
21. Cruet: 10 points for date within ten years of 1810; deduct 2 for each year outside the stipulated period.
22. Salver: 10 points for date within ten years of 1720; deduct 2 for each year outside the stipulated period.
23. Salver: 10 points for date within ten years of 1785; deduct 2 for each

year outside the stipulated period; add 5 extra if recognising Scottish origin.

24. Porringer and cover: 10 points for date within five years of 1685; deduct 2 for each year outside the stipulated period.

25. Candlestick: 10 points for date within ten years of 1765; deduct 2 for each year outside the stipulated period.

26. Candlestick: 10 points for date within eight years of 1740; deduct 5 for each year outside the stipulated period.

27. Sugar basket: 10 points for date within ten years of 1797; deduct 2 for each year outside stipulated period.

28. Cream jug: 10 points for date within ten years of 1760; deduct 2 for each year outside the stipulated period; add 3 extra for recognising Irish origin.

29. Wine taster: 10 points for date within twenty years of 1660; deduct 1 for each year outside the stipulated period; add 3 extra for recognising London origin.

30. Snuffer and stand: 10 points for date within ten years of 1715; deduct 2 for each year outside the stipulated period.

31. Candlesticks: 10 points for date within 10 years of 1785; deduct 2 for each year outside the stipulated period.
Basket: 10 points for date within 10 years of 1795; deduct 1 for each year outside the stipulated period.

32. Cup and cover: 10 points for date within ten years of 1710; deduct 1 for each year outside the stipulated period.
Candlesticks: 10 points for date within ten years of 1695; deduct 1 for each year outside the stipulated period.

33. Cup: 10 points for date within ten years of 1705; deduct 1 for each year outside the stipulated period.

34. Chamberstick: 10 points for date within fifteen years of 1815; deduct 1 for each year outside the stipulated period.

35. Porringer and cover: 10 points for date within ten years of 1670; deduct 1 for each year outside the stipulated period.

36. Monteith bowl: 10 points for date within five years of 1685; deduct 1 for each year outside the stipulated period.

37. Tobacco box: 10 points for date within ten years of 1720; deduct 1 for each year outside the stipulated period.

38. Chamberstick: 10 points for date within ten years of 1710; deduct 2 for each year outside the stipulated period.

39. Caddy: 10 points for date within five years of 1770; deduct 2 for every year outside the stipulated period.

40. Caddies: 10 points for date within ten years of 1790; deduct 1 for each year outside the stipulated period.

41. Inkstand: 10 points for date within ten years of 1810; deduct 1 for each year outside the stipulated period.

42. Salver: 10 points for date within ten years of 1760; deduct 2 for every year outside the stipulated period.

43. Cream jug: 10 points for date within five years of 1735; deduct 1 for each year outside the stipulated period.

44. Jug: 10 points for date within ten years of 1745; deduct 2 for every year outside the stipulated period.

45. Sauceboat: 10 points for date within ten years of 1750; deduct 1 for each year outside the stipulated period; add 5 extra for deciding that the crest is not contemporary (it's nineteenth century).

46. Two-handled cup: 10 points for date within ten years of 1750; deduct 1 for each year outside the stipulated period; add 10 extra for recognising Channel Islands origin.
Pair of cream pails: 10 points for date within ten years of 1740; deduct 1 for each year outside the stipulated period.
Pair of salt cellars: 10 points for date within ten years of 1815; deduct 1 for each year outside the stipulated period.

47. Marks on spoon, Newcastle, 1872. 10 points for date within five years; deduct 2 for every year outside the stipulated period; add 5 extra for recognising origin.

How did you do?

Score (maximum 561)	If you are a collector	If you are a dealer
550+	Brilliant. Honours.	If you are honest and not greedy you must be an excellent person for the collector to buy from.
475-549	Graduation. Congratulations.	Glad you've learnt something from the book.
375-474	Bad luck. Revise the chapters/areas which let you down.	Not very good.
275-374	Your mistakes were probably spread pretty evenly. Anyway revise.	Awful. I hope your customers have been lucky.
100-274	I'm afraid you haven't got too much out of this book. Re-read.	How long have you been in business?
99 or less	Have you read this book?	At a loss for words.

Fill in the points you obtained and the date each time you take the examination

Points obtained at
1st examination........................on.........................
Points obtained at 2nd
examination 2 months later...............on ....
Points obtained at
3rd examination ....on ....
Points obtained at
4th examination ....on ....

Those of you who have come through the quiz with colours flying may rightly feel proud. It would please me to believe that, along with the absorption of the facts and suggestions contained in this book, a genuine love of antique silver for its beauty, qualities and historical association has also been engendered in my readers. Those of you more prone to human error, who may not yet have 'graduated', will doubtless do so soon and already you must surely be more keenly aware of the dangers concealed in the silver jungle.

If, as I hope, you are already competent to differentiate between intentional deceits and genuine mistakes you will find plenty of honourable traders at all levels of the trade, and of varying degrees of expertise, with whom you will do mutually enjoyable business. There is little point in approaching me because, much as I would like to help, I am painfully taxed trying to keep my regular customers happy. In writing this book for you I have negected them.

Bibliography

Kurt Albrecht, *Nineteenth Century Australian Gold and Silversmiths*, 1969.

G.B. Barrow, *A Genealogist's Guide*, 1977.

Douglas Bennett, *Irish Georgian Silver*, 1972.

Frederick Bradbury, *Guide to Marks of Origin on British and Irish Silver Plate,* 10th edn. 1959.

    A History of Old Sheffield Plate, 1969.

    Bradbury's Book of Hallmarks, 1st edn., 1927, revised every year.

Boutell's Heraldry, ed. J.P. Brock-Little, 1978.

Sir Bernard Burke, *The General Armory of England, Scotland, Ireland and Wales*, 1884, repr. 1961, 1962, 1966, 1969.

Burke's Peerage Ltd., *Burke's Family Index*, 1976.

    A Genealogical and Heraldic History (Dictionary up to 1906) *of the Peerage and Baronetage,* 105 edns., 1826-1970.

    A Genealogical and Heraldic History of the Landed Gentry, 18 edns., 1843-1972.

    Irish Family Records, 1976.

J.W. Clarke, 'The Copper Plate of the Goldsmiths of Newcastle upon Tyne', Archaeologia Aeliana, 4th series, vol. XLVII, Northumberland Press Ltd., 1969.

Michael Clayton, *The Collectors' Dictionary of the Silver and Gold of Great Britain and North America*, 2nd edn. 1985.

G.E. Cokayne, *The Complete Peerage of England, Scotland, Ireland, Great Britain and The United Kingdom, Extant, Extinct or Dormant,* 2nd edn., 1910-1959.

John Culme, *The Directory of Gold & Silversmiths, Jewellers and Allied Trades, 1838-1914*, 2 vols., 1987.

Eric Delieb, *Investing in Silver*, 1967.

    Silver Boxes, new edn.

V.F. Denaro, 'Maltese Silver and Red Hand of Ulster', *Antique Dealer and Collectors' Guide*, September 1968.

Dictionary of National Biography.

Elvin's Mottoes Revised, with a supplement by R. Pincher, 1971.

Fairbairn's Book of Crests of the Families of Great Britain and Ireland, 4th edn. 1905, ed. by A.C. Fox-Davies, repr. 1968.

A.C. Fox-Davies, *Armorial Families*, 1895, 1925/30.

Julian Franklyn, *Shield and Crest*, 1967.

Arthur Grimwade, *London Goldsmiths 1697-1837*, 1976.

J.B. Hawkins, *Nineteenth Century Australian Silver,* 2 vols., 1990.

David Heller, *A History of Cape Silver 1700-1870*, 1949.

C.R. Humphrey-Smith (ed.), *General Armory Two*, 1973.

Sir Thomas Innes of Learney, Lord Lyon King of Arms, *Scots Heraldry,* several edns.

Sir Charles Jackson, *An Illustrated History of English Plate,* 2 vols. 1911.
  Jackson's Silver & Gold Marks of England, Scotland & Ireland, ed. Ian Pickford, 1994.
  Pocket Edition Jackson's Hallmarks, ed. Ian Pickford, 1991.
Patrick Kennedy, Herald Painter, *Kennedy's Book of Arms, sketches collected chiefly from the records in Ulster's Office and other authentic documents,* 1816, repro. 1969.
G.W. Marshall, *A Genealogist's Guide,* 2nd edn. 1903, repr. 1967.
Richard H. Mayne, *Old Channel Islands Silver,* 1969.
Sir Iain Moncrieffe, *Simple Heraldry,* 1979.
Charles Oman, *English Domestic Silver,* 1968 edn.
J.W. Papworth and A.W. Morant, *An Alphabetical Dictionary of Coats of Arms belonging to Families in Great Britain and Ireland,* London, 1874 repr. 1961, 1977.
Sir James Balfour Paul, Lord Lyon King of Arms, *An Ordinary of Arms contained in the Public Register of All Arms and Bearings in Scotland,* 2nd edn. Edinburgh 1903, repr. U.S.A. 1969.
Rev. M. Ridgway, *Some Chester Goldsmiths and Their Marks,* 1973.
Col. H.C.B. Rogers, *The Pageant of Heraldry,* 1957.
M. Stuart, *Scottish Family History,* 1930, repr. 1978.
Victoria and Albert Museum, *Small Picture Books* nos. 17, 24, 25, 27, 28, 29, 33, 37, 46 on English silver.
Sir Anthony Wagner, *English Genealogy,* 2nd edn. 1972, 3rd edn. 1983.
Peter Waldron, *The Price Guide to Antique Silver,* 2nd edn. 1992.
Patricia Wardle, *Victorian Silver & Silver Plate,* 1964.
Stephan Welz, *Cape Silver and Silver Plate,* 1976.
J.B. Whitmore, *A Genealogical Guide,* 1953.
Who's Who in History.
Wynyard R.T. Wilkinson, *A History of Hallmarks,* 1975.

Index